TRANSCONTINENTAL OVERLOAD

STEPHANIE X COOK

TRANSCONTINENTAL
OVERLOAD

First Printing, 2025
This book mainly follows British English spelling and punctuation rules.
For privacy reasons, some names have been changed.
The quote by Milan Kundera on the page after the dedication, as well as the excerpt in the last 'California' chapter, are taken from Kundera's *The Unbearable Lightness of Being*, translated by Michael Henry Heim, published by Harper & Row, New York, 1984.

Paperback ISBN: 979-8-9994888-0-0
Ebook ISBN: 979-8-9994888-1-7
Cover design by Xenia Kreativ LLC.
Published by Get The Boots LLC.

To my children –
cycle breakers
and my greatest teachers.
I love you.

'If I'm an advocate for anything, it's to move. As far as you can, as much as you can. Across the ocean, or simply across the river. The extent to which you can walk in someone else's shoes – or at least eat their food – it's a plus for everybody. Open your mind. Get up off the couch. Move.'

—Anthony Bourdain, *No Reservations*

'We can never know what we want because, living only one life, we can neither compare it with our previous lives nor perfect it in our lives to come.'

—Milan Kundera, *The Unbearable Lightness of Being*

'Life should not be a journey to the grave with the intention of arriving safely in a pretty and well-preserved body, but rather to skid in broadside in a cloud of smoke, thoroughly used up, totally worn out, and proudly proclaiming, "Wow! What a Ride!"'

—Hunter S. Thompson, *The Proud Highway*

'If you are always trying to be normal, you will never know how amazing you can be.'

—Maya Angelou, *Rainbow in the Cloud*

Author's Note

This book started as a blog with the same name, and I had no idea what an immense sense of overload I would face when I first set out to document our experience of moving from England to California. *Nomen est omen*, I guess. I remember how thrilled I was when I combed song lyrics and poems for appropriate titles and came across this line from James Brown's *Living in America*. It sounded cool and catchy, just what I wanted for my blog, which was going to be an entertaining yet informative journal-style log of our temporary stay in the US, a fun occupation for a couple of years during which I planned to drink a lot of Starbucks lattes, learn some weird American expressions, drive a big car, write down my observations about those crazy Yanks and then return to civilisation.

Life had other ideas. More than fifteen years later, I know the true meaning of transcontinental overload. After a total of seven moves – two of which across the country, from California to Texas, and from Texas to New Jersey, and three intercontinental, from the UK to the US, back to the UK, and back to the US again – I'm battle-hardened, exhausted and filled with gratitude and a sense of wonder. I've been told more than once how brave and resilient I was to live a life like this. Brave? Try foolish, impulsive or maybe, at a push, adventurous. Resilient? To be honest, I have lost all sense of what that word actually means.

I was diagnosed with ADHD a few years ago, after both my children were diagnosed, and psychiatrists finally compared symptoms. I had begun writing this book a long time before my diagnosis, and once I knew, I stopped for a while because I didn't know whether or how to incorporate this into my story. Leaving it out would mean omitting an essential part of my story and maybe even confusing or alienating readers, but neither did I want to make the diagnosis the primary focus nor, most importantly, the reason for my struggles. Moving to another country is a significant undertaking that will challenge even the most resilient and optimistic person, with or without neurodivergence in the mix.

Neurodivergence is a vast and hugely complex field that's only now receiving the depth of attention it deserves, especially when it comes to diagnosing adult women. I hope you can read my story simply as a glimpse into how this can affect someone's already heavily challenged expat brain.

I use the term 'expat' liberally in this book and in my personal and professional life. I'm aware this term can have specific connotations for people and is often negatively associated with a privileged lifestyle amongst privileged fellow countrymen and women or those of similar backgrounds. To me, being an expat simply means being someone who lives, whether temporarily or more long-term, 'ex patria', ie outside the country in which they were born and/or raised. I use the term in this literal sense, for lack of a better word, and I don't use the term 'immigrant' as much as it sounds too final to me. I don't feel like a true immigrant in the US because I don't think I will stay long-term. The word 'expat' retains a delicious sense of uncertainty.

Madison, New Jersey, September 2025

Contents

Prologue

It's early October; the oppressive heat of the summer has finally receded, and we're sitting at a long wooden table in one of Austin's many beer gardens. I tilt my head back and admire the gnarled branches of the Texas live oak trees that form a canopy above me. I love those iconic trees of the South with their long, tentacle-like limbs so fiercely, and wonder how I could ever have left this place.

I close my eyes and listen to the soft swishing and rustling of the leaves and the jangly screech of the grackles and marvel at how these ubiquitous shiny black jaybirds with their mean beady eyes and jarring song have become an almost calming presence in my exhausted mind. I can hear the odd clang and trill of music as the band starts to pick up their instruments again. The earthy smell of barbecued meat is wafting over from the food truck – the sounds and smells of Austin.

'How's y'alls' day goin'? Have y'all decided on food?' The soft voice of the waitress brings me back to earth, and I have to smile. I love the drawl of the language in this part of the world, the long vowels that seem to go on forever, so different from the clipped, almost harsh sounds I got so used to when I lived in England. A lifetime ago.

My husband orders some food, and I drift back into my thoughts. What is it about this place that keeps drawing me in? I've tried to run away from it more than once, but somehow it keeps pulling me back with a fierce tug. When I drive along the city's streets, even now that I don't live here anymore, it amazes me how well I know my way around it and how easy it feels to come back.

How does a place you never even wanted to live in become the place you find impossible to leave?

One thing is certain: this city has got under my skin, probably more than any of the many other places I've called home. Is this what it feels like to be home? Do I even know what the word means? I think I've lost all sense of 'home', and it's become something abstract, like when you stare at a word for too long and it becomes just random letters that have been jumbled up and don't make any sense strung together anymore. It's a strange feeling, moving to a new place and knowing it's not forever. Somehow, living a liminal existence has become the story of my life.

Texas was definitely not on my agenda. Not that I ever had one, not really, not since I left my home country over half a lifetime ago. The one thing I knew was that I wanted to live abroad for a while, but I never expected to leave and not return.

With a sigh, I open my eyes and stretch my arms out overhead as if trying to hold on to the branches above me to give me the hold I so desperately need.

PART 1: CALIFORNIA

'It's good-bye. But we lean forward to the next crazy venture beneath the skies.'

—Jack Kerouac, *On the Road*

A New Life

'So, how about San Francisco?' my husband Scott asked casually, his back to me as he poured me a glass of my favourite white wine. I stared at the back of his head, decided that his short dark hair needed a trim, and wondered if I had heard him correctly. He turned to me and raised his eyebrows, and the cogs in my mind started to whirr. I had to admit that this question wasn't a huge surprise. He had spent the previous couple of years working with a Silicon Valley-based company and had consequently been on numerous work trips to the West Coast metropolis, which had clearly captured his heart. An 'I love San Francisco' fridge magnet had mysteriously appeared one day, beaming at me when I stumbled into the kitchen each morning, and our cupboard was filled to the brim with Ghirardelli chocolates. Still, I needed to confirm that he was actually asking what I thought he was asking. 'As in....' I probed, frowning. It was like my lips didn't want to part to release the words. 'Moving there?'

He just smiled and nodded, and I closed my eyes. I felt the familiar tug at my heart, my impulsive inner adventurer fighting my inner scaredycat, one bursting to yell 'yes!', the other desperately pulling me back from the abyss of change. An inner contrariness I was very familiar with.

I could feel Scott's expectant gaze on me and sighed. *Damn you*, I thought, and smiled involuntarily. My husband knew me too well, and I would have bet my favourite pair of shoes that he had waited for precisely this moment to ask this life-changing question. Just this morning, I had been bitching to him about the fact that I didn't feel like I belonged in the very suburban, very neat, very desirable and very English small town we currently lived in.

We had moved to Kent when I was pregnant with our first child, Amelie, and we felt like we needed to leave our one-bedroom flat in south London to find a place with more space for a growing family and within easy reach of my parents-in-law. Since my own parents lived a whole flight away in Germany, and we wanted our children to grow up close to at least one set of grandparents, the small town we settled in felt ideal. A few years later, Maya was born, and our family of four now lived in just the sort of place I had envisaged when we were both working in London and dreaming of the future. A family home with a garden and an extra bedroom for guests, just a few steps from a great primary school, within commuting distance to the city and surrounded by other young families. The perfect place on paper. And yet... Now that we were more or less comfortable, I could feel the familiar itch for something new. It was all too *predictable*.

Impulsivity was my Achilles' heel. For some reason, whenever it came to making big life decisions, I tended to close my eyes and ears and jump, often to the shock and surprise of those around me, who usually perceived me as a calm and measured person, unaware of the raging impulsivity lurking beneath.

When I had applied to pursue a Master's degree in England a few years earlier, for example, I upended my life within just a few weeks. I had expected to be admitted as a student for the following year, but the University of Kent at Canterbury offered me a place to study European literature right there and then, and I said yes and left my hometown, my relationship and the life I had seen play out in front of me. I hadn't had a very concrete plan, but it definitely didn't entail staying abroad, meeting a new partner in this new country, and then moving in together after only a few weeks. Oh, and marrying him just a year later. Of course, Scott's impulsivity had matched mine in that respect; I think we surprised most of the people around us with our joint sense of irreverence, although I like to think his was always a more 'grounded impulsivity' than my more panicky approach. It was like my rational brain, frightened by the prospect of uncertainty and upheaval, couldn't override my instincts, and surrendered to whatever this feeling was; the pathways of my brain scattered in a thousand directions and ended up in a big tangle the minute I tried to be rational.

And now, with this new, exciting and terrifying opportunity – who could resist California? – I felt the same way. To sit down and calmly think through my options was out of the question. My brain had already given in; I had to follow my gut.

On the other hand, though, did I really want to move to America? America had never been on my radar; my focus always firmly set on Great Britain, ever since I discovered the *Black Beauty* books as a little girl. I preferred books and horses to people and loved to disappear into the worlds writers created for me; if I wasn't hiding in my room reading or drawing, I was at the stables. My favourites were horse-related novels by British authors, who brought the sweeping landscapes of Cornwall, the foggy Scottish highlands and the peaceful pastures of the Cotswolds to life right before my eyes, while introducing me to different cultures and history. To this day, I could easily give a lecture on life in 19th-century England, simply based on the combined works of the Pullein-Thompson sisters.

As I got older, the horses made way for more teen and then adult-related content. My life as a young horse girl abruptly came to an end when I suffered a pretty severe riding accident, which meant that I spent my transition into puberty at home or doing physical therapy, with plenty of time for reading and listening to music. I found that I truly loved the English language, devouring lyrics and novels in their original versions and teaching myself the basics of the language even before it became a subject in school. Later, I discovered Jilly Cooper, whose naughty romps through British society gave me an excellent introduction to the country's bizarre rules and foibles. When I was fourteen, my mother took my sister and me to London for a long weekend. Scraping marmalade on my hotel toast, marvelling at the famous red double-decker buses and gawping at the opulent food halls in Harrods and the daringly eccentric outfits of the Londoners, both young and old, I fell head over heels in love with this quirky city. I vowed that I would come back and live here one day.

My feelings about America were very different. While most of my peers during adolescence and when I was a student at language college, gravitated towards US culture, I never felt the same pull. At eighteen, I travelled along the East Coast with my oldest friend and spent time in New Orleans, Pennsylvania and New York City, but while I enjoyed my trip, the country never held the same fascination for me as London.

California, however, was a different story. I took a deep breath, my inner adventurer gleefully jumping up and down, and said yes.

As expected, I panicked immediately. Once I started to imagine what life in the US might look like, or rather, how scared I was to give up the safety of my surroundings, I cursed my impulsivity. Why did I keep doing this to myself? Making impulsive decisions might have served me well so far, but the emotional extremes this required were quite substantial. What was it about this contrariness that had been part of my personality for as long as I could remember?

I had always been at odds with myself. Growing up in Germany in the 80s and 90s, I was a naturally shy and serious child who turned into an awkward teenager, so risk-averse that I was probably the only girl in the nineties who didn't pluck her eyebrows into oblivion.

And yet I craved change as much as I loathed it. While I never stopped loving my idyllic Bavarian hometown with its scenic backdrop of lakes and mountains, I knew from a young age that I wanted to escape and explore life beyond the borders of my home country. Travelling was a big part of my childhood and was actively encouraged. I always had a globe or a world map in my room as a child and hungrily absorbed every detail, mouthing city names and mountain ranges, my little fingers eagerly tracing borders and rivers, as I travelled all over the world in my mind. I like to think that the thirst for adventure and other cultures was part of my genetic heritage; there were numerous adventurers in my family, both on my father's and mother's sides, from those who emigrated from Germany to the US in the 1800s as well as after the Second World War, to those who studied and worked abroad in the early 1900s and spoke several languages.

The first of many forays into independence abroad occurred when

I was nine years old; I spent a week without my parents on a horse farm in Austria. I was supposed to do this with my friend Maria, but she decided to return home after a couple of days; she couldn't stand being away from her parents. I insisted I wanted to stay, and my parents – sceptical but ultimately swayed by my insistence – agreed, even though the place was not exactly a horse riding camp in today's terms, but simply a hotel accommodating pony-loving kids in addition to their regular guests.

Headstrong, conscientious little me must have spent her days quietly going about her business, studiously setting her alarm clock each night and then taking herself down for breakfast each morning, going to all the riding and horse care lessons and finishing the day eating dinner by herself. I'm sure somebody checked in on me occasionally, but I don't remember anything from that week except just wanting to be around the horses and feeling calm and in control.

That week must have planted a seed – some deep knowledge that I could always take care of myself and that even when I felt lonely, I would be able to overcome my fears and be okay.

When I was eighteen, I became obsessed with the 1988 Philip Kaufman movie *The Unbearable Lightness of Being*, based on the book by Milan Kundera. I was at that teenage stage when you're full of idealism and self-importance and would sneer at people who only ever watched the film rather than read the book, but I made an exception for this one. I found myself inexplicably drawn to the character of Sabina, played by the beautiful actor Lena Olin. This gorgeous but troubled free spirit, who always wore a bowler hat and black underwear, was always on the move, either coming from somewhere or going somewhere else. I loved her. I wanted to *be* her. Something about her restlessness appealed to me, even at that age.

Sabina's energy was all around me that night in my English kitchen, when my husband dangled a new version of my life in front of me.

For a while, the idea of moving to California floated around our minds like an invisible veil. Scott kept describing the adventure ahead of us, while I mentally deconstructed what I had built here in the UK. My husband had already left England in his mind, I could tell, his own spirit of adventure pulling him westward, away from the confines of his way too familiar environment. I understood only too well how he felt, and I couldn't hold it against him.

Neither could I resist his energy and his enthusiasm, and how much his eyes lit up whenever he talked about this new place he'd found. A place that could take him away from the commuter hell that was Greater London and the six am alarm that meant leaving at the crack of dawn and often not returning until after Amelie and Maya had gone to bed. He was seriously approaching burnout and missed out on a lot of time with the kids while I held the fort at home, focused on being a mum first and foremost. The ultimate separation of chores. Now, he'd been offered a once-in-a-lifetime opportunity that he wanted to grab with both hands. Not only was this a new job in a new country, offering a wider range of career options, but it also had the potential to give us a whole new outlook on work and life in general.

I tried to analyse my thoughts and feelings, and was surprised by how much resistance I felt. I wasn't ready to upend my life again; I had already done this, not that long ago. I had left the familiarity of my home country and settled in a new place – a place I loved. England had become home. But there was no denying the fact that, after twelve years of living in this country, doubts had started to creep in. Was this very predictable, very suburban, very convenient life really the life I wanted? Was I really happy here, in this little town we'd made our home? Did I feel like I belonged? I was definitely feeling restless. As much as I was fixated on my little bubble of motherhood with its relentless routines, routines I felt comforted by but also tethered to, I knew I needed something else. Something new.

Over the next few days and weeks, Scott and I weighed up the pros and cons of living in the US, keeping this new idea to ourselves at first, then sharing it with friends. The idea became a more solid concept; we created a tentative timeline. We would consider going for two or three years, leaving as soon as possible. It was September now, and the company wanted him over there in Silicon Valley as quickly as we could make it happen. I didn't want to wait until the end of the school year because I was scared I'd panic and change my mind if I thought about it all for too long. Amelie was seven years old and Maya only three, so leaving mid-year didn't feel totally implausible.

I pushed my doubts to a far corner of my mind and told myself to be rational. I had already left home once, so naturally, I could do it again. I had just started to think about a way to increase my work hours; I was freelancing for the publishing house I'd worked for during my time in London, but I was also hoping to start some new projects. In addition to my writing and translation jobs, I had trained as a reflexologist during my second pregnancy, and I had recently obtained a qualification as a kids' yoga instructor – all activities that allowed me to set my own hours around my family. I was hoping to simply carry on doing what I was doing in the US if my visa allowed it. And if not, delaying any thoughts of a proper career for a couple of years didn't seem like the worst thing in the world. My main focus was still on my family, and I felt that I owed it to us, and in particular to my husband, not to let this opportunity slip through our fingers.

Living in America for two or three years would be an adventure not to be missed. After all, it wasn't just any place in the US; it was California! The Golden State, land of stunning nature and perfect weather, a place where you could go skiing in the morning and sit on the beach in the afternoon. My German friends approved. 'Wow! About time you got to see some sunshine again!' Our English friends and family were a little more restrained, with comments such as, 'Oh well, if it's only for a couple of years, you won't completely lose your manners,' and 'Good God, I hope your children won't end up speaking like Yanks'.

It would be fascinating to see what living in a country none of us had been born in would feel like, where we'd be on equal footing, both of us diving into a new culture, a new society. How would an experience like this shape us as a family, our views, our values, our whole way of life and our long-term plans? And what about our kids – would they turn into little Americans and speak with a drawl? Would they learn to play baseball and demand ice in their drinks and love air-conditioning?

Of course, a couple of years, that's all it is! I tried to placate the nagging voice in my head. If it didn't work out, we could just come back sooner. Our kids were still young, and I knew, deep down, it was now or never. I didn't want to wake up one day and regret not having jumped at the chance.

Sightseeing

It took a whole six months from the day I said yes to the day we actually boarded our plane to San Francisco.

Before we gave our definite and final yes to Scott's boss, and before actually telling our kids what was about to happen, I needed to see the place for myself. The company agreed to send us on a week-long look/see trip to the Bay Area. A week of staying in a nice hotel in the middle of San Francisco, car rental and all meals and expenses paid for – what was not to like? We left our unsuspecting children in the care of their grandparents and packed our bags.

I had spent the past few weeks researching the Bay Area online and had already established that living in the city was not going to be ideal. We were craving city life after years of living in suburbia, but San Francisco didn't really fit the bill. At least, not our bill. Living costs were famously high and had ballooned over the previous few years. Moreover, our expat contract, while covering the cost of our relocation as well as an additional flight 'home' each year, didn't include an allowance for private education. The public school system was a total lottery, which meant that there was a risk that the kids might be assigned to any local school and not necessarily the one closest to where we lived. I wanted to make sure it was a good school, as we needed them to slot back into the English school system without major issues after our two or three years in the States.

Another issue that put us off San Francisco was the weather. My initial excitement about life in California was dampened by various ex-San Franciscans who warned us about the notoriously gloomy summers in the city. If I had been thinking palm trees, sunny beaches and golden California Girls, I was just as misguided as someone who believed Germans wear *Lederhosen* on a daily basis. Apparently, San Francisco had its very own microclimate, and from June to September, you wouldn't even be able to see the Golden Gate Bridge through all the fog and icy wind that descended on the city. There's that famous quote, often attributed to Mark Twain, that sums it up: 'The coldest winter I ever spent was a summer in San Francisco.'

The reason, of course, is geographical. The cold current that runs along the West Coast from the north cools the warm breeze blowing up from the south in a rather abrupt manner, which causes the air to condense and leads to fog. In the dry and warm areas further inland, the fog doesn't stand a chance and immediately dissolves, but near the coast, those misty tentacles rarely budge during the day. Places like San Francisco that are surrounded on at least two or three sides by water cannot escape it.

We knew we would never be really happy if we spent our summers wearing woolly jumpers and socks while knowing that only twenty minutes down the road was beautiful California sunshine. We came to the conclusion that we needed to move to the 'burbs again.

Thanks to my extensive school research and some friends' suggestions, I was able to pinpoint a few areas that might be acceptable to live in, and I felt I had a pretty good idea of where we needed to live. Or so I thought.

By the time our plane touched down in San Francisco, my stomach felt like it had moved up to my throat. A mix of excitement, nerves and the unnerving pressure of having to like a place even though everything inside me wanted to turn around and go home. Scott's company had hired a relocation agent to show us some of the areas we had earmarked, but we had a whole day to explore the city by ourselves before embarking on our scouting tour. I was keen to play tourist for a day, but found I was way too fidgety to pay attention to the cable cars and the Golden Gate Bridge, as my mind was already racing ahead to where we should live.

The next day, Scott and I ventured out of the city to meet our relocation expert. First stop: the East Bay, the area east of San Francisco, accessible via the Bay Bridge or, further south, the San Mateo Bridge. We had earmarked Oakland and Berkeley, as well as a couple of less urban, but highly praised, suburbs that had been recommended to us by various acquaintances and San Francisco aficionados. We were very excited to finally lay eyes on them in person. It became apparent very quickly, however, that none of those people had recently lived in this area, or actually taken into account that Scott would be working on the Peninsula and thus on the other side of the Bay. Living in the East Bay would continue the brutal commuting lifestyle we hoped to leave behind.

The places further outside the city to the east were a shock to my European sensitivities. We drove for ages, and everything around us, while very picturesque and California-rugged, looked the same. The houses were big, surrounded by even bigger gnarly oak trees and wide roads snaking up golden hills, endlessly meandering past more houses, more trees, and more hills.... My brain, fresh out of England, just couldn't relate it to anything; there were no town centres or even sidewalks to walk on. We didn't see anybody walking around anywhere, and there didn't even seem to be any places you'd want to walk to. Every few miles, there was an accumulation of commercial buildings, so-called 'strip malls', with an obligatory Starbucks and maybe a couple of other shops, but I couldn't get a sense of what any of these places were like, and I couldn't see myself and my family in any of them.

I knew I had to muffle the panic that was beginning to rise in my stomach. I had said yes to this endeavour; I had to find a solution. With a clenched jaw, I continued my online research once we got back to the hotel. The next, and most sensible, option was the area near Scott's workplace south of San Francisco, an area which I had hoped to avoid: the Peninsula, which included places like San Jose, Palo Alto and Mountain View. Facebook, Google, Apple. *Silicon Valley*. I felt sick. I knew from combing online forums that this was a very polarising area; some people loved it; others detested it. What I could glean from people's comments was this: huge pressure to perform, rich kids, everything ruled by the tech giants, eye-wateringly high cost of living, and miles away from the city.

I was seriously regretting my brave 'yes' to California. That same afternoon, as we strolled down Market Street, a homeless man spat at me, and I didn't even try to feign any more enthusiasm. But we had another day to explore, and the pressure of a final decision was looming, so I gritted my teeth and we jumped into our rental car for our final drive south.

There are two options to get from San Francisco to Silicon Valley: you can take Interstate 280, which winds along the Pacific coast through some of the Santa Cruz Mountains, or US Highway 101, which runs along the Bay further east. Our GPS told us to use the quicker route via 101, and so we missed out on what I now know is one of the most scenic drives along a freeway in the US, inviting you to admire the golden Californian hills and even a few peeks of the Pacific Ocean. 101, on the other hand, is a ten-lane monster of a road, flanked on both sides by industrial buildings, huge billboards, and mountains of trash and roadkill.

We stopped for a coffee in Mountain View, which at least seemed to have something resembling a town centre. It was impossible to tell one town from another down here on the Peninsula, as everything seamlessly merged together. Our next stop was Los Altos, which one of Scott's new colleagues had praised as a very cute little gem of a town.

Los Altos looked very different from the other places we'd seen so far. A real, somewhat quaint town centre with actual sidewalks, people sitting outside pretty coffee shops, plenty of dogs on leads, smiley faces and kids riding bicycles. *Well, there you are*, I thought, and after a little stroll, I was sold. I knew from my research that Los Altos had extremely high scores as far as public schools were concerned, and that was all I needed to know. We were too exhausted to fully acknowledge the fact that such a high school ranking equalled extremely high house prices, but it dawned on us that expat life might not be as glamorous as we had originally hoped.

We returned to England with a little dent in our enthusiasm, but still determined to make it happen. It felt like going through with this move was non-negotiable at this point. Scott really wanted this new position, and in fact, would probably find it hard to stay with the company if he changed his mind. I knew he understood my hesitation on some level, but he didn't really understand how panicked I felt inside. Plus, l had said yes. I had to follow through. To refuse to go would feel like a failure to me. Crumbling at the first hurdle? Not me. I would not admit defeat. Now we faced the gargantuan task of telling the kids.

I was way too emotional and cowardly, so I let my husband take the lead. He decided to get it over with in a very brusk and practical way and just blurted it out at breakfast: 'Kids, I have exciting news!' Two sets of hazel eyes widened with anticipation. 'We're moving to America!' A few seconds of deadly silence ensued. I will never forget the horrified expression on our firstborn's face, who had probably expected 'I'm buying you a pony', or at least 'You can finally have a dog'. I promptly burst into tears.

Amelie started howling, and with a withering, 'That's not exciting news, that's terrible news!' she bolted the two flights of stairs up to her bedroom and slammed the door shut. Her little sister promptly ran after her. Scott and I looked at each other in shock. I shook my head in despair, unable to speak because of the tears, and he sighed. We could hear wailing from one corner of the house and then a small voice from another: 'When are we going?' Maya was standing at the top of the stairs, her whispy, light brown hair freshly brushed and her hands clutching the handle of her little pink Angelina Ballerina suitcase, which she had clearly just packed, her favourite toy, a black horse, peeking out from the top. Slowly, she bumped down the stairs on her bottom, her little face alight with excitement. This tipped me over the edge; tears and snot were now streaming relentlessly down my face. What had we done? What the hell were we thinking?

The Big Journey

After a disastrous first experience with American bureaucracy, we spent the whole winter on tenterhooks. Our initial attempt at applying for our visas failed due to someone misplacing a comma in the salary bracket, which then didn't match Scott's job description, and we had to restart the entire application process. I got very close to calling the whole thing off. Patience had never been a strength of mine, and I loathed not knowing what was to come next, so I found this phase unbearable on every level. I was reminded of those last few weeks of pregnancy, when people constantly look at you with eager, sympathetic eyes and ask how much longer it's going to be. What I really wanted was to close the door on the world, bury myself under my duvet and wake up in America. Or be able to turn back time and make the whole idea disappear.

In March, we finally got the go-ahead from the embassy and frantically set about reorganising our lives. We found tenants for our house, watched a relocation crew cram our belongings into a big container that was going to sail across the Atlantic Ocean for two months, via the Panama Canal, and had an extremely teary goodbye party at the local pub. The girls had their last sleep-overs with their besties, swearing eternal friendship, and after a final roast dinner at my parents-in-law's, the four of us, full of excited trepidation, waved goodbye to England and boarded our Virgin Atlantic one-way flight to San Francisco. The company had splurged on business class tickets for us all, and the girls squealed with excitement when they saw their little pods that could magically turn into beds. Scott was shaking his head, mumbling something like 'Ruining them for life with this stuff', but his relief at their genuine laughter and beaming smiles was visible. Even Amelie had succumbed to the general sense of excitement and was busy lining up her favourite books and her Nintendo for the flight.

Scott's English colleague and his wife, who had made the same journey a few months before us, were waiting for us at arrivals – after all, we were bringing nine suitcases plus copious amounts of hand luggage, which weren't going to fit into our rental car, even though we had booked an SUV to tide us over the next few weeks until we could buy or lease our own car. Feeling too stressed to make any further decisions, I had let my husband handle the rental; of course, he had taken advantage of my disinterest and reserved a true monster of a vehicle – a black Chevy Suburban. I almost fainted when I set eyes on it. *Never ever will I be able to drive that thing*, I thought, but to my total surprise, I made friends with the beast pretty quickly and ended up missing it when we eventually had to return it.

We headed off to locate our temporary apartment in Mountain View, our home for the next few weeks until we'd found a house to rent. Luckily, Mountain View's main shopping and restaurant scene, Castro Street, was only a few steps away, and we dragged our exhausted bodies to the nearest pizza place before collapsing into our massive American beds.

The first day in our new country started with a trip to the supermarket. After we missed the turn for Trader Joe's, a small and more economical chain, which I'd already decided was going to be my favourite during my first trip to San Francisco, we decided to give in and try our luck at Whole Foods. This supermarket was conveniently located on El Camino Real, the main road between Mountain View, Los Altos and Palo Alto. We needed pretty much everything, which was a slight problem, as we knew from hearsay that Whole Foods was called 'Whole Paycheck' for a reason.

As soon as I entered the hallowed halls of this gorgeous behemoth of a supermarket, however, I knew there was no stopping me. What. A. Paradise. Of course, California's reputation in terms of health, fitness, organic food, etc. was well known, but to see so much *goodness* in one place was almost too much, even for me. So much variety! So much beauty! I almost wept when I saw a few items that I had only been able to buy in speciality shops or online in the UK. Here they were, invitingly presented in a mouthwatering way, on shelves or behind counters, begging you to reach out and buy, buy, buy. Everything looked more enticing, more healthy, more wholesome than anything you'd ever seen in your life. Purple cauliflower, giant avocados, live lobsters, expensive organic skincare, never-before-seen vegetables that looked so beautiful you wanted to grab them and cook them even though you had no idea how – in short, I felt delirious. The bill at the checkout counter brought us back down to earth, and we decided to save Whole Foods for special occasions from now on.

The next day, Scott had to go to work. This was America, after all. As soon as he'd kissed us goodbye, telling the girls to be good, and the door had closed behind him, the girls looked at me with glinting eyes. 'Can we go to Starbucks?' Laughing, I told them to get dressed and promised them they could choose whatever fancy concoction they desired, trying to start our life in America on the right foot.

After a few hours of exploring our surroundings, we headed back to our apartment to give the swimming pool a try, which the girls had discovered immediately upon our arrival the day before. I found it hard to relax, my head filled with a giant to-do list, and I begrudgingly accepted that we needed a second car as soon as possible. Without at least one car per driving family member, you couldn't survive in this country. Public transport, while available in and around San Francisco, only existed in a rudimentary way down here on the Peninsula; it wasn't going to work for a family of four. I realised very quickly that a huge portion of my day would be spent behind the wheel.

Buying or leasing a car in the US, however, wasn't an easy undertaking at all since we didn't have any credit history in this country. Nobody cared about our impeccable credit history in another. Anyone planning to live in the US needs to start building their credit history from the very beginning. It's recommended that you buy everything using your credit card and then pay it off the minute you get the bill in order to build up good credit fast. The fact that you can't get a credit card easily without an existing bank account is another matter. American logic. Luckily, Scott had been able to open a bank account on one of his previous visits; I'm not even sure how, but it definitely saved us during those first few days.

When he came home from work that first evening, he instantly sat down and scoured Craigslist, the infamous American bulletin board for local classifieds, where you can buy everything from garden furniture, records and drugs, to pets and cars. He found a car he could buy in cash, an old, beat-up black Audi that was covered in huge patches of what I learned was damage caused by the relentless California sun. Now, I didn't have an excuse anymore not to get behind the wheel. It was time for my American life to get real. If I wanted to get started on my to-do list, I needed to brave the outside world.

Scott gave me a thumbs up and drove off in his Audi, and I stood in the parking garage of our apartment building with a huge Chevy and two excited little people next to me. I was terrified. Silently cursing my husband's persuasive powers and my own impulsivity that had made me say yes to all of this, I took a deep breath, helped the kids clamber into the back seat and slipped into the driver's seat. I had never driven an automatic car before, let alone one where the gears were located on the steering wheel rather than the middle console. *At least I'm driving on the right side of the road*, I thought, gritted my teeth and hit the ignition button.

First Impressions

To secure a place at one of the highly coveted 10/10 Los Altos elementary schools, we needed to find a house within district boundaries. I wanted my children to be enrolled in school as soon as possible, as school meant making friends, and making friends was the only way to help them settle in and be happy, which in turn meant I would be happy too. The pressure was on; it was April, and school here ended in June, which meant we only had a few weeks left in the school year. The thought of enrolling them in another district and then changing again was out of the question, but homeschooling and waiting until August and the beginning of a new school year was equally unimaginable. A summer without friends? No, thank you.

Once we had a home address and school would begin for Amelie, we needed to think about Maya. Once school started for her older sister, Maya would be home alone with me for a lot of the time. She had gone to preschool on a daily basis in England and would have started 'big school' this coming autumn, but here in the US, she would have to spend another year at preschool. This was a bit of an issue. I had done thorough research as far as elementary schools were concerned, but finding a nice local preschool proved to be a huge and very expensive problem. It was pretty much impossible to find availability this late in the term, and any place that did have a spot for her was sadly unaffordable. I managed to look at a few places, but they were less than inspiring. My heart was aching when I thought of our small, lovely, welcoming and perfectly affordable preschool back in England.

Maya and Amelie had been really good little adventurers so far and seemed to actually enjoy each other's company rather than squabble over little things. Maya bounced up to me as I stood in the kitchen one morning, trying to decipher the alarming-sounding ingredients list on a cereal box, and announced: 'Mummy, Amelie and I are going to be best friends now, and not just sisters!' To demonstrate this new spirit, she ran off to grab her sister's hand, and they both danced a little ceremonial dance around me. I smiled at my beaming, almost-four-year-old. Spending so much time with her older sister, whom she adored so much, was a dream come true for this little love bug, and Amelie was indulging her a lot more than back home. I wasn't kidding myself, though; this was never going to last.

Maya's words made me contemplate my own situation. Similarly to the kids, Scott and I needed to add a new layer to our relationship; we needed to be more than just partners and parents. All we had in this strange new environment was each other; we were on equal terms and had to build new relationships from scratch, together as a couple and also separately. I hadn't had a huge circle of friends in the UK, but I did have my mum tribe, totally separate from my husband's friendships, which he'd built over a lifetime, and which I had automatically gained access to when we became a couple. They were still much more his friends, however, and while

I really liked most of them, I had relished building my own network.

'Will you be my friend?' I chirped, batting my eyelids, when Scott returned from work that night, and I told him what Maya and Amelie had decided. With a big grin, he pulled me into his arms. 'Good job I like you, Mrs Cook,' he laughed. 'Let's see if you can make us some decent friends here.'

I swallowed hard. My husband was the people-person, not me. It was one of his biggest strengths, something I noticed about him the very first time we met. He was excellent at meeting new people and making connections, and had a vast network of friends and work colleagues who ended up knowing each other, often even working together. A true gift. I always felt *recognised* by him, and like he was encouraging me to bring out my true self and my best qualities. Right now, he knew that I desperately needed to have a place I could call my own. A cocoon I could retreat to after being new all day; a place I could invite people over for coffee when I felt like company.

Scott took a day off to join our next house-hunting trip with another relocation agent. Starting our search at the lower end of our budget and working our way up, we realised very quickly that we needed to adjust our expectations. I had already googled enough places to know that a California swimming pool wasn't likely to be part of the equation, even though the girls hadn't given up hope yet. We saw depressing-looking houses that had clearly not even seen fresh paint, let alone new kitchen or bathroom fittings, since the 1960s, some with equally neglected swimming pools; houses that weren't even located in the right school district as well as remote places in the hills that were miles away from school and looked like they were haunted. Just as we were giving up hope, the agent turned onto Whitham Avenue, a leafy road that led up a slight hill, to view the last house of the day. Bingo.

It was slightly too big for our needs, but it was modernised, in the right neighbourhood and within cycling distance to one of the desirable Los Altos schools. Its style and furnishings were a different matter, reflecting a weirdly old-fashioned grandeur that seemed at odds with the relatively young age of its owners. In Europe, you'd expect a simpler yet more modern IKEA look in the home of thirty-somethings; the typical upper/middle-class American style was very different. Kind of more *grown-up*. Opulent heavy velvet curtains adorned the living room and bedrooms, imposing solid oak furniture added gravitas, the bathrooms were floor-to-ceiling marble, and a huge chandelier dazzled in the dining room – to sum it up, not at all to our taste, but with plenty of bedrooms and bathrooms for us and the many visitors we were expecting, a decent sized garden, a quiet street and beautiful surroundings. Of course, the rent they asked for was way above our budget, but we were exhausted, and I couldn't stand another day of uncertainty. We decided to cut our losses and signed the lease. After all, it was only for a couple of years, and we wanted to enjoy our time here in a nice place.

As soon as we'd decided on the house, spring break started, which meant we had another week to kill until Amelie's first day of school. The weather was a dream, just as we'd hoped California would be, and perfect for some initial excursions into our new world. At the top of the list was finding a new horse riding place for Amelie. This was a non-negotiable part of the moving experience; while I knew that living in this part of the world was a privilege that came at a price, I needed to ensure our children could continue doing what made them happy. Horses were what made

Amelie happy, and so I signed her up for some trial lessons at various stables nearby. We fell head over heels in love with Webb Ranch, nestled in the hills above Palo Alto, a reassuringly low-key and slightly dilapidated establishment. The spotless, competition-orientated stables we'd seen before, which felt like military-style academies, didn't appeal to us at all, but Webb Ranch reminded us of the small and welcoming stable we'd left behind in England. Amelie's beaming face after her first lesson with 'Dylan' was worth all the hassle and heartache of the past few months. Thank god for horses and horse-crazy kids the world over.

Amelie felt instantly at home, adored her warm and gentle riding instructor, Ronnie, and quickly bonded with a few other horse girls of various ages. The countryside up here was absolutely beautiful; a dirt road was flanked on both sides by wide open pastures set against a backdrop of mountains covered in evergreens, and gnarled blue oak trees provided shade for the herds of roaming horses, which looked extremely relaxed and well cared for. To make the day even better, when we got back to our apartment that afternoon, there was a welcome letter from a preschool for Maya, and not just any preschool, but the one right next to Amelie's elementary school. Oh, the relief! Everything was going to be okay.

We discovered Mountain View's weekly Farmers Market, with its piles of fresh produce, artisanal breads, spreads and delicacies on display, which you were even allowed to sample. Every Saturday morning, we felt like greedy, hungry caterpillars, munching our way through the buzzing market square. We knew instantly that California would ruin us and that we would never ever be able to eat strawberries, lemons and oranges from any other place again.

Even the supermarkets were impressive, although there was a clear quantity-over-quality bias going on. Until I had learned to navigate my way through the sheer amount of what was available, grocery shopping was going to take me hours. Why did Americans need to have so many choices? Utterly unnecessary and yet also quite wonderful once you knew your way around. I usually felt overwhelmed in a supermarket, preferring smaller shops to the giants. I even struggled at Starbucks, unable to choose between whole milk, 2%, 1%, non-fat, almond, oat, coconut or soy milk. We were told about another chain, Peet's, the original California coffee shop, which was founded in Berkeley in 1966 and had served as a template for Starbucks. If you were a Peet's patron, you wouldn't set foot in Starbucks and vice versa. I couldn't really see a big difference between the two, but of course, I learned pretty quickly to keep my mouth shut and not ruffle any feathers. When in Rome...

Like any self-respecting traveller in a new country, we were endlessly fascinated by grocery shopping. Everything was new and interesting, and during every shopping trip, I brought home things that we'd never heard of before, such as milk chocolate-covered potato chips, peanut butter-filled pretzel nuggets, chocolate-covered if desired, shaved ice, root beer, spray cheese, and corn dogs.

We enjoyed the wonderful sushi on offer as well as plenty of colourful, tasty Mexican dishes, and even found an Indian restaurant, so that we didn't have to give up our beloved Friday night curry, much to my English husband's relief. All that, and we didn't even have to head up to the city! San Francisco, of course, was known as foodie heaven, and we knew we'd never be able to sample all that was on offer in the two years we would be living here, even if we tried.

The cultural diversity of California wasn't only in its culinary offerings. This area was home to numerous international companies, attracting an equally diverse workforce. I knew from scouring the Internet that both Mountain View and Palo Alto were home to

German schools, and we even considered enrolling our girls at one of them to strengthen their language skills. The fact that we were planning to return to England put us off, but we went to visit the German International School of Silicon Valley (GISSV) in Mountain View nonetheless, just to hear some German voices and sign up for a library pass. I couldn't suppress a smile when I saw all the flyers on the noticeboard in the school office: a Swabian all-male choir, numerous adverts for local 'Oktoberfests', a Bavarian dance group called 'Almenrauschen' looking for members, and – hooray – ads for a German butcher and a German bakery. This place was clearly made for me! Of course, we had to investigate, and the girls filled a few shopping bags with their beloved Bavarian pretzels from 'Esther's German Bakery' on our way back home. The German lady at the checkout was so refreshingly hostile that I took an instant liking to her. I realised how much I had missed some good old European grumpiness over the last few weeks.

On some days, I had to stop myself from making a cynical remark when the omnipresent cheerfulness was annoying me. When I ordered my first Starbucks latte in San Francisco, for example, apologetically asking for almond milk, the barista gave me a huge grin and said, 'Sure, honey, I can make that happen for you!' and I just thought, *dear god, just make the damn coffee!* But it was early days, and I was fresh off the boat.

Of course, nobody had any reason to be miserable in this beautiful environment – sunshine galore, attractive, healthy-looking people and stunning scenery made it pretty unacceptable to show any displeasure. I had already noticed that the people here never joined in when you started complaining about things. Comments such as 'Isn't it grey today?' or 'Wow, gas prices have gone up!' usually just elicited confused smiles. What on earth did people do when they had a bad day?! For us hardened English or German people, the whole 'don't worry, be happy' state of mind could be pure torture. I was so used to a constant barrage of irony and making sure that you never said anything too exuberant or complimentary, and was struggling to find an appropriate way to interact here in the US. This was going to take some getting used to.

California is, without a doubt, a paradise for nature lovers. If you're prepared to ignore its inauspicious location right above tectonic plate activity, its extremely dry summers and fire danger, and the depressingly monotonous agricultural plains of the Central Valley, there's not much to dislike about this stunning part of the world.

We wanted to see it all: Lake Tahoe, Yosemite, Big Sur and Highway One, Napa Valley, the giant Redwood trees – our list was endless. We were ready to explore, knowing our days would soon get sucked up by the daily grind, children's sports events, birthday parties and other activities each weekend.

We ventured over to the coast, to Half Moon Bay, for our first weekend outing to meet Scott's colleague and his wife for dinner at the famous Sam's Chowder House. Even the drive up scenic I-280 and then across to the coast, cutting through the golden hills and lush green woodlands of the Santa Cruz mountains, was beautiful. This mountain range runs from the south around Salinas Valley all the way up to San Francisco and forms the border between the Pacific Coast and the San Francisco Bay. There are numerous hiking and biking trails, nature parks and vineyards along the way, and if you manage to venture up to the top on a clear day, you can glimpse the city of San Jose to the south, the Bay to the east, San Francisco to the north, and the Pacific Ocean to the west. Our first proper view of the ocean that day in Half Moon Bay took our breath away. It was a beautiful April evening, cool but sunny, and the kids, far from reverent silence, were screaming with delight and cartwheeling across the beach below while we watched the sun go down from the restaurant's patio, a glass of delicious chilled Californian Chardonnay in hand. I had to pinch myself; this was our new life.

For our second weekend – we were still in our apartment in Mountain View, after all, waiting for our belongings to arrive and the beginning of our lease – we decided to drive the five hours up to Lake Tahoe. Even though it was late in the season, it had recently snowed, and the kids thought it was hilarious that we were able to enjoy the mountains in bright sunshine while wearing t-shirts instead of our warm winter coats. Having grown up with a view of the Alps, being in Tahoe felt a little bit like home, and it really struck me how much I had missed being close to the mountains during all those years in the UK. Instead of simply enjoying the scenery, however, I felt overwhelmed by homesickness; I wasn't even sure which home it was that I missed. The newness of my surroundings and the enormity of what we had begun were hitting me hard. To counteract this, I posted a smiley family photo on Facebook and cried inside when I read comments such as 'You look so happy!', and 'Lucky you!' I felt so ashamed that my feelings couldn't match the outside.

Having crossed Tahoe off the list for now, we wanted to see more of the nearby coastline. We decided to give Santa Cruz a try. It was only a 45-minute drive away, and we had heard that there was a longboard competition happening – the perfect opportunity to get to know a town famed for its surfing credentials and several movies.

First, we checked out the famous Boardwalk, which looked just like in the *Lost Boys*, with all its decidedly knackered yet nostalgic rollercoasters and arcades. Then we drove past the very pretty harbour and its lighthouse until we got to the contest location, a place alluringly named 'Pleasure Point'. Apparently, there used to be a famous brothel in this location in the 19th century.

I am convinced that there are places on this planet that simply wait for you to visit, just to say: 'Well, there you are! What in the world took you so long?' Some voice was definitely whispering these words into my ears when I set foot on the cliff at Pleasure Point. It was love at first sight. I could finally feel a sense of ease. It was like the smell of neoprene, suntan lotion and jasmine lulled me into a feeling of total belonging and relaxation. All around us, there were long-haired girls in shorts and bikinis riding skateboards, little kids with bleached blond hair, gorgeously carved male and female bodies in wetsuits, older tanned guys, a little less sharp around the edges, but their shoulders still broad, eyes slightly reddened by the salt water and that very special surfer smile on their lips. We even saw a surfing dog. Add to that the absolutely breathtaking view of Monterey Bay, which sparkled and flickered from the rays of the afternoon sun, and I could feel how a big chunk of my heart was being wrenched out of my chest, soaring high up into the air with a delighted sigh and then plopping deep into the Pacific Ocean.

Time for School

O nce spring break was over, it was time to register for school, and after another week of bureaucracy, we were ready for the first day. Both kids were excited; Amelie was going to join Ms Mastropietro's second-grade class at Loyola Elementary and was already practicing her new teacher's quirky name, while Maya was going to spend two mornings a week at preschool, a pretty big change from her five days a week back home, but better than staying home with me and not meeting other children.

The first day was a full success. Even on our way to school, I couldn't help but be impressed by the many bike lanes, speed limits, zebra crossings with huge signs everywhere, crossing guards in fluorescent vests waving and smiling, and cars actually going slow. And then the absolute shocker: a drive-thru lane right in front of the school! How brilliant – and how lazy? – was that?! You could actually take your kid to school without having to get out of the car. All you needed to do was get in the line of slowly moving cars in the drive-thru lane and wait until you reached the drop-off zone, where somebody – usually a teacher or volunteer parent helper – opened the car door for your child to jump out. No need to find a parking space, and you could literally stay in your pyjamas after breakfast. Or, for the more career-oriented Silicon Valley dweller, you didn't have to interrupt your morning conference call in the car on your way to work. Of course, this option was incredibly popular, and so there was a long line of cars each morning snaking around the neighbouring streets. The smart ones obviously knew this and got in line at least half an hour early so they didn't have to wait so long, but I baulked at the idea of waiting in a car for that length of time, especially when it was hot and you had to keep the engine running for the necessary air-conditioning. I decided to keep the drive-thru lane strictly for emergencies. I was definitely too European for that kind of environmental ignorance, and would usually just park a few streets away and walk the rest of the way.

I dropped Amelie off at her new classroom, where a tall girl greeted us with a big smile, introduced herself and dragged Amelie along to meet a few other girls, while I watched her happy face disappear into the crowd. A blond woman stepped next to me and beamed: 'Welcome to Los Altos! You must be Amelie's mom! That was my daughter Alex just then, and I'm Amanda.' She explained that she was Classroom Mom for our class and, ignoring my questioning face, informed me, 'Just FYI, it's Teacher Appreciation Week this week!' I smiled a confused smile. What on earth did that mean? And what was a 'Classroom Mom'? Apparently, each class had a mother – or sometimes, more rarely, a father – who took on the role of volunteer liaison between teacher and parents, always up to date with everything, which explained why she already knew who we were. Classroom parents were elected right at the beginning of each school year, and, by the sound of it, were constantly busy organising things. A very popular role, and some classes even had to elect two Classroom Moms or Dads, because neither of them wanted to give up this prestigious position.

One of the roles was organising Teacher Appreciation Week. Every elementary school in the US – and sometimes even the middle and high schools, if you're lucky – dedicates a whole week towards the end of the school year to their teachers. It means that one day of that week, the kids bring their teacher flowers, another day, a poem or a painting, or maybe some cake, and the parents are on a constant rotation of providing breakfast, coffee, and lunch. The Classroom Mom ensures the whole thing runs smoothly, so the teacher doesn't have to be left without their favourite beverage from Starbucks or end up having to eat two lunches. What a concept! *Oh, to be a school teacher in America,* I thought, at that point still totally unaware of the atrociously low pay and general lack of support teachers in this country received. I also had no idea about the immensely generous Christmas and end-of-year presents that were expected in addition to Appreciation Week. And if a teacher was expecting a baby, it wasn't uncommon for the parents of her class to throw her a mini baby shower. I was floored. After another few minutes of chatting to my new friend, we realised that she lived just around the corner from our new house, and we would actually be neighbours. Bingo!

Next stop: preschool. Maya ran off as soon as she spied the pristine playroom where she was meeting her group teacher. I was relieved that she was so eager to start playing, as I had to take care of a mountain of bureaucracy. I almost fell off my chair when I saw the summary of the fees for the measly nine hours a week Maya would be spending here; it dawned on me that those nine hours I would be able to dedicate to my translation work wouldn't be enough. If I wanted to find something more lucrative, however, I would have to wait until my work permit came through, which

I'd been warned could take up to nine months. We'd just have to tighten our belts for a while. Goodbye, Starbucks and a new expat life of leisure.

After about three hours, during which I barely managed a supermarket run and a visit to the bank, it was time to pick Maya up. The same drive-thru process was applied at preschool, but the system was even more refined. I pulled up, wound down the passenger window and called out my child's name to the woman waiting at the curb, who promptly relayed this information via walkie-talkie to the group teacher inside, who then appeared with my child a few seconds later, opened the car door and ushered Maya inside. Then she gushed about how wonderful it had been to spend time with my absolutely delightful, clever and oh so polite daughter, and how she couldn't wait to see her again in a couple of days. She waved, and we drove off. The daughter in question smirked at me, tired but happy, and proceeded to tell me all about her new friends. Her group teacher had even put a handwritten note in her school bag, which told me in beautiful cursive handwriting – so much more elegant and flowery than German cursive letters – how much she loved having Maya in her group. Once I'd overcome my very British, cynical first reaction, I allowed myself to be blown away by the thoughtfulness.

It was a bit of a pain to have to make the car journey so many times a day, as we needed to get Amelie after a mere two hours, but we were going to move into our new house soon, and I was looking forward to being able to walk or cycle to school.

Two hours later, a beaming Amelie left her classroom clutching armfuls of welcome cards and what looked like intricate art projects. The teacher had obviously given Amelie's classmates a heads-up the previous week, and they had promptly spent the weekend making things for their new friend from England. I was really touched. What an unforgettable welcome!

Amelie unceremoniously dumped the bounty into my arms and sprinted off to the school playground to join some new acquaintances, her little sister hot on her heels, and I was left by myself, feeling a little lost.

'Well, now we all have friends except you, Mummy!' Amelie concluded half an hour later, when I rounded them up to go home. 'We need to get you some friends soon!' Point taken. They were right, of course, and I knew it was time for me to get proactive. I still felt like I hadn't really arrived yet, and the person doing school runs and trying to get ready for our new home was merely a robot, while the real me was cowering in the fetal position somewhere high above the Atlantic, too scared to come out of hiding. It had been a while since I'd had to make new friends, and the thought of venturing out with a beaming smile and introducing myself to new people made my introvert's heart constrict.

On her second day of school, Amelie was invited to a 'playdate'. A playdate usually happened after school, allowing the kids to do their homework together and then play before being picked up for dinner at home. I really liked that concept – in England, playing after school invariably meant feeding the child visitor, which never failed to stress me out, as I was terrible at coming up with universally approved dishes. Knowing I was safe from having to cook whenever we would return the favour, I delightedly swapped phone numbers, addresses and allergy advice with the other girl's mom. I was amazed at how quickly Amelie had become an expert at this.

When I picked her up, I was impressed by the family's house – it was modern, not too big, but with high ceilings, and was very tastefully decorated with stunning art on the walls. I felt all American when I started gushing about how much I liked the house, but the girl's mom laughingly dismissed my compliments: 'Oh no, this is only our little dive while we're waiting for our house to be finished.' I really couldn't see anything 'dive' about this place, but my years in England had obviously influenced my perception of size and style.

On the whole, our family felt very welcomed in our first few weeks of living in California. Had I feared to stick out as the obvious foreigners, I needn't have worried. A community of so many internationals, as was found here in Silicon Valley and the Bay Area overall, was an incredibly welcoming place for expats. Here, we were a very normal international family, one among thousands of others who experienced the same moments of fascination, bafflement and sometimes frustration we did. It seemed to me that most of the people who lived here loved being in such an international environment, whether they had grown up here or chosen to move here.

Our reception wasn't always that easy and welcoming, though. I had already felt surprised a couple of times when I experienced some sort of 'renters' discrimination'; some people instantly lost some of their enthusiasm when meeting us upon hearing that we were here only temporarily and were renting a place rather than being homeowners, or at least looking to be homeowners. While there were definite financial connotations – property in this part of the state was eye-wateringly expensive – there was another kind of bias. One of the moms at school told me she actively discouraged her children from making friends with 'temporary' kids, as they would leave again, and she didn't want to deal with all the heartache her own children might experience. Apparently, they had already had a few incidents like that – her kids were nine and five years old at the time – and she was simply done with all the pain that came with saying goodbye. She just shrugged and said she lost interest the minute she heard somebody was 'only' renting. I had never doubted our decision to choose a local school for our kids, but for the first time, I realised why expats preferred international schools over local ones. The shared experience of a transient life was clearly a plus.

Our New Home

F our weeks after our arrival, we learned that our container had almost reached San Francisco. A day later, however, we received a call from customs to inform us that it had been selected for a random check, which would result in a delay of another week or two; unfortunately, nobody could tell us exactly how many days this would be. The problem was that we had to move out of our apartment and into our new home in exactly three days. I was so desperate for a sense of 'arriving' in a home to get settled into, and the kids were eager to welcome their toys and clothes. This news didn't improve my mood in the slightest. But contracts were contracts, and so we borrowed a few air beds and sleeping bags from one of Scott's work colleagues, bought some new towels and kitchen utensils – to my relief, IKEA was only a 15-minute drive away – and we moved into our new home on Whitham Avenue as planned.

Thank goodness we had plenty of distractions. My mum arrived from Germany, her suitcase filled to the brim with Haribo gummy bears, German chocolates and her sleeves rolled up, ready to jump in and help us set up our home. Since there was nothing to help us with yet, we decided to make the most of our time together by being tourists. This was California, after all, and her very first time in the US. We drove along the coast, sat on the beach in Santa Cruz and admired the majestic redwood trees at Big Basin State Park, ate Clam Chowder at Fisherman's Wharf and explored San Francisco by cable car.

Maya's fourth birthday coincided with the arrival of our container, which meant that she didn't miss her friends at all as she was too busy reacquainting herself with her toys and happily set about finding homes for them in her beautiful new bedroom. It was a very surreal feeling watching the container being unloaded on our massive drive, and remembering how huge that very same steel box had looked only a couple of months ago in our narrow street in England. Opening everything and trying to decide where to put things felt like Christmas, but 287 boxes later, our enthusiasm was starting to wane. I worked obsessively, desperate to create some sense of home, and was grateful to have my mum there to make sure everybody was fed and watered.

Word must have got out that a container was being unloaded in the neighbourhood. We had already noticed how friendly and chatty the people who lived around us were, and a few days after moving in, we experienced our first slice of *Desperate Housewives*. The doorbell rang, and we excitedly raced down to our big front door and found a blond woman and a skinny girl about the same age as Amelie on the doorstep. With a big smile, the woman extended a hand and then a tray towards me, which smelled delicious and lemony. 'Welcome to the neighbourhood!' she exclaimed. We thanked her profusely for this amazing gift, but she just laughed. 'Oh, it's just a few lemon slices. And lemonade. We don't know what to do with all the lemons on our tree right now...' A lemon tree in the garden! How absolutely wonderful. I felt like I was in a movie. We exchanged some more information – where are you from, which of the neighbours are nice or not so nice, etc – and then she shrieked: 'Oh my god, your accent is sooo cute! You *must* meet my friend Gemma, she's English too.' I smiled politely, not being English at all, but so grateful for the contact, and promised to meet her friend and join her book club.

Of course, having my mum with us meant that Scott and I were able to go out, just the two of us, which we badly needed. Back in England, we were used to dropping the kids off with my in-laws on a regular basis. On Fridays, I would usually hop on a train to London and meet my husband for drinks and maybe a concert before heading back to enjoy a long lie-in on Saturday morning, feeling like the luckiest new parents in the world. Or rather, not like parents at all.

During those last few weeks in California, however, and actually also the last few months of planning and stressing about the move and our visas, we'd barely had time for a decent adult conversation, let alone one that didn't consist of arguing about how we were going to manage. A night out on the town sounded irresistible. San Francisco without the kids! We wanted to see a band, have a drink or two at a bar and just enjoy some grown-up time.

In our enthusiasm, we sprinted off like young horses after a long winter cooped up in their stalls, and committed the typical newbie faux pas: we neglected to bring our IDs with us. Neither of us had got our American driving licences yet, which meant that we were supposed to carry our passports with us – and who wanted to remember those bulky documents when they were desperate to leave the house?! Feeling more than a little stupid, we spent the whole night sipping Diet Cokes and water, as the barman just ignored our wrinkles and unmistakably older-than-21 physiques.

The next morning, I called the DMV, the Department of Motor Vehicles, and made an appointment for my driving test. As a foreigner in California, you're required to take both the theoretical and the practical driving test within 90 days of setting foot in the country. Whether you have had a clear European licence for the last 20 years doesn't make any difference. With a groan, I opened the *California Highway Code* and started studying the various rules and regulations of this state. I was fine with the theory, but the practical test caused me numerous sleepless nights. I had always suffered with terrible nerves when taking tests, and when I drove to my test – in my own car, my blemish-free European driving licence in my pocket – my hands were shaking so much that I worried they would run a drug test on me. Luckily, the driving instructor assigned to me was friendly and very happy to chat about German freeways and non-existent speed limits, and the twenty minutes passed pretty quickly and more or less flawlessly. I drove home as the proud owner of a California Driver's License.

We felt a bit lost when my mother left; now we were really on our own, in our new house, our new life. Showing my mum our new surroundings and playing tourist had been fun, and not real life at all. I had to be a grown-up now and deal with all those grown-up things that were waiting for me. I had to go out and talk to new people. It's daunting to be the new person somewhere, at any stage in life, especially for an introvert like myself. I knew I had to do it, but I felt so exhausted by the move and just wanted to head out to meet a friend for coffee, or go to the playground with my children, where I was guaranteed to bump into someone I knew. I missed my old life. I wasn't the only one; Amelie had a tough time too, even though she made new friends daily and always seemed so happy and cheerful on the outside. A perfect facade. I could hear her crying herself to sleep at night, and it broke my heart. 'What if the people in England forget about me?' she sobbed one night, and I promised to arrange more Skype calls and to make plans for the summer when we'd see our friends again. Maya, who'd been woken up by the tears, climbed into bed with her big sister and hugged her so hard that the snuggling turned into tickling, and the tears gave way to giggles before long. A fleeting success, but I knew it would take a while until we all felt more settled.

Luckily, our next visitors were about to arrive: my parents-in-law were coming to spend two weeks with us and inspect our new home and surroundings. This was a first for us. I was used to having my parents stay with us in England for a few days at a time, and sometimes even a week, but I had never hosted my in-laws. Having only just started his new job, Scott couldn't take any time off, which meant that it was down to me and the kids to play entertainers and present California in her most delightful way.

Of course, I needn't have worried: California delivered. The weather was beautiful, and the granddaughters deliriously happy to be able to hug their grandparents and show off their new home, school and neighbourhood. We had plenty of ideas and energy for excursions. We were unable to convince their sensitive English ears that the American accent was fun, but a trip to Napa wine country and lunch in the sun at the *Crow's Nest* restaurant in Santa Cruz won them over. I could see how California was sneakily chipping away at their preconceptions about the US.

Aha Moments

It was strange to hear everybody talk about the summer when it was only May, and it felt like we had only just started school. In England, it was half-term now, and the children still had school until the middle of July, so this new timetable took some getting used to. There were numerous end-of-year events in need of volunteer helpers, and I bravely signed up for Amelie's class's Hawaiian-themed party – the perfect opportunity to make friends. As it turned out, it was also the perfect opportunity to encounter a new species: American *Super Moms*.

In England, I had mostly held back when it came to helping out at school; it simply wasn't required of us parents to spend hours of our time volunteering, and it never went beyond a few reading sessions or baking a cake for a school sale. It was a very different story here.

The organiser of the event was a mom who didn't really fit into the Super Mom mould, which meant that the Hawaiian luau for the second graders was not planned with military precision. This did not go down well with some of the other mothers. Fascinated, I listened to a 20-minute discussion on whether the pasta salad should be placed right next to the chicken nuggets, and whether it was wise to open the cookies already or wait until the 'main course' had been consumed. One mother grabbed a pack of tortilla chips from my hands, just as I was emptying them into a big serving bowl, and then started pouring the chips back into the bag. 'We want the children to eat the real food first.' I was silently shaking my head at the description of chicken nuggets as real food, but managed to bite my tongue. Later, when the desserts came out, I watched in horror as another mother wrestled a melting mini ice cream cone from a little boy's hand and threw it in the trash, since apparently he had already had one, and it was 'unfair to give some kids second helpings'. I realised that some of these women had clearly been professional powerhouses at some point, used to precision organising and getting their way, who felt the need to demonstrate those abilities in their role as mothers.

After this exhausting day, my social batteries were completely drained. The effort of trying to navigate my new surroundings and hoping to connect with some of the local mums had taken every ounce of my energy. I felt like I had done well; I hadn't affronted anybody too much or upset any children with my 'Europeanness'. Yet I still felt very out of place, not sure what role to step into as a newcomer to California. I only knew that my life here would be very different. In England, I had just got to the point where my kids, at seven and four, were old enough to be more independent, going to school and preschool respectively; my in-laws were nearby and happy to help out, and I had a brilliant network of friends and other parents of kids of similar ages, which meant support was available in every way. After spending the last few years mainly as a stay-at-home mum, juggling family life and part-time work, I had reached a point where I needed to think about my career again, and whether I wanted to keep working the way I did, or take a new direction. I wasn't planning on changing things drastically, at least not until the kids were a bit older.

So while I didn't feel like I'd interrupted a brilliant career for this move to the US, I had hoped to pick up more or less where I left things back in England. I realised that there was no chance of that here, with these incredibly limited child-free hours and no family support. I had to start from scratch again.

To my surprise, this situation, which could have been incredibly unsettling, proved to be the opposite. I secretly felt immense relief about not having to throw myself into the world of employment in a new country, and I was grateful for the fact that my husband's new position meant I didn't have to contribute financially, at least for the time being. I loved being a homemaker, able to pick up my kids from school and spend time with them doing their homework or baking cookies, and exploring this new world together. The lack of financial freedom and sense of independence was another story, and I could hear the faint sound of alarm bells at the back of my mind, but I felt that it was a small price to pay considering what an incredible opportunity this was for us.

If I were perfectly honest, I had never truly loved my previous work in various London offices, but fell head over heels in love with motherhood as soon as Amelie arrived in our world eight years earlier. I had never considered myself a very maternal person or even someone who likes children – I loathed babysitting when I was a teenager and was so bad at it that nobody ever asked me back; I never felt the urge to hold someone's new baby, and the first nappy I ever changed was my own child's – but I fiercely adored my own children and felt a sense of purpose, serenity, and pride in what I was doing. For once, I felt like I was *good* at something. I had never really figured out what I wanted to do professionally;

everything I had studied or trained for felt more or less like something I should be doing, but not necessarily something that truly lit me up from inside. Until I became a mum. Sure, sometimes I missed being a professional person and the banter with work colleagues, but I always hated being in an office, and had no desire to go back to working in one unless absolutely necessary. I had always found it incredibly difficult to share space with others while working; glaring office lights and ongoing noises, such as phones ringing, loud conversations and the general hubbub of office life making it excruciatingly hard for me to concentrate on my tasks, and while I never missed a deadline, I often brought work home with me to complete in the calm of my own surroundings. Working from home as a freelancer was perfect for me. And now, with this American adventure, I was being given an extension to 'just' being a mother and housewife. I just wasn't sure if I was cut out to be a proper American elementary school mom. It scared me a bit.

Keeping everybody in the family involved in activities was a good start to feeling integrated. This being America, there were infinite options in terms of clubs, organisations and activities, but somehow, everything felt like one giant competition. It would take me ages to fight my way through this jungle and find out where and when to register for what league or class, which ones were a good option and which ones were best avoided, and, above all, how much it would all cost. Parents were required to not only spend an indecent amount of time being involved in their kids' school and social life, but also an even more indecent amount of money. It seemed like all parents, even the ones working full time, were constantly signed up for a volunteering gig at school, and everything, absolutely everything, was geared towards their offspring.

Because of the huge distances between home, school, sports clubs, etc., it was normal to spend what felt like years in your car, taking, waiting for and picking up kids. In an attempt to make some connections, I registered the girls for various activities and got used to always carrying an arsenal of entertainment for myself, such as books, my laptop, headphones and my knitting bag.

Standing in the school yard on a bright sunny day, right at the end of the school year, I realised how much more familiar my surroundings began to feel to me. It had only been two months since our arrival, but I already couldn't imagine life without the incessant buzz of the cicadas, the blue-tinged hills of the Santa Cruz mountains in the background, and the smiley faces of all those tanned Californian children around me. I was waiting to pick Amelie up from her art class, where they'd been painting a flowery landscape with real watercolours. I mentioned to the mother I was standing next to how lucky we were to be able to send our kids to school in California. She cocked her head as if to gauge whether I was being serious, and then just said, 'Oh, that's just because of all the rich people here. You should see the schools in east Palo Alto'. Then she proceeded to explain the secret of our wonderfully high-achieving school district to me.

All that equipment, the speciality teachers and classes other schools in California could only dream of, didn't just appear by magic or the taxpayers' money. Every family was encouraged to pay a hefty amount per child per school year. This was all voluntary, of course, and meant that our kids had the luxury of music, PE and art education, which would simply not exist without those donations. California had no budget for these luxuries, battling decades of debt stemming from outdated property tax laws, corruption and political inconsistencies. To imagine that one of the most creative powerhouses in the world couldn't pay for any music, art and sports at school came as a real shock. It started to dawn on me why there was such a never-ending array of fundraisers to entice parents and local businesses to donate money for our kids' education.

These fundraisers came in many different guises. Each school held an annual auction – essentially a lavish themed party for the parents, which was a shameless ploy to get us drunk and part with our hard-earned money, and during which we were asked to bid on tickets for even more themed parties, hosted by parents. Then there were 'bake sales' – usually student-led sales of more or less delicious creations – and, one of the favourites, an annual 'walkathon', where students walked or ran laps around the school's athletic field and collected money for each lap they completed from sponsors they had hounded during the weeks running up to the event. A wonderful way of supporting the community, but extremely exhausting for our wallets. Every year, the Los Altos School District determined a donation goal, and that intimidating number was proudly displayed in front of each school with the 'suggested' 'voluntary' contribution in small letters underneath. And then there was the district newsletter thanking all the donating families by name. If you weren't on the list, you had to brace yourself for 'The Call' from one of the volunteers taking part in the annual 'phonathon', cold calling all those families who hadn't donated yet.

Luckily, this was Silicon Valley, and there was always some anonymous donor who pledged to match, double or even triple the amount of whatever the parents managed to accumulate. New sports equipment, music and dance instructors, landscaping of the school grounds and an iPad for every student – all courtesy of this wonderful, blessed bubble.

After all, living in such a special, privileged part of the world, one of the wealthiest areas of the United States, came at a price.

It just took us a while to adjust to the massive difference in price range when it came to those generous donations. $100 teachers' presents at Christmas and again at the end of the year were no rarity, which was baffling to our European mindsets. However, after all those culture shocks, which could easily be sneered at as showy-offy gestures and detachment from reality, we came to realise how generous and self-aware most people here actually were, fully acknowledging their privilege and committed to doing their part for the community and sharing their wealth in a much more philanthropic way.

Generosity, community spirit, and the willingness to take action to improve things rather than wait for the state to lend a hand, were such a vital part of the American mentality anyway, and we realised how vastly different our own European socialisation had been. Our tendency to complain at the slightest irregularity made us look extremely grumpy and entitled, and I felt a profound sense of shame on numerous occasions.

Maybe this willingness to step up and take matters into your own hands is part of the original American pioneer spirit – forefathers who had no choice but to get things done on their own accord, with their own hard work. It is precisely this spirit that still attracts so many people to this country even in today's highly controversial and polarised climate. The *American Dream*, at least in theory. Even young Americans exhibit a huge readiness for hard work, and the workload expected of kids, both young and older, is intense, not just for school but also for extracurricular activities.

Getting up at 5 am every weekday to go to swim training, followed by school, followed by a volunteering slot at an animal shelter, followed by soccer practice, plus band or piano lessons, before spending at least two but more often four hours on homework, is expected and supported by the whole family, who will then split their time on the weekend attending various games or performances. As an average European with a 40-hour work week, you might be aghast and shake your head at this routine, but asking an American when they have time to just sit and relax usually results in a shrug or questioning look.

Summer Back Home

F inally, the last day of school arrived. With the long summer
holidays ahead of us, we were looking forward to spending a
few weeks in England and Germany, but when the time came to
pack our bags, doubts crept in. We had booked these flights back
in March without thinking about how it would feel to disrupt our
new flow so soon after moving. Would it be too emotionally drain-
ing to see friends and family, too painful to say goodbye again? Of
course, we were very excited to catch up with everybody, tell them
all our stories and recover from the stress of moving in the company of the people we had missed for the last three months. So
much had happened; it felt much longer than that.

I tried to quench my tendency to worry and overthink things
and to look at it from a practical point of view: we had ten weeks
off school, without any summer camps booked since we had arrived so late in the year, and we desperately needed something to
do. Plus, we probably wouldn't see our friends again until next
summer.

As I watched the English countryside roll by from the window
of our taxi, tired and disorientated after the eleven-hour flight

from San Francisco to London, I marvelled at how familiar and yet how different everything looked. My eyes had adjusted to the technicolour skies of California, and England looked decidedly more pastel-toned. The familiar shapes and textures of the Kent countryside felt almost soothing to me, and I surrendered to this strange mix of nostalgia and foreignness. We enjoyed every minute of our stay; it felt like we'd earned our break from being the new person all the time. The one thing that really baffled us was how much we noticed the differences in behaviour, as well as the general grumpiness, both in England and Germany. Things that had always been normal parts of our daily lives now seemed incongruous, from the outrageous amount of 'sorrys' and 'pleases' and 'would you minds' to the much less glamourous TV presenters and gruff airport staff. And our kids with their healthy Californian tans and their light brown hair now streaked with natural highlights looked amazingly out of place next to their pale English friends.

Heading to Germany after consuming indecent amounts of baked beans, Cadbury's chocolate and Marmite sandwiches, as well as gallons of tea and Pimms, felt much more normal; after all, this had been our usual routine each summer since the girls were born. Whether we arrived from America or England didn't make much difference here. In contrast to our time in England, where we spent hours showing photos and confirming or refuting clichés about Americans – yes, *everything is bigger*, no, *they aren't much louder than the people here* – our weeks in Germany were more like a holiday where we did what we always did: swim in the lake, eat Spaghetti ice cream and sit in beer gardens.

I wasn't sure if it was harder to say goodbye this time or easier. Easier because we knew what to expect at the other end; we knew we had already mastered the initial difficulties, such as bureaucracy and starting school, and we had a ton of plans and were returning to a place and people that were now familiar. But it was also harder because we knew it would be a whole year until we'd see our English and German homes again. So much happens in the course of a year, especially in the life of young children, and by the time we'd see everybody again, the girls would have been more and more integrated into their American lives and moved further away from their English mentalities. Somehow, it felt as though the first three months in California had been a trial period for us. Now it was time to get real.

Fall in NorCal

School started again at the end of August, and we quickly fell into our new routines. Maya started at a new preschool, which was more down-to-earth, flexible, and also less expensive than the first one, meaning we could increase her mornings to three. She loved her new teachers and made new friends immediately, clearly capable of handling yet another new environment. I needn't have worried.

Amelie was now eight, a third grader and, apart from her still very British pronunciation, acted like she'd never been anywhere but an American school. I still hadn't received my work permit, but I managed to find some freelance writing work through a previous employer in England. Things were slowly falling into place.

Summer seamlessly turned into autumn, or rather *fall*, which wasn't really noticeable down on the Peninsula. San Francisco was another matter. Maya and I decided to have a mother-daughter day and hopped on the Caltrain that took us from Mountain View right into 'the City'. We learned that you weren't allowed to call it anything else, and I made an effort to unlearn saying 'San Fran', the version preferred by British people. We wanted to see the sharks at the Aquarium of the Bay and the seals at Fisherman's Wharf, and since it was early September, I was expecting less fog and warmer temperatures than in July.

Since the weather on the Peninsula had been unexpectedly hot over the last few days, the San Francisco fog, however, hadn't shifted, much to our despair. It felt like we were time travellers: we boarded the train in flip-flops and only a light sweatshirt, but even during our journey up, we started to regret our choice of clothing. The train dived into a wall of fog, and when we debarked at the Caltrain station in San Francisco, the fog had lifted a bit, but it was definitely autumn, and everybody around us was wearing boots and coats. We shivered like complete idiots in our summer outfits, and I realised why you always saw so many people wearing San Francisco hoodies – they were all bought at Fisherman's Wharf, where the shop owners could spot a freezing tourist at a mile's distance.

We were told that there was no better place to be than northern California in September and October, and so far, we agreed wholeheartedly. My parents were due to visit, and I was excited to show off our new surroundings in such perfect weather conditions. We decided to venture further and headed to Yosemite National Park, which was high on our list of places to see. This park was one of the very first National Parks in the United States; in 1864, while the Civil War was still raging on, President Abraham Lincoln found time to sign a bill granting Yosemite Valley and the Mariposa Grove of Big Trees to the State of California 'upon the express condition that the premises shall be held for public use, resort, and recreation, and shall be inalienable for all time'. In 1890, it officially became part of the National Park system, my favourite institution in the United States.

Yosemite was breathtaking. Of course, we had seen documentaries and countless pictures by Ansel Adams, but I had always been slightly dismissive when people told us how spectacular it was; after all, I had grown up near the Alps and wasn't sure anything could rival their scenic beauty. But when we drove along the winding roads through gently swaying fields and colourful woodlands in bright sunshine, with an azure blue sky and dramatic cloud formations adding some special touches, we all fell silent, awed by the incredible beauty surrounding us. Even the kids, who usually had their noses deep inside a book or whatever device they were allowed to handle, stopped what they were doing, their faces incredulous and legs itching to run around and climb onto whatever rocks they were able to scale when we took breaks.

On our second day, we celebrated my dad's birthday, and our festive picnic on a pebble beach right next to a picturesque creek in the middle of Yosemite Valley, with the dramatic rockface of El Capitan in the background, is one of my most cherished memories of all time.

That afternoon, the sky turned black and the most almighty thunderstorm came down on us, lightning dividing the sky like giant sabres and thunder reverberating from the massive granite rocks around us. Time to leave the park, for now. We promised ourselves to come back soon, maybe in springtime, to enjoy the park when the wildflowers were out and the waterfalls full of snowmelt. We had discovered a new favourite.

Halloween

If it hadn't been for the pumpkins, we probably wouldn't even have noticed that autumn had arrived. We were still enjoying summer temperatures, while our jackets and boots were gathering dust in their still unopened boxes in the garage. It was blissful. Until the pumpkins took over.

As if the golden California sun wasn't enough, the landscape was transformed into a sea of orange and yellow, and vast stretches of farmland were turned into pumpkin patches. I had never seen so many differently shaped and sized gourds in my life.

Whole weekends were spent exploring pumpkin patches and posing for family photos amidst the yellow and orange globes. Of course, we joined in. We picked a local patch, just around the corner from Amelie's riding stables, and enthusiastically grabbed a wheelbarrow from a friendly volunteer who was dressed like a scarecrow and posed next to some neatly stacked hay bales. The kids ran off, choosing a variety of pumpkins, until Scott wandered over to the checkout line to enquire about the price of one of those beauties, and we promptly upended our load back into the field. To appease the disappointed girls, we stopped at Safeway on the way back and bought a whole assortment of pumpkins for a fraction of the price, although I felt horrendously guilty for not behaving in a Californian, politically or organically correct way.

Everything here had to be organic, fair trade, locally grown, supporting the community – yes, those were the buzzwords of the white upper-middle class. Though this was true worldwide, it had never seemed so extreme and so competitive as here in California. Healthy food was everything in this state, which wasn't surprising, given that everything you could possibly dream of could be grown here.

Our pumpkins, albeit not organic, looked the part, and we even invested in a fancy carving set to turn them into grisly artworks. After proudly displaying them outside our front door, however, we discovered that the squirrels were equally appreciative of our art, but more in a culinary sense, and our carefully carved grimaces kept getting increasingly deformed by the rodents. A mother at school suggested drizzling chilli sauce on the cut surfaces in order to keep them at bay, and I instantly followed her advice. I should mention at this point that while I adore the dainty, elf-like squirrels in Europe, my feelings about their larger grey cousins on this side of the pond are more complicated.

The next morning, about to leave the house, we were alarmed to hear hair-raising retching and gagging noises from above. One of those grey tree rats was perched on a branch right above our front door, doubled over in pain and clearly trying to throw up whatever piece of pumpkin he had swallowed. Amelie instantly started sobbing, and I could barely stop the kids from pummeling me to death and accusing me of animal cruelty.

Finally, it was Halloween. We were beyond excited for this event, knowing from numerous American movies what a big deal this very special day was. Even in the UK and in Germany, it had become normal to spend the last day of October celebrating the undead, dressing up in gruesome costumes and going Trick-or-Treating. But we knew that nothing would beat a real American Halloween. We were so ready for this.

Halloween decorations had been on display since early September. Witches and ghosts were dangling from windows and trees, and some houses were covered in huge spiderwebs, while giant inflatable black cats and skeletons lurked on rooftops or on top of trees. Maya, a devilish glint in her eyes, was in her element and cackled like a witch at every opportunity. She had prepared a total of four different costumes, including make-up and accessories, for Halloween week. There was a Halloween Parade at her preschool, another at Amelie's school, a party at a school friend's house, the actual night of trick-or-treating and a party at one of our neighbours' houses. Christmas clearly had nothing on Halloween.

In the middle of October, we received our official Halloween guidelines from school. Here in California, the most litigious state, everything had to be spelt out explicitly, so that nobody should get so scared by their neighbour's grisly decorations that they would fall and break a bone and then take the neighbour to court.

Scott and I had a good giggle about the over-the-topness of the list, which, amongst other things, reminded us parents to make sure to remove our children from the scene if they got too scared, to make sure to have them wear thermal underwear in case their costume was made from thin material and it was a chilly night, and to pack extra hats, gloves and socks, which you should put at the bottom of their trick-or-treat bag, in case you were wondering where to place them.

This wasn't even the whole list. Of course, it was absolutely forbidden to wear anything gruesome for the school parade. The newsletter explicitly asked for 'age appropriate attire', with no violent themes, no excessive blood or gore, and no weapons – basically, nothing that would be scary to a child in any way. We were baffled. Wasn't this the whole point of Halloween?

That year, Halloween was celebrated for a total of three days, because the actual holiday fell on a Sunday. Friday's festivities were relatively relaxed. First came Maya's preschool Halloween parade, which lasted a total of ten unspectacular minutes. Once I'd sung the required songs and howled like a witch with my little daredevil, we raced over to Loyola Elementary so we wouldn't miss their clearly more impressive parade. And what a spectacle it was. Halloween is to Americans what carnival is in other cultures, such as *Karneval* or *Fasching* in Germany. It seems that we humans just have an innate desire to dress up, regardless of age or occasion. But where a European Halloween was strictly adhering to blood, gore and general scariness, American Halloween was a different story. I shouldn't even have bothered to come up with gruesome but guideline-conforming Halloween costumes. Wherever I looked, I saw princesses, sphinxes, Teletubbies, cowboys, pirates – of course, without a toy rifle or knife in sight – and hardly any witches or vampires. Some parents had obviously spent considerable time, effort and money to create outrageously good costumes. One child was dressed as a helicopter, complete with cardboard rotor blades, and another was a catamaran, including a billowing spinnaker. Maya was wearing costume number one, a purple and black witch outfit with long black hair, and Amelie was dressed – extremely creatively, I thought – as a headless horseman, wearing her riding boots and a denim jacket buttoned up on top of her head, with a red scarf aka blood squirting from the neck opening. Needless to say, none of her friends, dressed as Cleopatra, a glitter fairy and a baseball star, could guess her costume.

On Saturday, it was time for our neighbourhood Halloween party, a few doors down from our house. I had bought a special mould in the shape of a brain and made a truly gruesome-looking green jelly, adding a few plastic spiders on top for effect. On a trip to *Party City*, a giant costume supermarket, the kids and I stocked up on make-up and accessories, and we spent the whole afternoon turning ourselves into witches and ghouls. Scott, who had just returned from a business trip to London, didn't really need a ton of make-up to look like a zombie, but we added a few special touches for extra effect. He refused point-blank to wear a costume, which only highlighted the contrast between his blotchy, greenish-white face, blood-splattered cheeks and his usual jeans and T-shirt combo. The girls and I were all wearing crazy wigs and could hardly contain our excitement. We hadn't really met many of the neighbours yet and were very keen to make a good impression.

Within a few seconds of arriving, we realised our mistake. Nobody, apart from the children, was wearing a costume. One woman wore a blue wig, another one a T-shirt bearing the slogan 'this is my Halloween costume', and someone else sported vampire fangs. We were clearly and embarrassingly overdressed. The sight of my zombie husband making small talk with his new and decidedly not made-up neighbours still haunts me to this day. Luckily, there was plenty of delicious California wine to take the edge off our faux pas.

By the time Sunday night, actual Halloween, rolled around, I was utterly exhausted. But buoyed by the unwavering enthusiasm of my children, I pulled my wig over my hair for a final time and set out to accompany them on their trick-or-treating quest for candy.

The kids decided that they had had a great Halloween and tumbled into bed exhausted and with massive, chocolate-smeared grins.

Luckily, I wasn't a fan of the typical American Halloween candy and wasn't even tempted to steal their bounty; instead, I poured myself another glass of Russian River Chardonnay and sent a silent prayer to the vampires and ghosts, grateful that this was over.

Of course, we learned how to 'do Halloween' properly over the years: by finding the best neighbourhoods for trick-or-treating, and then leaving the kids to roam with their friends while we gathered on some other parents' patio or front porch for a glass of wine.

The Holidays

As soon as the last skeleton was stuffed back into the closet, it was time for 'the Holidays': Thanksgiving at the end of November, followed by Christmas and New Year. We couldn't wait for our first festive trilogy.

Wreaths made of autumn leaves, inflatable turkeys and a palette of reds, oranges and browns replaced the ghouls of the previous weeks, and we started to feel excited about our first 'Christmas without religion and presents', as Thanksgiving had been described to us. We were told it was *the* big family day, more so than Christmas, when the whole family gets together, which means that the whole of the US comes to a standstill. Unless you work in retail, of course, in which case you have to brace yourself for the craziest day of them all – Black Friday, the day after Thanksgiving, which counterbalances any of the 'we don't do presents' restraint.

Our school district gave the kids the whole week off school, which was badly needed, since they hadn't had a single day off since Labor Day back in early September. We decided to make the most of our week off to drive up to see a friend in Portland, Oregon, our first road trip to another state.

After the never-ending sunshine of the Californian summer and fall, we were ready for some rain and cold, which we deemed much more appropriate for this time of year. We crammed our snow jackets and boots in the car and set off on our twelve-hour drive north. Since it was raining relentlessly, we opted for the less scenic and slightly quicker inland route; I was disappointed because I really wanted to see the stunning Oregon coastline, but had to accept that this wasn't the best time to do that.

We started Thanksgiving by watching the Macy's Thanksgiving Day Parade in New York on TV. I had thought that the Brits were pretty impressive when it came to parades, but this American extravaganza with giant inflatable turkeys, never-ending bands and elaborately decorated wagons, so-called 'floats' was spectacular on a whole other level. Our turkey dinner was equally impressive, and our hosts clearly decided to give us 'all the trimmings', with buttery mashed potatoes, baked yams with marshmallows, green bean casserole and more. And of course, the most famous dessert of all time: pumpkin pie, a mix of delicious crumbly crust and slimy, mushy brown mousse. I'm not a fan of pumpkin and pumpkin spice at the best of times, and was supremely grateful for the pecan pie alternative. The kids didn't care; they tried everything with gusto.

Despite the below-freezing temperatures and persistent rain, we explored Portland as best we could, which made up a little bit for having missed out on the state's coastline. I fell in love with this city immediately. Full of small, local shops, a very laid back artsy vibe, plus tons of green spaces and excellent food – Portland was very much my vibe. We wandered around shops, hiked through the enchanted greenery of Forest Park in sub-zero temperatures, drank beer at local craft breweries and enjoyed the much more wintery and definitely more Christmassy feel of the Pacific Northwest before heading south again.

Christmas was getting closer, and I started to worry about pretty much everything. How would it be for us to celebrate this holiday without our families? I was already aware of the fact that a lot of expats experience an extra dose of nostalgia and patriotism for the places they've left behind, especially at this time of year, but I was still surprised how much it affected me. Somehow, Christmas time added another layer to this nostalgia. The consequence: a major bout of homesickness.

One of the most significant contributors to homesickness was the gruesome time difference: Germany is nine hours ahead of California, and England eight. We practically lived our lives in exactly the opposite order to our friends and family back in Europe. This meant no more spontaneous phone calls. We tried to set up regular Skype sessions, but it took a long time until we were able to establish the perfect time slots for these events. It was almost impossible to talk to anybody during the week. When the kids came home from school at three in the afternoon, it was midnight in Germany, but mornings were out of the question. Anybody who has ever tried to have a sensible conversation between breakfast battles, cleaning teeth and making lunches knows what I mean. Which left the weekend, although that was tricky too, as we could either talk to Europe early in the morning when it was afternoon for them and meant that they were usually out and about, or we could wait until it was evening over there, which interfered with our own day, since we loved exploring our surroundings, and the kids often had birthday parties or sports events to attend.

If I felt like picking up the phone after an exhausting day during the week, in desperate need of some kind words or just a good old rant with a friend or my sister, tough luck. They were all fast asleep. Of course, I could stay up until midnight to catch them when they got up in the morning, but that usually meant that while I had been drowning my sorrows in wine, they'd be sipping their morning coffee and getting ready for their day, unable to empathise very well. And vice versa: it wasn't easy to have important conversations with our parents, for example, as by the time we got hold of them mid-morning our time, it was evening over there, and they were in the middle of dinner or watching TV, more often than not already halfway down a bottle of wine themselves, and consequently not very receptive to our woes.

If there was one good thing about the time difference and the subsequent lack of communication with old friends, it was the fact that it forced us to go out and make an effort to meet people instead of weeping on the phone. For someone like me, who wasn't naturally extraverted and gregarious, this was very daunting, but I discovered that having kids was a marvellous tool. I made an effort to talk to other parents in the playground, accepted each and every invitation, kept signing up as a volunteer helper at school events, and always, *always* made sure to plaster a big smile on my face, indicating an outgoing, interesting personality. That way, I made a lot of connections early on, which meant I never had to be really lonely, at least not during the day. I usually crumbled with exhaustion in the evenings, having spent every ounce of energy on relationship-building, but at least I could pretend that I was making friends. For my husband, things were a bit different. At first, I felt jealous of him heading off to work, where he was surrounded by people all day. But when I berated him for having an easier time meeting people because he was able to mingle at work, he just looked at me dejectedly and pointed out that it was actually much easier for me, as I had time to turn my acquaintances into friends.

He missed the English pub culture, where it was normal to go out for a pint after work, especially on a Friday; this concept didn't seem to exist here, and if you wanted to get to know your colleagues outside of a work environment, you had to be extra crafty. He also missed his friends; this was a new situation for him, whereas I was used to always missing people, having left my home country and my oldest friends over a decade ago, and knew the feeling only too well.

We somehow experienced more homesickness during winter than during summer, for which I blame the temperature. I have never felt as cold as I felt in our first house during our first winter in California. This state was simply not made for the cold. In my clearly homesick mind, I craved the familiar: I wanted cold outside temperatures and cosy inside temperatures, but I got neither. With the outside temperature actually higher than inside our badly insulated house, I couldn't get warm at all, in spite of wearing warm clothes, thermal socks and sometimes even a woolly hat. I tried to spend as much time as possible during the day away from home, which didn't really help my sense of pre-Christmas festiveness. Starbucks, with its relentless combination of *Jingle Bells*, *Rudolph the Red-Nosed Reindeer* and Eggnog Latte, didn't provide the cosiness I craved.

In an attempt to overcome my grinch-like mood, we baked *Plätzchen*, German Christmas cookies, put up our first American Christmas tree, and ventured out to the German school's Christmas Market in Mountain View. This didn't enhance my mood either; the weather was too California nice, and they didn't sell any

Glühwein, only non-alcoholic, overly sweet punch. I found something to complain about in absolutely everything. Luckily, Trader Joe's carried *Glühweingewürz*, a special spice blend to mull your own wine, because in my sullen mood, I had decided it simply wasn't Advent without this festive beverage. I even missed all the obnoxious nativity scenes and nativity school plays I was so used to from England and Germany, because there were no nativity scenes or other Christian displays to be seen in this very politically and religiously correct part of the country. I realised my hypocrisy: I wasn't religious at all, and yet, like a petulant child, I craved the Advent and Christmas elements I had grown up with.

I had to accept that I wasn't going to get a European Christmas; here, Christmas seemed more like an afterthought, once Halloween and Thanksgiving had sucked up all the attention and energy for big celebrations. I told myself that a small, relaxing Christmas, with just the four of us, was probably the best thing anyway, after the turmoil of the last few months. It was hard to believe that just a year earlier, we had been sitting on our packed bags waiting for our visas to be granted.

In the end, Christmas and New Year came and went exactly like that, in an unspectacular and quiet manner. It rained the entire time, and we didn't even venture out for drinks with the neighbours, who'd kindly invited us over. I was amazed to find that it was indeed what I, and in fact the whole family, needed. It had been such a busy and exhausting year, and we really needed some downtime to reflect on these adventurous last few months.

Earthquake

J ust as I was wading through the quagmire of my Christmas
blues, wallowing in self-pity and painting my toenails a festive
red to cheer myself up, it happened. A loud rumble, just like a massive truck or train was driving past, followed by shuddering and
shaking that lasted for a good fifteen seconds *Clink*, a little orna-
ment fell off the Christmas tree. Our first earthquake.

It wasn't a very strong one, 4.8 on the Richter scale, not
even mentionable by California standards, but it was very discon-
certing nonetheless, with its epicentre just around the corner, and
a definite indicator of what a bigger one would feel like. A quick
survey of the scene revealed that there was no damage. Scott, who
had been on a Skype call with his parents when the quake hit, said
the walls warped in and out like a ghostly optical illusion, but luckily, I didn't see it myself, since I was bent over my toes. The quake
made me jerk my hand, and I spilled some polish, which I now had
to scrape off the marble floor. It made me question anyone's desire
to undergo surgery in California.

Of course, I knew that all the major buildings, especially the high-rises in the city, as well as hospitals and schools, were earthquake-proof and could withstand even bigger shaking of the ground. High-rise buildings are built to be able to sway up to two metres to each side, and some buildings are put on giant rolling systems, which means they don't sway but rather roll from side to side to avoid any shaking. This is called 'seismic retrofitting', making older buildings structurally sound by adding special features, and there are numerous other technologies depending on the type of structure. None of this alleviated my fears.

In fact, earthquakes were the first red flag for me when we were thinking about moving to California. San Francisco has obviously been the victim of more than just one earthquake, and is sitting right on the infamous San Andreas Fault. I extensively 're-searched' earthquakes by watching videos on YouTube, scaring myself to death with footage from the Loma Prieta quake of 1989, with its epicentre just north of Santa Cruz, which was incredibly close to where we lived now. I was absolutely convinced that California was just waiting for our family to disembark the plane in order to roll out the 'Big One', which had been predicted for years. In an attempt to be ready, one of the first things I did after our arrival was to prepare an emergency survival kit for the whole family, which consisted of a backpack filled with emergency clothing as well as flashlights, batteries, tins of food and a first-aid kit. I also placed a pair of shoes and a flashlight underneath each bed, so that we would be able to see and walk across broken glass in case a quake struck in the middle of the night and the power went out. I tucked the emergency backpack into the boot of my car, which I also made sure always had a full tank for a quick getaway, and which I also vowed never to park inside our massive garage, but outside the house. Our garage was located right underneath our generously sized kitchen and living area, and I'd decided that this part of the house would clearly collapse during an earthquake and bury our escape vehicle. I recognised an old phobia of mine that I'd always been able to suppress: ever since I can remember, I've had an irrational fear of the ceiling caving in or the floor collapsing when a room is 'too big'. I need to see some structural support, whether that's a wall or a beam supporting the ceiling, otherwise I panic. The large garage located on the ground floor had no such supporting pillars. Of course, I couldn't share this with anyone; phobias don't make sense, and I had always been too ashamed to talk about mine. I have left concert venues before where I had to stand underneath a massive balcony, for example, and I've missed the plot of a theatre production because my seat was up on the balcony, and all I could focus on was that I wasn't safe. It's not an easy thing to admit, and explaining, 'hey, I need to stand somewhere else because I'm afraid the ceiling is going to crash down on us', doesn't exactly make you appear sane.

My poor, overthinking mind flew into overdrive. Often, I would get up in the middle of the night and check under each family member's bed that all the flashlights and shoes were in place. I was also replacing every single glass picture frame with lightweight plastic frames to avoid glass breakage wherever possible, even though we hadn't even hung any pictures, as our landlords didn't allow us to put holes in the walls.

The bottom line was this: I intended to be as ready and prepared as I could be and wanted to avoid any possible pitfalls. In an attempt to calm my nerves, I also attended an educational emergency preparedness course, which was offered for free by the local council and run by the local fire department. What I learned, however, only confirmed my deepest fears. There was no doubt that the Big One was about to happen. All I could do was be ready.

The kids were dealing with all this in a much more relaxed and definitely more Californian manner. Every few months, there was an earthquake drill at school, where they learned what to do in case of such an emergency. Our kids were very well-prepared and extremely happy to share their knowledge with us, demonstrating how to drop and roll underneath a table and what an emergency family plan should look like.

The Californians in our vicinity didn't seem to be ruffled by this constant threat in the slightest. One of the neighbours casually mentioned that there was a fault line just about 30 metres from our house, and that in case of the anticipated megaquake, the whole West Coast was going to be submerged under water anyway, so there was no need to stress about elaborate emergency kits or any such thing. Needless to say, none of this made me feel any calmer.

Divided by a Common Language

January arrived with blazing sunshine. While our friends back in Europe were still drowning in grey doom and gloom, we headed to the coast. Sitting at Lighthouse Beach in Santa Cruz, my bare toes drawing patterns into the fine golden sand, I marvelled at what we had accomplished over the last twelve months. We definitely felt closer as a family; without the gruelling commute he had had to endure during his work week in England, Scott was able to spend a lot more time with the kids. He was a lot happier and more relaxed, and our weekends became opportunities to be active and explore our surroundings, rather than needed to recover from a stressful week. We had also learned a multitude of new skills; it boggled my mind that there were so many things we hadn't know, just nine months earlier.

One example was the language. Language is always the key to a culture, and American English was no exception, even though it wasn't a totally new language for us, at least on paper. Having studied English, I thought I had a pretty good understanding of the differences between British and American English, but in truth, I had barely scratched the surface. One of the two Irish writers – sources disagree whether it was George Bernard Shaw or Oscar Wilde – was definitely on to something when he claimed that England and America were two countries divided by a common language.

We embraced the Americanisation process somewhat half-heartedly, forcing ourselves to use American versions of words in public, such as 'vacation' instead of 'holiday', 'restroom' or 'bath-room' instead of 'loo' or 'toilet', or 'trash' instead of 'rubbish'. We learned that an 'entree' is not the starter, but the main dish, and that cheese is served as an appetiser and not as a course after or in-stead of dessert.

The kids were frightfully good at their American accents, al-though they tended to use them just for fun, and usually stuck to their familiar British pronunciation. Often, this led to misunder-standings, as some words were pronounced very differently. One day, Amelie slumped in the car after school with a big frown on her face, furious because the teacher had deducted points from her test for spelling 'colour' with a 'u', rather than 'color', and for not rhyming 'vase' with 'case'.

Maya, who started her new preschool with so much enthusiasm, grew quieter and quieter during her first couple of weeks. When I asked her what was wrong, she sighed and told me that she wasn't invited to any of the parties that the other kids seemed to be hav-ing every day. 'What do you mean, they're having parties?' I asked her, frowning. 'They always tell the teacher to go party!' she ex-plained, bottom lip wobbling. 'And they never ask me to come!' After a moment of confusion, it hit me. Of course! 'To go potty' was American kid-speak for 'to go to the bathroom', ie 'to go to the toilet', and Maya, unfamiliar with this expression, heard a slightly Australian-sounding version of 'party'. She was so relieved when we got to the bottom of this and she realised she wasn't missing out on any fun after all.

As a non-native English speaker, I faced an additional conundrum. I knew that adapting my language was a necessary tool for daily survival, and that sticking to my British pronunciation was a choice I made rather than one I was born with. It didn't really make sense to have a pronounced English accent when I wasn't actually English, but it felt the most natural to me.

In the end, I decided that switching accents would be too weird and too complicated, like I was acting, and so I adapted just a few things whenever I was in the company of Americans. Some words felt really strange to me, or even wrong, when pronounced the American way, but I thought it was a small price to pay if I wanted to be understood. Over the years, my accent has certainly changed; it is now a reflection of the many places I have spent time in, something that would have bothered me enormously once upon a time, but I have come to embrace.

Culture Clash

It wasn't just the language we had to get used to. My nerdy inner anthropologist adored exploring this new culture. Having studied the English for over a decade, I was now becoming an expert in American social norms and etiquette and loved observing the little nuances and expressions that were so different from both England and Germany. I found myself in the unique position of a neutral observer who could understand the antics of all three nationalities from an outside vantage point. I didn't feel particularly German anymore, but also definitely not British or American.

All of a sudden, in this new environment, I had to reassess the way people communicated with each other. After almost twelve years of living in the UK, I was used to communicating Brit-style; now, I had to unlearn it all. I had already trained myself to stop adding an 'x' or 'xx' to the messages I sent to non-English people; it's rude to omit these little kisses at the end of a text message or email when communicating with a friend or even just an acquaintance in the UK. This is not the case in the US. You can use 'xoxo' instead of 'xx', but only when it's a message to a dear friend, and even then, only if the message is expressing something heartfelt.

Here in the US, I often found myself rearranging in my head what I was going to say, in order not to be misunderstood, especially in the early days, and especially when humour was involved. Sometimes it felt like being split into several personae. Just as I had conquered the English way of communicating, I had to switch gears again and hold back from using my arsenal of flippant comebacks, choosing more carefully when those would be appreciated. While Americans in general adore the irony and ambiguity that comes with British and English humour, it can be utterly confusing when it's used in a more challenging context.

This realisation hit us rather painfully one night, when we were invited to a friend's house for dinner. Those familiar with the British style of chatting will know that when you have two Brits in a room, they converse as if playing tennis: it's a constant lobbing of the ball back and forth, the ball being witty and ironic remarks, and the longer the ball stays in the air, the better. Sometimes it's out, and sometimes it hits the net, but it's a game nonetheless. British people love to play on words and generally say things by saying the exact opposite. This can be infuriating, especially in business situations, because it can look like they can never be serious, but it's great fun when you're aware of it, or know how to play the game.

At my friend's dinner party, my husband, the proprietor of a very sharp and quick-witted English sense of humour, was being himself and started his usual tennis match of conversation instead of just boring chit-chat. This wasn't a work situation, and he was only here because I had made him come with me and the kids. One of the guests, who was seated opposite Scott, was a non-native speaker of English, who seemed funny and engaging, but started to become more tight-lipped as the night went on. We were all eating, drinking and laughing, when all of a sudden, she pushed back her chair and stormed out, shouting, 'I'm not taking this any longer! I am not an idiot!' There was stunned silence at the table, and we all looked at each other in confusion. Finally, I realised what had happened and ran out to find her and explain why all of this was a misunderstanding. Scott had been making conversation English-style, by asking her questions and then using what she'd said, putting an ironic spin on it and lobbing it back over the net at her, while she didn't even know she was involved in a game. As a consequence, she felt like he was making fun of her by turning what she had said into a joke, and accused him of insulting her and criticising her lack of English proficiency. She came back to the table eventually, but the mood was ruined.

Anyone moving to a new country will find it helps to be open-minded when it comes to manners; it's so important to not only learn the language, but also which behaviours are appropriate and which are not. Measuring another country by your own country's standards, which is so tempting when it comes to another Western culture, must be avoided at all costs.

I learned that Americans had their very own code of manners and customs, just like the Germans and the British had theirs. Expressions were used differently or omitted altogether, which could be perceived as rude or impolite when it was simply the country's way of doing things. We Europeans are overwhelmingly raised to think of the Americans as uncultured and boorish, but they're just not adhering to the same codes. For example, Americans aren't very lavish with the word 'please', whereas they're excellent at saying 'thank you'. Whenever I asked one of my kids' friends if they wanted a juice or a cookie, for example, I'd get a 'Sure' instead of 'Yes, please', which was what most of their friends in England or Germany would say. The first few times this happened, I bristled a bit, but I realised soon enough that this wasn't a lack of manners; it was simply the appropriate code that was used here.

I also discovered that 'excuse me' and 'sorry' were used differently. In England, you say 'excuse me' when you want to pass someone in a crowd or narrow supermarket aisle, or when you intend to ask someone a question but also want to be polite and give them a warning that you are indeed about to ask a question. This procedure is similar in Germany, although there, it is also totally fine to just squeeze by somebody without saying anything – something I still do, which drives my British husband to despair. If you bump into someone in the UK by accident, or – god forbid – tread on somebody's toes, you have to say 'sorry' at least five times, in a variety of tones and expressions. In Germany, one mumbled 'sorry' is acceptable. And if somebody bumps into you or makes you stumble, you still have to say 'sorry', even if the other person is at fault. In this case, one or two 'sorrys' are sufficient. If you do that in Germany, people will think you're crazy, so I don't recommend it. In the US, you never say 'sorry' in accidental physical contact situations. 'Excuse me' is used as a blanket expression.

This took some getting used to. Whenever I realised that I was in somebody's way, or even if there was plenty of room but somebody wanted to pass me, I needed to say 'excuse me' instead of 'sorry' and step aside. And if somebody bumped into me, they would also say 'excuse me' instead of 'sorry'. To my British-trained ears, this sounded very impolite at first, as though it implied that I was the one who should have stepped aside, or as if it were my fault that that person bumped into me in the first place.

I really struggled to get used to this, and I still find it bizarre when people pass me at a distance and say 'excuse me', even though there is plenty of space. It's almost too courteous.

If all fails, a cheerful smile will solve anything and is, in fact, *de rigueur* in the US, whereas in Europe, people might look at you as though you've lost your mind.

Identity Warps

Something else was happening to my culturally expanding mind: I found that I was slowly reconnecting with my German roots. Maybe it was a subconscious attempt to reclaim some of my inner core, or maybe it was because I was suddenly thrown into a more international environment.

I had always spoken German with my children, from the moment they were born. 'I'm so glad I can speak German with you,' Amelie told me more than once after our move. 'At least I don't have to change my accent in German!' English was our family language, but as soon as it was just the kids and me, we communicated pretty much exclusively in German. Another huge reason why I had chosen not to go back to work full-time. Scott, who had taken some German classes in the early stages of our relationship, found that, if not his speaking skills, his comprehension had improved drastically just by listening to our chatter over the years. He regularly indulged the girls in heavily-accented, hair-raising German word constructions, which usually resulted in uncontrollable giggles.

We made it a regular event to pop into the German bakery whenever we passed it on our way back home from some outing; I found that I enjoyed listening to German conversations in the café section of the shop, while the kids always pounced on the pretzels and chocolate treats you couldn't find in the local supermarkets. Sometimes, we'd head to the park afterwards for an impromptu picnic.

'*Wie schön*', a voice piped up behind me. 'I love to hear German voices; it always makes me think of my grandma.' I turned to the elderly lady who sat on a bench near our picnic spot. She was now smiling apologetically. 'Unfortunately, I don't speak the language myself,' she continued. 'But whenever I hear it, I feel a connection. Where are you from?' We proceeded to tell each other our life stories, another connection formed. This sort of thing was a regular occurrence.

It was a totally new experience for me to be met with so much enthusiasm and interest when I mentioned where I was born. This was in stark contrast to all those years in the UK, where I had basically trained myself to erase my German accent and any vaguely Teutonic behaviour because I had got so sick and tired of being mocked or having to endure the endless 'war jokes'. I felt liberated here in the US, and thoroughly enjoyed communicating in German with my children in public. I realised how much of my heritage I had repressed and even hidden when I lived in England.

It was exactly this open-mindedness and genuine curiosity that made me begin to embrace the Californian attitude and abandon my standard English superciliousness when it came to American culture. Yes, I missed Europe and its diversity of cultures and languages a lot, but I was impressed by the openness of the people here.

I found that Americans, on the whole, were a lot less confrontational than the society I had grown up in. Germans can come across as very aggressive in their blunt and direct style of communication, often appearing a lot more combative than they actually are. As a highly sensitive child and teen, I had struggled with this a lot, and now, after such a long time abroad, I felt rather non-German. I really enjoyed the non-judgmental attitude I had encountered in this part of the country so far. This was probably due to the fact that California was a true melting pot of cultures, maybe even more so than other states. There were so many different people here that you didn't have a choice but to accept a lot of differences in the way things were done and different types of upbringing and backgrounds. And not only to accept them, but to embrace and celebrate them, too.

Of course, this laissez-faire attitude had a giant flipside. I had to admit that while I appreciated the agreeable, non-judgmental tone, I missed a certain amount of friction and the willingness to defend one's opinion, especially in controversial matters. I was European, after all, and still German. To express your opinion, whether solicited or unsolicited, is a highly German characteristic, which non-Germans often perceive as impolite or insensitive. I had had such a hard time during my years in England, trying to defend, appease, negate and explain why Germans act the way they do. And I can't help cringing just as much as others when I hear a strong German accent or see German tourists behave in a 'typically German' way, reciting loudly from their guidebook at a point of interest, for example, or complaining about having to tip twenty per cent. I want nothing to do with it.

So now I faced a dilemma: sure, it was wonderful not to be expected to offer your opinion or engage in arguments all the time, but occasionally it could be a little bit bland to always keep things 'safe', and politically, culturally and religiously correct. California is known to be the most litigious state; people are quick to sue each other, and everybody seems really careful not to upset anybody. This is even reflected in the language. Because there are so many different nationalities here, with varying degrees of command of English, the language has become something that has to be easily understood without any power to upset.

I loved that I was learning to navigate all these different methods and styles of communication; it meant that I was keeping myself mentally agile, switching codes whenever necessary. My inner chameleon had a lot of field days.

It fascinated me how I could sense subtle changes in personality, depending on what code was being used. I had mostly avoided expat groups when I lived in England, with only a few German acquaintances crossing my path from time to time, mostly so that I had an opportunity to expose my children to other speakers of my mother tongue. Somehow, I had never felt truly comfortable in the company of other German expats, and I still had reservations.

And yet, now that I lived even further away from my home country, there seemed to be an invisible force that made me ease myself back into my German roots. There's always an unspoken code among your fellow countrymen or women that is understood on a subconscious level; it's a code that has been deftly constructed through shared references, linguistic experiences and childhood socialisation, which means a lot of things don't need any explanation. Just like an English person knows that 'Do you want a cuppa?' means that 'a cuppa' will be black tea with milk, the only variable being 'no sugar, one sugar or two', you won't get questioning looks from a German when you serve the kids Nutella sandwiches for dinner.

Anniversary

Our first California anniversary was fast approaching, and we had to make some decisions. Our rental contract was up for renewal at the beginning of May, and as much as we'd enjoyed having the extra space, we hated feeling 'house poor'. Our money was spent on rent rather than fun. After all, we'd come to California to experience all that this gorgeous state had to offer, rather than sit in a big house with all those empty bedrooms. We wanted to explore further afield, go on more weekend trips and spend time in Mexico and Hawaii, since we'd never get to live closer to those dream holiday destinations.

We found a second-floor apartment right in the centre of Los Altos. It didn't have a garden but two large balconies facing out to some enormous eucalyptus trees, which acted like giant air fresheners, their bluey-green leaves especially fragrant after it rained. It also had an office space that could be turned into a guest room when needed. This made so much more sense to us, and we happily signed the lease and waved goodbye to Whitham Avenue.

The kids weren't that bothered about moving to a new home. Since they were able to stay in their respective schools and old hands at moving, they just shrugged their shoulders and enjoyed the fact that we were now within walking distance of 'downtown' and Peets and Starbucks, with a new budget that decidedly allowed for a few more coveted double chocolate chip frappuccinos.

One day, soon after our move, as I was sitting outside 'our' new Starbucks with my laptop, I caught sight of myself in the window across the street and almost did a double-take. The woman I was staring at looked so different from the one who had set foot in this country just a year earlier. Gone was the short pixie cut, her mid-length bob scrunched into a messy bun underneath a baseball hat. She didn't wear a scrap of make-up, not even lip gloss. The jeans, T-shirt and flip flops combo wasn't quite the ubiquitous leggings-all-day look favoured by American women and their daughters, but it was decidedly less London and more California. I wasn't sure I recognised her; there seemed to be something off, as if she was playing a character in a movie, rather than living a real life. She looked healthy and at ease, but when you looked closer, the smile on her lips didn't quite reach her eyes.

Tiger Mom Territory

In addition to more treats, our new budget also meant more extracurricular activities: Maya started taking karate and rock climbing classes, and Amelie swam and rode horses twice a week. I deemed this amount of activity enough for my girls, since it left some downtime for reading or just going to the park, but it seemed that we weren't nearly as busy as everybody else.

After all, we lived in Tiger Mom territory. I had just read the notorious *Battle Hymn of the Tiger Mother*, which had been published a year earlier and caused a massive outcry among parents. It was still a constant topic of conversation. Amy Chua's story was not a singular case of a pushy parent. There were a lot of pushy parents in this area. The contrast between my own childhood and the way children were brought up in this part of the world was becoming more obvious to me every day. It was entirely normal here to have a full schedule for children of all ages, not only during the week with after-school activities, but also with additional weekend classes, competitions and tutoring. To me, it felt like an attempt to raise little super robots, used to performing and delivering, and to being entertained at all times, without any time to just 'be' or any room for imaginative play and creative thought. People sent their kids to creativity workshops for that. I, on the other hand, loved having my kids at home where they had to come up with their own entertainment, only going to scheduled activities a few times a week. We loved sleeping in on weekends and enjoyed lazy breakfasts, or going off on day trips to explore our surroundings. But of course, that was my very privileged view. I realised how incredibly ignorant I was being when, at some school event, I voiced my concerns and disapproval of overscheduling and general pushiness, as displayed by the Tiger Mom. I was swiftly put in my place by another parent, not in a critical or negative manner, but enough to make me reconsider my one-sided view. He pointed out that while he shared my concerns, I needed to consider the author's background, upbringing, and, of course, the country she was living in. The United States, country of endless opportunities and the American Dream. But for whom?

The concept of the American Dream might have been realistic once, but it certainly had a pretty hollow sound to it now. There was no room for losers in this culture, no room for non-achievers. There was no real social system. You had to be successful because if you weren't, you fell through the cracks.

So who was I to judge someone like the Tiger Mother? I was a privileged white upper-middle-class woman who lived in one of the most affluent areas in the world, and who worked for her own fulfilment rather than to make ends meet, someone who had grown up listening to classical music, eating organic home cooked food and enjoying piano and horse riding lessons, and vacationing in Italy and France, who had no idea what it felt like to be a social outcast, who had no idea that in other countries students had to take out horrendously high loans to go to university if they even had the opportunity.

Looking back at my family's history, I realised it was full of academia, peppered with doctors and lawyers, both on my dad's and my mum's side, but it had never occurred to me that that sort of background had influenced my choices. When I pointed out to a friend that I never felt like I had to become a doctor, too, she just laughed at me and said, well, maybe not, but certainly something comparable. She told me that her parents, both immigrants, had signed her up for a multitude of extracurricular activities, all because they wanted her to achieve more and better things in life than they had. Compared to today's standards, however, the activities she listed seemed incredibly modest.

In this society, simply doing a lot of things wasn't enough any more. You had to be the best at whatever you are doing, strive for more, hustle, *always*. I was starting to understand how the American mind works and why American parents are so ambitious for their children. If your child shows any aptitude for a sport or instrument, for example, and if you are prepared to put in the hours and money, there is a chance to qualify for a scholarship to get your offspring through college. In a country where it isn't unusual to pay upward of $30,000 a term for higher education – and this is the lower end of the spectrum – this is a hugely attractive prospect. American parents usually set up a college fund as soon as their child is born, or even earlier, just to be prepared. I know plenty of people who are still paying off college loan debt well into their forties.

All this eye-opening information scared me profoundly, and I was starting to worry about what effect this environment was going to have on my own family. I didn't want my kids to turn into little performance miracles, yet I also appreciated the many opportunities they were being given here. It was going to be tough to keep the balance between what was too much and too little pressure. What really bothered me was how life here in this 'Golden State' looked very much like a hamster wheel on steroids. All I could see was people frantically rushing around, scheduled around the clock, filling every possible minute of their day with stuff. No time to think, to relax, to just *be*. It was unacceptable to stand still, unless during specially assigned times such as yoga or meditation class.

I could already see how this attitude was very successfully being passed on to our children, who were being kept so incredibly busy that they didn't even know what to do with themselves when there was nothing to do. Being bored was not an option; it seemed like children weren't taught how to deal with the feeling of being bored, let alone how to use tools to overcome it. On some occasions, when my kids' friends were over for a playdate, and they ran out of ideas, they would come over to me and whine about feeling bored, and when I told them to come up with their own game or suggest an idea that involved too much creativity, they sometimes even asked to go home, and expressed their displeasure at not being entertained. I found the lack of boredom tolerance very concerning, and secretly loved how my own kids didn't seem to feel that way at all. Maybe I was kidding myself, but I definitely felt like we had managed to preserve some of their own resourcefulness.

Here in California, it seemed normal that each day after school and homework, there were at least one or two more activities, usually sports, sometimes music lessons, plus language classes and more school-improvement activities such as studying with a tutor. Everybody was always learning, working, *doing* something to improve their skills. To be better, quicker, more efficient. I loved learning myself, but I couldn't understand why there was such a huge emphasis on it, even for this young age group.

But school and work were everything, and if you didn't join in, you automatically felt like a failure. At eight years old, Amelie began to worry about her math skills. She told me that she wasn't as good as her peers, and I was baffled. As a bright, happy eight-year-old, she was totally capable of doing the work required in her grade, sometimes maybe not as quickly as she'd like, but it was all there, and I was happy with what she could achieve. And yet she was worried. It turned out that most kids received extra tutoring, or the parents themselves set them extra tasks. What was taught at school didn't seem to be enough anymore. I couldn't wrap my head around this. Yes, I wanted my child to be able to do her homework well, but did she really need to be able to do it more quickly, more easily? I felt very strongly that I'd rather have her spend that extra hour playing, reading a book that was not on her school reading list, or doing something she wanted to do. If it was normal that everybody had extra tuition and spent extra time on school stuff, wasn't that a sign that the system was broken? No, I did not want my eight-year-old child to sit up and work on school stuff in the evening, and then maybe get some downtime, and go to bed later than was good for her.

My frenzied thoughts were whipped up even further by thinking about the summer. In England and Germany, people looked forward to a fairly manageable six weeks, a relaxing break from school that was partly used for maybe a two-week holiday and an opportunity for the grandparents to spend time with their grandchildren and help out with childcare. In the US, we had to jump into the race for the best summer camps. Even though our family was lucky enough to be able to spend half of our summer break in Europe, there were still quite a few weeks to kill.

I picked up some brochures about summer camps and immediately put them down again. There was so much pressure on picking the right camp for your child, and the best ones got snapped up so quickly that you needed to know exactly what you were doing, very early on. One academic camp offering maths and writing improvement classes was advertising with the slogan 'Your kids forget up to 80% of what they've learned during the year – don't let them!' Of course, there was a whole range of really exciting offerings too, art and music camps, dance workshops, proper overnight camping, and so on. All fun, as long as you were able to afford them, of course. And all designed to not give your child a single second to get bored.

Exasperated, I threw the brochures away. I felt stifled by pressure. Was it just me, hypersensitive to stress and pressure, and unable to cope with it all myself? Why couldn't childhood be more relaxed? Of course, we all mourn the freedom we had ourselves, growing up in the seventies and eighties, playing outside all day and riding our bikes everywhere from a young age, without any parents in sight. The reality of 21st-century childhood couldn't be further from it, and it seemed to me that it was even more extreme here in the US.

One afternoon after school, we decided to go to one of our favourite places, Cuesta Park, so the kids could run around while I got to sit on a blanket with a book and enjoy the sunshine. There was another park within walking distance of our house, but we preferred Cuesta because of its fabulous climbing trees. The kids ran off, and Amelie decided to climb a different tree this time, one where the branches started higher up on the trunk, which made it more challenging than the almost horizontal one that was her usual choice. Maya had seen a friend of hers and ran off to the nearby playing structures, where I could hear them giggling. I settled down on my blanket and closed my eyes, listening to Amelie's constant chatter – she was one of those kids who always had to talk about what she was doing, 'thinking out loud', and she was moaning and groaning to let me know how much of an effort it was to climb this tree. I just glanced up from time to time and told her to stop complaining when I noticed a woman on a nearby bench watching us. Amelie made it further up the tree, and I managed to read a few pages. After a while, I heard her calling me to come and help her down. I had just reached a captivating section in my novel and really didn't want to be disturbed, and so I just told her that since she had climbed up the tree herself, she could surely get down by herself too, and that I was too busy reading my book. At this point, Amelie started to complain loudly, and I promised her I'd watch her climb down. All of a sudden, the woman from the bench got up and strode over in our direction. I gritted my teeth, thinking 'oh no, here we go, she'll tell me what an irresponsible parent I am!' and sat up straight. She stopped in front of my blanket, a big grin on her face, and just said, 'You are my hero!' Then she waved at Amelie, and with a 'You got this, kid!' she took off, and I sank back onto my blanket, feeling as though I'd just won a prize. I was still chuckling when a very disgruntled Amelie turned up next to my blanket just a few minutes later, a face like thunder and a little scrape on her knee.

Detached

I'd been in California for over a year now, but I still felt disorientated. Dismissing advice from other expat friends that it would take at least a year or even two to feel more settled, I hated the fact that I couldn't seem to adjust. Patience had never been my strong suit.

Despite the friendliness of the people around me, I hadn't worked out how to fit in. I was craving something more, something deeper, even though rationally, I knew that real friendships take time. There were a couple of people whom I had got closer to and who I really felt could become friends – even our husbands seemed to like each other. And there were a few I would meet for a walk or a coffee, although it often stressed me to arrange these events. There was some underlying code of behaviour I just couldn't grasp properly. Inviting someone over for a coffee, for example, wasn't necessarily an invitation for coffee; often, it was just a polite thing to say. I, on the other hand, always took everything that was said at face value, and if someone said 'Let's meet for coffee', I would then want to commit to a date and time, or follow up with a message confirming it. I never seemed to know when it was 'real' or just empty words. Just the other morning, I was supposed to meet someone downtown, but they cancelled at the last minute, claiming that they felt too tired to come out. I felt rejected and, being the perpetual overthinker that I was, tried to pinpoint a mistake on my part. This sort of thing happened regularly. I just couldn't seem to get it right; as a consequence, I feared that I came over as too intense.

In an attempt to claim some sense of feeling anchored, I persuaded Scott to try for another baby, not 100% certain that it was the right time to add to our family, or indeed the right idea. All I knew was that I was in such a state of confusion and dislocation, not truly finding my footing in this strange new country, and I was craving a new task I knew I could accomplish: being pregnant and looking after a newborn. I desperately needed to feel competent. Having another baby at this point felt like the missing link that might give me a deeper connection to my new home. Scott, although desperate for me to feel happier, was seriously questioning the practicality of this endeavour and probably felt relief when we remained unsuccessful for several months. The faint pink line that appeared on the test I took just after we'd given up trying surprised us both.

The pains started while I was at Whole Foods, perusing the aisle of pregnancy supplements. Scott was due to go to London for an important meeting and had just left for the San Francisco airport. As much as he had had to travel from London to San Francisco when we still lived in England, it seemed like our situation was becoming reversed now, and he had to go back to London almost every month.

I had a rare day to myself; the kids were staying at my friend Nicole's house after school, and I was spending the day looking after myself and trying to process what was happening. I wasn't sure how I felt about it all. I had only just taken the test, but I didn't fully trust this new situation yet. Having suffered a miscarriage before, after Amelie was born, I refused to let my mind jump ahead to the image of a new family member. I hadn't made any early doctor's appointments or announcements yet.

The Whole Foods I was in happened to be close to the small hospital where my doctor was located, and so I decided to take the pain seriously and drove by to see if a doctor could take a closer look. They gave me an emergency appointment on the spot, and I called Nicole.

'Listen, I'm not sure when I'll be back to pick up the girls,' I told her. 'I'm at the doctor's having an ultrasound because I'm having pains. I'm pregnant.' When you're an expat, without family or a big circle of friends around you, your acquaintances have to stand in from day one. Your emergency contact for school, for example, will probably be your neighbour or the mother of one of your kids' friends. The lines blur quickly.

'Oh my god! Are you okay?' she exclaimed. 'Isn't Scott travelling today?' I reassured her that I was fine and then went into the ultrasound room. I felt utterly calm and detached from this moment, as though all of this was happening to somebody else. And I knew even before the cold gel was spread over my lower belly that it was going to be bad news. All they could find were remnants of embryonic tissue, not even a single mass of cells.

'Looks like it wasn't developing at all,' the sonographer informed me, a concerned look on her face. 'You might experience more pain tonight and tomorrow.' I felt numb; all I could think was that Scott's plane to London was just about to take off, and that I would never try to have another baby.

'Can you please call your husband?' She put her hand on my arm. 'I don't think you should be on your own tonight.' I nodded and told her I was going to call him on my way out, and she accepted that, probably somewhat perplexed by my calm demeanour. 'I'll give you some good painkillers, but at this point, there is nothing we can do but wait. There isn't that much tissue; everything will resolve itself.' Resolve itself? Tissue? Flushing out bits of baby, rejected by my body, again.

I don't recall any further details. Scott was heading to London, so I either didn't tell him what had happened, or I must have convinced him I was fine. There's a giant gap in my memory. It was as if things were erased from my mind and my body within hours. I must have driven back to Nicole's, collected the girls, made dinner and gone through our usual routines, but I don't remember any pain, nor any tears.

I couldn't help but wonder if all that worrying about living in this new society and the stress about not fitting in caused me to lose this pregnancy. Rationally, I knew that it didn't; statistically, miscarriages happen a lot more frequently than people think. When I had my first miscarriage all those years earlier, I tried to dismiss it in an outwardly matter-of-fact way; internally, however, it messed with my mind for several years. I never truly processed it, not even after Maya was born. As a woman, regardless of what the statistics say, and regardless of how much you look after yourself when you're pregnant, there's always that tiny flicker of doubt that it was, somehow, your fault.

This American Life

The new school year began, and it was finally Maya's turn to start 'big school', aka Kindergarten, the equivalent of Reception Year in the UK. As our apartment was located within a new catchment area, we were assigned a new elementary school, which meant we had the choice of leaving Amelie at her school and getting Maya in because of the sibling factor, or we could opt to switch to the new one. I definitely wanted to keep Amelie at her school, where she had settled in so nicely, but we thought it might be nice for Maya to have her 'own' school, a place where she could be completely herself without being compared to her sister – I vividly remember how my sister and I hated those comparisons during our own childhoods. I also hoped that it would be the perfect opportunity for me to find new mom friends – this time, from scratch, starting my child's school journey along with everybody else, and not as the newcomer who joined mid-year. This time, I would be able to experience the American school system right from the beginning and observe how and by what American kids are shaped. This process started literally on day one.

Every Friday, our new school, Gardner Bullis Elementary, held a 'flag salute'. All kids and teachers as well as those parents who had the time and inclination to join, assembled in front of the stage outside the multi-purpose hall in order to recite the Pledge of Allegiance, which was always led by the principal and one or two students, followed by important announcements, tributes, awards, etc. Once the star students from each class had received their star studded certificates – achievements could be anything from being the teacher's helper that week to finally spelling a word correctly – and all the necessary photos had been taken for posterity, the principal vigorously animated everybody to join her in some stretching and then singing and acting out a song like 'head, shoulders, knees and toes' to get everybody moving. And boy, did everybody move, including us parents.

I was beyond impressed. All I could think was that any German or English person who happened to find themselves in a situation like this would just panic and most likely be too embarrassed to display their national pride so openly and unashamedly, and to wiggle their arms and legs and pull faces along with everybody else, most of them dressed in business attire, as they were on their way to work.

Every school and college in the US has a mascot, which is meant as a symbol to unify and foster a sense of belonging – brand awareness is taught very early on. Amelie's school's mascot was a lion, which meant the students at that school were the 'Loyola Lions', and Maya's was a grizzly bear, making the kids 'Gardner Grizzlies'. Once the usual praises and awards were granted and events announced, the principal would ask the big question: 'What time is it?' and the kids chorused their reply: 'Time to learn!' To add a little oomph to this very laudable response, everybody from kid to parent then joined in a loud and enthusiastic 'Grizzly Grrrr' and pawed the air with their imaginary bear claws. After suffi-cient growling, the principal wished everyone a great day and dis-patched the kids to their classrooms.

After my initial shock, I decided to join in with gusto, and so did my parents, parents-in-law and friends whenever they hap-pened to visit and come along to this joyous, over-the-top Ameri-can ritual.

While I knew that choosing two schools rather than one meant that I had to handle two drop-offs and pickups, I didn't consider the fact that I now also had to deal with two parent evenings, two PTAs, two fundraising committees and two places to volunteer at. There was only one creative solution: as soon as anybody wanted to pin me down for an activity that I really didn't want to be part of, I claimed that I was already volunteering at the other school, which was often true but saved me from some boring tasks a fair number of times.

Of course, volunteering meant that you felt much more part of the community, and it was a great way to make friends. But reading once a week and sorting books in the school library didn't quite hit the spot for me. I wanted to do something I was passionate about and decided to use my creativity, and joined the one-year training programme offered by the 'Los Altos Art Docents' in order to be-come an art teacher. I used to love painting and drawing as a child, but had more or less abandoned this hobby as I got older. Now was my chance to let my inner child play.

The Art Docents were a group of wonderful women and occa-sional men, one more interesting and enthusiastic than the next, without whom the California elementary school students would probably never know what it felt like to swish colour from a paintbrush onto real paper, rather than draw a line on an iPad.

Every Wednesday morning, I attended a three-hour training session, painted, drew, sculpted and learned about art history, until I 'graduated' and was unleashed onto the tech-savvy but artistically and creatively disadvantaged Silicon Valley brood.

I loved how this volunteering activity allowed me to get to know the children and teachers, and to see how school life in this country took place and shaped its citizens, from Kindergarten to the early teenage years.

All of a sudden, I had a new task, a new identity, a new circle of interesting people to talk to and something I thoroughly endorsed and enjoyed. Every time I dragged my huge art portfolio and supply box into a new classroom, setting up workstations with paintbrushes, paper, clay, and texturing tools, I felt a surge of excitement. Talking to the kids about art and guiding them through simple and more challenging art projects, seeing their creativity come through, made me feel useful. I had arrived.

As soon as the summer temperatures eased off and the air and leaves turned autumn golden, we opened our doors to a flurry of visitors. First came my in-laws, who provided a breath of fresh English air, free babysitting, and fantastic cooking. My mother-in-law delighted Maya's Kindergarten class with tales from the Queen and Buckingham Palace, my father-in-law enhanced Amelie's presentation about the UK with a good dose of Cockney rhyming slang, and they both looked after the girls while Scott and I disappeared to San Diego for a blissfully child-free wedding anniversary weekend. We'd been married for eleven years and marvelled at this accomplishment and the journey we'd had while tucking into mountains of seafood in La Jolla. Fully embracing our American environment, we claimed it was our anniversary every time we went for lunch and dinner, and were presented with a free celebratory dessert every single time. Americans definitely love, and know how, to celebrate.

Our next arrivals were a couple of my friends from Germany, who were on a road trip through the US, followed by my sister-in-law, and then, finally, my own sister with my niece and brother-in-law. We absolutely loved sharing our new home with friends and family, even though we had to laugh at the irony that when we had the big house with lots of rooms, nobody showed up, and now our apartment was spilling over with people, every bed, sofa and sleeping bag occupied.

California presented her beauty with dazzling autumn colours, gorgeous weather and friendly, laid-back people, and we spent whole weekends at the beach, ate oysters fresh from the sea, saw more redwood forests, visited some more wineries and survived another Halloween, our family and friends in tow. Everybody was very loath to leave, and when they finally did, the house felt eerily quiet.

Luckily, my parents were able to join us for Christmas, and we enjoyed a typical California winter equally split between the mountains, the city and the beach. We discovered new ski resorts around Lake Tahoe, explored San Francisco, and started the new year by whale watching off the coast of Santa Cruz with a family from Finland, whose daughter had joined Amelie's class a couple of months before. As I stood next to my new friend, wrapped in my warmest winter coat, the icy January sea air whipping my face, dolphins and whales jumping in and out of the waves around us, I wanted to pinch myself. It was amazing how different I felt compared to a year earlier. We would reach our two-year mark very soon, yet the thought of leaving this place and returning to England was slipping further and further away.

After one year in our apartment without our own outside space, we decided that we needed a place we could go to that wasn't the local park. There were plenty of parks and recreation areas nearby, but we missed something a bit more private. We decided to do something I never in a million years expected to agree to: we joined a country club.

Everything inside of me bristled at the idea of becoming a member of what I perceived to be the epitome of white, upper-middle class living, as depicted in movies such as *Dirty Dancing*, but I let myself be persuaded – the kids' excitement at being able to spend whole days in a pool won me over. We found a club that didn't charge an annual Silicon Valley salary as a joining fee and turned out to be less expensive and a million times more attractive than our old health & fitness club back in England.

Located a twenty-minute drive from our apartment amidst the incredibly picturesque hills of Saratoga, the club offered beautiful vistas, a great swimming pool, and – my favourite part – guests I didn't know from school and our daily life. It meant that we were able to truly relax here and be as social or as private as we wanted to be. We were becoming proper members of upper-middle-class American society now, and mentally another step further away from our old European life.

Being proper Americans also meant taking part in local sports. Every family was deeply invested in the comings and goings of at least one football, basketball and baseball team, whether that was due to location, college affiliation or simply because it was part of family lore. It seemed to me that if you weren't into sports, finding and making connections in this country could be a real challenge, certainly for someone like me, who was so glaringly disinterested in sports. There was simply no option to opt out; I gritted my teeth, knowing I needed to work on my attitude.

Kids were introduced to sports from the cradle, and it was a given that everybody participated in at least one or two sports, ranging from basketball and softball, a precursor to the real baseball, to soccer, ballet and swimming. You could choose from every sport imaginable, and there was also a team for every sport imaginable. I got the impression that even the three-year-olds were semi-professional, and it wasn't easy to take up a new sport as you get older. If you decided to take up soccer at age ten, for example, it was pretty impossible to find a team that would accept a beginner at this age.

Amelie started swimming in a team, but managed to opt out of the numerous swim meets, the team's competitive side, as she simply couldn't handle the pressure of competitions. This suited us as a family, as we were watching other parents frantically attempt to attend all their children's activities each weekend. Maya joined a girls' soccer team, but more because one of her friends had wanted to do it and egged her on rather than because of a real interest in the sport. Her fondness of pink also played a role – her first team was called 'Pink Lemonade', and it looked like the team members were more interested in eating ice cream during the breaks rather than actually following any soccer drills. It was a wonderful, low-key group activity that got us out of the house and chatting with other parents. I loved the fact that all the team sports had relatively short seasons – three months for soccer in the fall, followed by basketball in the winter and finally baseball in the spring – which meant that the kids could try out all the sports and didn't really have a chance to get bored and quit.

To support this enthusiasm for sports and foster team spirit, our school district held an event each April: the *Junior Olympics*, where the district's seven elementary schools competed against one another in various athletic disciplines. Apart from classics such as hurdles, sprint and long jump, they'd added activities like basketball, pull-ups and jump rope, and each child was allowed to choose their three best categories.

We turned up to our first Junior Olympics thoroughly unprepared, surprised to see that most families had already arrived early in the morning to set up whole 'stations', complete with a tent, picnic blankets, lawn chairs and coolers full of beverages and a huge spread of food, eager to celebrate their offspring and their friends, who would pop in and out of their families' stations throughout the day whenever they had a break from competing. As is the custom for any American sporting event, the National Anthem was played to kick off proceedings; it was performed beautifully by a 6th-grade school band, sometimes with, and sometimes without, a vocalist. This was followed by the Pledge of Allegiance and a little dance number performed by all the school mascots. It was a special honour to be chosen as your school's mascot for the day, but since it was the end of April in California, this meant committing to a sweaty day inside your furry costume. To conclude the day, the whole place erupted in cheers for the final event, the race of the mascots. I will never forget the marvellously insane sight of a lion, a coyote, a lynx, an eagle, a bear, and a bee – yes, really – racing each other on a track.

We continued our newly found enthusiasm for sports when we travelled to England that summer for our annual trip 'home' – 2012 definitely turned out to be the Year of Sports. London was hosting the Summer Olympics, and the whole country was uncharacteristically euphoric and welcoming. We loved every second of the

Games and spent the majority of our stay glued to the television, along with the rest of the nation, thoroughly enjoying the American-style pride that Britain was experiencing.

It surprised me how differently I felt this time compared to the previous few summers. The kids had a great time as usual, but it didn't feel like a 'going home' trip. Our life was now definitely happening in California. When a friend cancelled our long-anticipated get-together because her daughter had a tennis lesson at the time I suggested, and didn't offer an alternative during the week-long time frame she knew we had, I realised that my old friendships were starting to shift. People were moving on without us. I knew this development was inevitable, but it still stung. It almost felt like a personal rebuke and very unsettling. I was so determined to keep every single relationship alive, as much for my children as for my own sake, and I had to accept that it was an unstoppable pattern. If we stayed in the US, we would drift apart eventually; it was simply impossible to maintain every connection.

Over the years, I would learn to be less bitter and become even more appreciative of the moments we got to spend with those friends who genuinely wanted to see us. Some connections even deepened despite the distance, especially within our extended families, both in England and in Germany, not only with our parents but also with cousins, aunts and uncles. It made me incredibly happy to see that both Amelie and Maya held such firm and important positions within both their English and German families. They clearly still felt at home in both, happily munching baked beans on toast in England and confidently riding their bikes around my little German hometown. Maybe we hadn't ripped their roots from the ground after all.

The Giants

Perfectly befitting our year of sports, we finally made it to a baseball game. I'm not sure how I had managed to avoid it during the two and a half years I had lived here, since Bay Area residents lived and breathed this sport.

The San Francisco Giants, a team consisting of a very eclectic mix of players, had just got into the playoffs of the ultimate American tournament, the interestingly named 'World Series'. There was no stopping the enthusiasm for baseball, and for weeks, people seemed to wear nothing but black and orange, the Giants' team colours.

Maya and Amelie were boasting new baseball knowledge on a daily basis, and I realised that the American language was bursting with expressions derived from this sport. As an English language learner, you just take them on, even if they don't make any sense unless you're familiar with baseball. 'Ballpark figure', 'home run', 'let's take a raincheck', 'throwing a curveball', 'major league' – all these and many more idioms pepper the everyday language. And I guess, even in Germany, people know what 'getting to second base' means...

Although I loved the general enthusiasm for the Giants, I struggled to understand the rules. Each time someone tried to explain them to me, my eyes started to glaze over. An Indian mum at school just laughed at my cluelessness and quipped, 'It's not that hard – it's just like cricket!', which didn't help a great deal, since I had similar difficulties with the rules of that sport. It's not baseball's fault; I just suffer from a general inability to understand game rules. It's like my brain is lacking an essential little screw somewhere and just freezes as soon as it has to deal with a set of rules or instructions. I can just about handle an IKEA leaflet to build a bookcase, but only because it's on paper, and it's in pictures and doesn't include tons of written instructions. Any verbal explanations pass right through me without finding anywhere to latch on. This applies to sports, but also to any other instructions, such as someone giving me directions when I'm lost. If I can't see a map with arrows, forget it. Equally, someone trying to explain to me how baseball works, especially *while* I'm watching the game, might just as well speak a foreign language. It's probably the biggest reason why I abhor playing games, even board games. And why I've never been very interested in sports.

Sports enthusiast or not, I knew there was no escaping this game, and so I feigned enough enthusiasm for my husband to buy tickets for the whole family to see the Giants *at home*. We grabbed our hats and headed to the train station, as the Giants' home stadium, the AT&T Park at the time, was located right next to the Caltrain Station in downtown San Francisco. As expected, the train was filled to the brim with baseball fans, a sea of orange-and-black clothing and accessories. There was no way we would get a seat, so we just scuttled along and positioned ourselves right in the middle of what turned out to be a big group of college students in party mode. Music was blaring from a portable stereo, conversations were shouted across the whole carriage, and alcohol flowed freely. This being America, there was usually not a chance for anybody to be seen with bottles that weren't 'hidden' in brown paper bags, but today, nobody seemed to care. The Giants were playing!

Bracing myself for an arduous journey that would feel much longer than the expected 45 minutes, I wearily smiled back at all those wholesome, tanned American faces beaming up at me. But within less than a minute, Scott was holding a beer, and a bucket of Chardonnay was pushed into my hands. No fuss, no awkwardness, no fighting, just friendly smiles and questions from every corner. What a wonderful group of kids. It turned out that most of them were swimmers from Arizona State University, in town for a competition, and they happily talked sports, wanted to know all about London and the Olympics, and engaged Maya and Amelie in conversations about hobbies and all sorts of things. Our kids were beaming with admiration and pride to be taken seriously by those amazing, larger-than-life college kids. Once again, I was absolutely stunned by the confidence, openness and positivity of young Americans.

Needless to say, the journey passed in no time at all, which is not what I can say about the actual baseball game... I can't remember much about it, only that I wished I had tried a little harder to understand the rules. It was a fun day, but even the Giants' win didn't convince me, although I have to admit that I still feel a sort of patriotic pride whenever I glimpse someone wearing the iconic black-and-orange SF Giants hat.

The Second Amendment

There are so many things in this country that I will always find confusing, but have assimilated without giving them much notice anymore. Saying 'Happy Holidays' instead of 'Merry Christmas', for example. Or having to expressly ask a server not to put ice in my drink. However, having a sheriff parked outside my kids' school all day is not one of those things.

It was the 14th of December, 2012. President Obama had just been re-elected for a second term, and his promise to tackle the gun control issue was still echoing in our ears when we received devastating news from the East Coast.

I had woken up with the usual pre-Christmas frenzy on my mind – school concerts, teachers' gifts, bringing in craft supplies and all the various seasonal obligations – but when we heard the news, my petty worries turned to anguish.

In utter disbelief, we followed a live account of one man in the process of shooting up Sandy Hook Elementary School in a place called Newtown, Connecticut. By the time I had got my children ready for school, we still didn't know the exact number of fatalities, but I don't think there was a single parent that day who dropped their kid off at school without experiencing profound nausea. We all felt it, collectively. There was no hiding or denying the insanity of this act. You could see it written all over people's foreheads, 'What if this happens at our school?'

We were well aware of how easy it was to acquire weapons in this country; school shootings were by no means a rarity. This time, however, twenty little elementary school children lost their lives, children the same age as Maya and her friends. All of a sudden, the danger felt very real, and it hit me like a punch in the stomach how immensely different our cultures actually were. When I picked my girl up from school later that day, still reeling from the gruesome footage on TV, there was a police car in the school parking lot. It became a fixture for the next few months, just one of the many new security measures taken to increase a sense of safety that never actually materialised.

Over the next few weeks, all our schools were surrounded by sturdy new fences; visitors to the schools had to go through various controls, and the number of emergency drills increased. Every few months, the kids had to undergo a fire drill, and since we were in California, the occasional earthquake drill, but in addition to these, there were two other ones: 'Code Yellow' and 'Code Red'.

The former meant that there was a potential threat, such as an approaching tornado, or if you lived near a coast, a tsunami. It was about a danger source outside of the school premises and meant that the buildings were locked and everybody waited for the danger to pass, or for other steps relevant to the danger to be taken. Lessons could and would carry on as normal. Code Red, on the other hand, meant an immediate danger, often from within the school grounds, for example, a school shooter. California schools had a different layout from schools in other parts of the country;

the classrooms weren't housed in one or more lockable buildings, but rather spread out individually across the school premises, usually around big open courtyards, and each with its own set of two doors. This meant that Code Yellow would be treated like Code Red. The doors of each classroom were locked immediately, the blinds drawn, nobody could enter or leave, and everybody had to remain completely silent and take up a protective position, hiding under their desks. Our kids usually seemed to take these drills in their stride and often didn't even mention that they'd had one, although I always wondered what effect these drills would have on their psyche in the long run, and whether they'd have nightmares and worry about danger too much.

Unbelievably, while security measures increased dramatically all over the country after Sandy Hook, nothing changed with regard to the acquisition of weapons. As I write this, several more school shootings have taken place, among them the more recent elementary school shooting in Uvalde, Texas, in May 2022, which claimed even more lives, and yet nobody seems to be able to stand up to the gun lobby.

The Second Amendment to the United States Constitution dates back to 1791 and grants each citizen the right to own and bear arms. I don't need to point out the fact that it is completely outdated and came into existence during a very different time in history and circumstances; it remains to this day the most baffling part of the American legislature and will never make sense to a European.

During my obsessive research on this subject over the following weeks, I learned that a staggering 45% of the American population owned at least one gun, and there were more firearms in this country than citizens. I thought of my new friends and acquaintances here and wondered who among them might be a gun owner. I only knew of one family at Amelie's school, where the dad, an ex-policeman, insisted on carrying a concealed weapon at all times. I'd always declined invites for Amelie to their house for that reason, although I knew that statistically, my kids must have spent at least some time since we moved here in the vicinity of a gun.

I knew plenty of people around me who felt exactly the same way about gun laws, but my safe little California bubble didn't feel quite so safe anymore.

Three Years In

To celebrate our third anniversary in the US, our green cards arrived in the post, almost to the day we had first set foot on American soil. I experienced a strange mix of emotions – on the one hand, this nifty little card, which was indeed green, made living here a lot easier, as it meant we no longer had to worry about renewing our visas every year. But on the other hand, it meant that we were now permanent residents. Permanent, as in, this was officially where we lived, where our main residence was. It was no longer a temporary adventure. If we left now, we would have to make sure to return within six months, unless we wanted to risk losing this precious document.

An expiring, possibly not renewable visa could have meant a return to England, and we would be able to point the finger at the company and say, 'well, we would have stayed in California but we couldn't'. The decision to stay or leave would be out of our hands. Now, it was entirely on us.

We never really sat down to discuss that the two years we had originally planned to stay had gone by, and now even a third year had passed. It was as though nobody wanted to confront the proverbial elephant in the room. Things were running smoothly, and we just carried on doing what we were doing; the kids were settled and happy at school, we all had our routines, things to do and people to spend time with. Scott had got into cycling and thoroughly enjoyed weekend rides with other biking enthusiasts. His position at work had changed, and he was embracing his new options as well as our West Coast lifestyle. California was home, and moving was something we'd consider at some point in the future, but not right now.

Looking at the powerful little card in my hand, I wasn't sure how to feel. It was as though I needed to build a new reality in my mind, one that was no longer fixated on Europe. I was still desperately trying to maintain our connections with friends back home, for the kids' sake as much as my own, but I could see them slipping away as time went on. The effort to do this while also giving my full energy to building my life in California was tearing me apart; I felt like I was failing at both, with nothing tangible to hold on to.

We decided to celebrate our permanent resident status with a family trip to one of the ultimate Silicon Valley holiday destinations: Maui. We had never been this close to Hawaii as we were now, and with the girls a little bit older, we felt like we could actually create some lasting memories.

As with Lake Tahoe, another favourite Silicon Valley dweller hot spot, you couldn't help but bump into people you knew. As we disembarked the plane at Kahului airport and stood in line to pass through the gates to grab our luggage, a little girl in the opposite line was jumping up and down, frantically waving at us and calling Maya's name. Someone from her school returning from her family's annual Maui getaway. Rather than getting really excited at this coincidence, her parents just smiled hello. This was clearly a very standard occurrence.

Travelling to foreign places was high on the agenda in the area where we lived. We noticed that it wasn't just us expats who left for Europe and other foreign destinations each summer. Unlike many of the residents of other corners of America who don't tend to leave their state or don't even own a passport, the wealthy and educated Bay Area dwellers seem to have an insatiable appetite for other cultures and a desire to impart this to their offspring. I was regularly blown away by people's knowledge of European history and culture, and had never met so many ten-year-olds who had already visited Tate Modern, the Louvre *and* the Prado Museum. To discuss artworks in my art docent lessons and find that half of the class had already seen the oeuvre in person wasn't a rare occurrence at all.

The genuine appreciation and love for history and other cultures I encountered among many Californians travelling within Europe truly amazed me, and I often felt embarrassed by their knowledge and the fact that they had visited far more historical and cultural sites than I had myself. It was hard to reconcile this with the image of the dumb American the rest of the world is used to, and I wondered, not for the first time, how misunderstood this nation really was. Or rather, how incredibly vast the gap between the haves and the have-nots really was.

To add to our more permanent attitude, we also acquired a new family member: 'Snowy', a jet black, half-Siamese kitten. We had talked about getting a dog since we first moved, but since dog-friendly rentals were hard to find, and we had decided it was too difficult to manage a dog with our frequent travel, we had abandoned the idea for the time being. The girls were desperate for a pet, and when a friend of mine found an abandoned mama cat with eight kittens behind a supermarket and promptly scooped them all up, took them to a veterinary clinic and then phoned every single friend of hers to find them all homes, I felt the timing was right. Once our landlord had given the go-ahead, we brought our little feline devil home. The girls were in heaven.

We had officially become Silicon Valley residents, hook, line and sinker.

American Girl

Pets aside, our family was always big on toys, which is probably something I passed on to my children from my own childhood. I loved my cuddly toys and strongly advocated for the continuous growth of Amelie and Maya's own collections. Numerous boxes containing a variety of Playmobil, Lego, fairy castles, cuddly animals and dolls have survived the many moves we've put them through over the years. Even a couple of my own childhood dolls are still hiding in there somewhere, squashed in a giant box with their English and American sisters.

While we shed a few things over the years, I've always felt too maternal to give the dolls away. Maya was the archetypal doll mummy, and I loved the thought that she might discover her babies again someday, when she opened one of the moving boxes. When I rifled through a couple of boxes during one of our last moves to check the contents, I had to smile: one whole box was dedicated exclusively to American Girl dolls. Oh, weren't we just the biggest suckers for American consumer culture?

Our blissful European ignorance of the rabbit hole that is American Girl™ came to an end one summer day when my in-laws visited California via New York. Two miniature dolls, one in traditional Mexican and one in Native American costume, were put in the care of our girls. Of course, being a gift from Nanny, they weren't just any dolls; they came with a story. American Girl dolls are never 'just' dolls: the range contains look-a-like dolls that can be customised according to their human mama's wishes in terms of eye and skin colour, hair length and style and choice of outfit and accessories, as well as historical dolls that each represent a certain point in American history and come with a multitude of educational toys, books and DVDs. To be honest, I think our family learned more about US history from American Girl merchandise than from any US history class in elementary, middle and high school combined.

The creepy thing is that all the dolls, regardless of eye, skin and hair colour, look *exactly* the same. Until you've visited an American Girl store and felt the cold stare of several hundred identical American Girl dolls on you, you haven't felt real horror.

'You know, the people in the store in New York said they would open a new California location soon,' Nanny informed us, eyes twinkling in anticipation.

Which, of course, they did. A brand new, two-storey American Girl™ store came to town, and Maya could barely contain her excitement. I resisted her begging for a good two weeks, forewarned by other parents about the massive hype, the huge queues, and the potential danger of having to remortgage your house as soon as you got sucked into the store. Of course, the inevitable happened. One of Maya's friends invited her to an 'American Girl™ birthday experience'. Maya: 1. Mama: 0.

We arranged to meet outside the store, a whole hour before it opened, to make sure we'd get in. I had heard about the store limiting the number of visitors, and we wanted to make sure our kids' dolls didn't miss their appointments. Each of the girls had chosen their favourite American Girl doll to accompany them on this visit. It felt like going to church. Surrounded by other mums and even dads and their daughters, many of whom were donning their Sunday best and were clutching dolls in matching outfits, we braved the November chill and waited for our turn to enter the hallowed halls of American Girl™ Palo Alto.

Inside, we were ushered to the spa area upstairs. Apparently, part of the 'birthday experience' was a doll spa pamper package. And so it happened that I stood in an American doll store, alongside my 40-something Google Executive friend, watching our six-year-old daughters as they, in turn, watched 'Kanani' and 'Rebecca' receiving a full body massage, a manicure and a hair treatment and styling session, before heading over to the jewellery section to have their ears pierced. Earrings came at an extra cost; my friend had splurged. Even Maya had had enough at that point and was demanding food. Luckily, the line for the in-store American Girl Café experience was too long even for the most ardent fans, and we were able to escape.

Maya loved her American Girl dolls, but at over $100 a pop, it was a habit that we couldn't quite sustain. 'Kit' joined us via eBay, a much more economical route, and she arrived in almost perfect condition, minus one shoe, which meant I was able to haggle for an even better price. Maya, ever the creative little problem solver, simply removed the other shoe, too, and declared: 'Kit is from the Depression era, so she's poor!', which was a very knowledgeable statement for a six-year-old. I was secretly impressed by the company's dedication to history.

Maya went to bed, happily cuddling Kit, and I felt very smug until I woke up to my daughter's blood-curdling screams the next morning. 'Mummeeeeeeeee! Kit's eye is broken!!!!' As it turned out, one of the doll's eyes was stuck, as the row of eyelashes had detached and slipped behind the eyeball into the dark abyss of the socket. Kit's wide-eyed, asymmetrical expression was certainly not a good look, and neither my attempts at wiggling the eye nor my suggestion of a 'Depression era' eye patch were successful. I googled 'dolls' eyelashes', drove to a craft store to buy new ones and did my best to make up for what I had obviously messed up by purchasing a second-rate doll on eBay. It was no good.

My mum, whom we consulted via Skype, suggested a doll doctor. *Did those even still exist?* In my desperation, I called the American Girl store, and indeed, they told me they had an in-house doctor who could take a look at Kit and possibly send her to the doll hospital. I neglected to point out that we had purchased her on eBay.

Maya and I bundled Kit into a plastic carrier bag and headed to the store. We were instructed to wait next to the spa area, as the doctor was apparently attending to a patient up there. And then he arrived. A man in his 40s, in scrubs and with an old-fashioned headlamp on his head, rushed in our direction, brows furrowed with concern. 'Where's the patient?' he demanded breathily, and Maya thrust the plastic carrier bag towards him. Clearly taken aback at the sight of such an unseemly receptacle, he pulled the doll out of the bag, a hardly suppressed tut escaping his lips. 'What ails you, poor angel?' he cooed and cradled the damaged doll in his arms. Maya and I exchanged a look of horror. 'Er, her eyelashes seem to be lost,' I explained, and his look of concern deepened as he examined Kit's eyes. Maya managed a perfectly executed eye roll. The doctor looked serious. 'Kit needs to go to hospital right away!' he concluded. We nodded in agreement, not quite appreciative of the gravity of the situation. 'But,' he directed his earnest gaze at my daughter. 'It's so close to Christmas, and, well, honey, this is a serious operation, and she might need to stay there over the holidays.' His eyes were as wide as saucers with concern. 'You probably won't see her again until January,' he delivered the final verdict. Maya shrugged, clearly unsure how to react and then glanced at me with alarm. *Does he know it's only a doll?*, her eyes seemed to say. We signed the release form, and the doctor, clearly unimpressed by Maya's distinct lack of maternal instincts, whisked Kit away to get her prepped for her trip to the hospital.

'That's kind of a strange job for a grown-up,' was Maya's only comment when we got back in the car to drive home.

As it turned out, Kit did make it back home before Christmas. She arrived in a big parcel, with two perfect new eyes complete with lashes and a 'note for Mommy' stuck to her AG hospital gown. 'I've been very brave, and all the doctors and nurses were really nice to me. I missed you so, so, so much and I'm so happy to be back home.' I placed Kit, still in her hospital outfit, on Maya's bed, so she could see her straight away when she came home from school. Then, I tore up the note.

Fundraising

Having mostly ignored the school fundraisers during our first few years in the Los Altos school community, we decided that our fourth year was the year to finally give in, and purchased tickets for our very first school auction. We needed to know what all the fuss was about.

The theme was Bond, James Bond, and the venue was the very sophisticated Palo Alto Country Club. Scott, who miraculously owned a tuxedo, dusted it off and was good to go. Still unaware of the lengths my fellow auction goers would go to when it came to outfits, I traipsed to good old H&M and found myself a trusty little black number, watched a YouTube tutorial to get my sixties eye makeup right – I had recently had my hair cut into a Twiggy-style pixie, which was begging for fake freckles, white eyeliner and fake lashes – and off we went.

We were shown to our table and then gazed in amazement at the crowd around us. People had really gone to town; everybody was glammed up, coiffed and ready to spend some serious dollars. Bemused and fascinated at the same time, we just leaned back and enjoyed the view. And then the auction began, at which point I humbly bowed to the auction committee's absolutely mindblowing fundraising skills. Prizes included a weekend in a ski chalet in well-to-do north Lake Tahoe, a week in someone's abode in Maui, flights included, day trips on a private yacht, gourmet food deliveries for a year, a party catering for 50+ guests with a private chef, exquisite jewellery, high-level tutoring for your brainy offspring, and so on. People didn't hold back when it came to bidding, and what appeared to be incredibly ostentatious and even vulgar to our European minds was expected and applauded in these surroundings. This was how things were done here.

By the time we got to the main prize of the night, three highly coveted prime parking spots in the school parking lot for one school year, I had to forcefully clamp my jaw shut. Bidding started at $1,000. 'For a *parking spot*??' I mouthed to my husband, who was almost choking on his goblet of Pinot Noir. Who would spend that amount on a lousy parking spot at their kid's school? Plenty of people, as it turned out. The bidding war progressed at lightning speed; people casually held up their paddles as the bids became ever more astronomical, until finally – 'to you, ma'am, for $23,000!'

The other two spots were auctioned off at similarly eye-watering offerings before the crowd descended on the dance floor. There was no holding back in any way, and when we got home at the end of the night, we felt like we'd just been on a movie set. What a night. What a totally different world.

Some of the other coveted auction prizes were theme parties, hosted by parents, for which other parents and even teachers had to buy tickets. This was a great way to contribute a prize when you didn't have a luxury yacht or holiday condo to share, but still wanted to make a donation to benefit the school. Since there was no shortage of international families in our area, there were always plenty of internationally themed parties, which everybody adored.

We happily joined forces with a few German-American families and organised an *Oktoberfest*. Hundreds of pretzels from Esther's German Bakery, vats of potato salad, serious amounts of sausages and tray upon tray of homemade *Apfelstrudel*, lovingly baked by my mother, who was visiting from Germany, were piled high on the beer tables we had hired, the perfect accompaniment to the gallons of authentic German beer. This being well-connected Silicon Valley, someone knew someone who knew someone at the Gordon Biersch Brewing Company, whose brewmaster happened to have studied brewing in Munich and was more than happy to donate two massive kegs. We found a German brass band that provided the perfect mix of Oktoberfest tunes and classic German hits, and moderated a few drinking games and German trivia. Everybody had such a blast that we committed to hosting another one the following year.

We ended up enjoying two more school auctions in California, one a lavish, Great Gatsby themed do, and one a barn dance in the style of *Footloose*, which was held at a local winery, Picchetti, in the hills above Cupertino, where most of the memories fell victim to the copious amounts of delicious California wine we drank like lemonade. We truly loved the wine in this state, from Mendocino and the Russian River Valley to Napa and Sonoma, Lodi to the east, down to Paso Robles in the south. We had already learned that California keeps the best vintages within state borders, and knew we had to make the most of this while we had the privilege.

As much as we enjoyed those lavish events, however, it became ever more apparent that this world was existing on another level. I knew that once we left California, it would feel like a dream, a dream that would never become our reality. I wasn't sure how to live here and enjoy all that the Golden State had to offer while always feeling like an outsider.

One day after school, one of Maya's classmates came home with us after school for a playdate, took a long look at our apartment with her seven-year-old Silicon Valley eyes, and then asked me: 'Are you poor?' I was too stunned to reply and then proceeded to scrape my worldview off the floor, where it had shattered into a thousand pieces. The disconnect was like a punch in the gut. I felt so lucky and privileged to be able to live in this very extraordinary place. It was the opposite of 'poor'. To this little girl, however, who had no concept outside of a world of big houses, an endless supply of tutoring, music lessons and family vacations in Maui, our not very modern and not very impressively furnished apartment must have appeared minute and shabby.

But what did we expect, choosing one of the country's most expensive areas to live? A place where children grew up in surroundings that were so very far removed from how the majority of people lived in the rest of the world.

One day, the sixth graders organised a bake sale at school to raise funds for their elementary school graduation party – Los Altos was one of the very few school districts that kept their students in elementary school until the end of sixth grade rather than the more usual fifth – and graduation parties were a big rite of passage, even if it was 'only' from elementary school to middle school.

The co-founder of one of the world's leading tech companies, who happened to live just around the corner from school, and whose young son was in the first grade, turned up just as the kids were laying out the cakes and cookies, all of various shapes and sizes and decidedly varying degrees of baking skills. At the sight of the very diverse offerings, he expressed his displeasure at the fact that the cupcakes my friend's son was setting down were obviously bought from a shop and not homemade. Raising his eyebrows, and looking at his five-year-old son, he informed us, 'well we always make everything from scratch, don't we buddy, and we actually even grind our own flour!' My friend looked him up and down and then coolly pointed out that not everybody had all the time in the world plus housekeepers and personal chefs, and was he going to buy one of the cakes or not? Flustered, he then mumbled something about not carrying any cash and, under the death stare of my friend, who was not letting him get away with this, called an employee at his house to bike over some change.

I look back at all this with a lot of fondness – the absurdity of making small talk at a school event, which invariably involved mentioning work, and seeing the other person's eyes glaze over the minute it became apparent that you didn't work at Facebook, Apple or Google. Living in a rented apartment. Somehow, because of this very inaccessibility and other-worldliness, I can look at this enchanted bubble like a child watching a Disney movie. With awe and yet knowing it would never be my reality.

Living the Dream

At some point, we stopped talking about going back to Europe altogether. Instead, we moved to a new house. After more than two years in our apartment, we were ready for a real home again. I found an acceptable rental, a typical ranch-style California dwelling from the sixties that hadn't seen any updates or modernisations since those days but fit our requirements. It was the perfect size, within walking distance to downtown Los Altos and equidistant from both of the kids' schools.

The minute the realtor opened the door, and I saw the evening sun hit the dark green tiles with their distinctly 1970s feel in the entrance hallway, I fell in love. It wasn't a pretty house, far from it, and so unlike anything we would have chosen all those years earlier: there was ugly linoleum flooring in the very outdated kitchen, a cracked concrete patio, as well as very old-fashioned bathrooms in salmon pink and a boxy, fully oak-clad office, but I didn't care. The beautiful original wooden floors were gleaming, and I did a silly little happy dance when I glimpsed a lemon tree and even an orange and a persimmon tree in the back garden. What was more, it was built in 'ranch style', all on one level, which made me feel safe and secure. No more thoughts about collapsing floors and ceilings.

I could feel the buzz of excitement I experienced every time we moved to a new place, that delicious temptation of new rooms, waiting to be filled with our belongings and with all the promise of new beginnings. A clean slate. I couldn't wait to move in.

Things were calm, at least for a while. Snowy, who had been an indoor cat up until this point, loved his new residence. He practically did a somersault the first time I let him out into the garden, and he discovered that there was a whole new world outside. And so did the kids, who were so happy to run and bike with their friends around our new and yet so familiar neighbourhood on Starlite Lane. Maya could now ride her bike to school and joined a few other kids in the mornings whose parents had decided to let them be equally independent and venture out without parental supervision.

I fully embraced my California housewife status, splitting my time between yoga classes, my hours as an art docent, some copywriting and reflexology work and running the kids to their various classes. I had pushed any thoughts about a career to the furthest corner of my mind and found that my brain was enjoying this new attitude. There was still a lot of multitasking, but as long as I was able to keep everything in various, neatly divided categories, it was manageable. Maybe I could finally enjoy this California lifestyle properly.

Fragmentation

It didn't take long for the calm to show cracks; I was kidding myself if I thought I could just 'go with the flow'. As much as our life appeared to have reached a smooth period, and I seemed to be in control of it, the many parallel facets of this lifestyle threatened to overwhelm me.

I realised it was the uncertainty of our future that I couldn't handle, while knowing I somehow had to learn to live with it. At this point, there simply was no certainty; we didn't have a real, tangible plan. There was a vague notion of returning to Europe, all depending on Scott's work, our parents' health, and what we wanted to do. We didn't even know what this 'Europe' would actually look like. Would we return to England, or maybe somewhere entirely different? We knew that we didn't want to settle in California long-term; it was simply too far from our families, both in terms of time zones and the distance involved in getting there in case of an emergency. Before long, our parents, while still fairly healthy and willing to travel at this point, wouldn't be able to keep doing this for that much longer. I felt it was vital to live somewhere closer, but the thought of deciding where that 'somewhere' would be scared me. I felt insanely jealous of those expats around me who had to deal with 'only' one place to go back home to; one place they missed. I was dealing with two already, and the splits I had to perform across England, Germany and the US were tearing me apart.

On the other hand, I knew we had to make a decision sooner rather than later. The longer we stayed here, the less likely the girls would want to be uprooted. Scott couldn't understand my anxiety; he seemed to be living fully in the moment, and I tried to bottle my fears for the sake of family harmony.

On the inside, however, I was running in circles, trying to find a coherent narrative that didn't consist of all these different pieces. It was like my life was somehow not real, or that it was happening elsewhere. That I was somehow only existing, but not actually living, waiting for my real life to begin. I just didn't know when or where. When I travelled to Europe each summer, I felt that it was my reality; my family and friends there were my *real* life, while California seemed to exist only as a concept. And yet, every time during my stay and before I returned to California, the narrative flipped, and my European friends seemed to become less real. Would this ever stop? I found that I was constantly thinking things like 'I don't have to worry about this now, I'll deal with it when I'm in California', or 'That's what I'll do when we live in England again'. Clear signs I wasn't fully present in the moment.

Did I have to sacrifice one reality in order to live fully in the other? Why couldn't I feel like one person, living one life, rather than this fragmented human being, flitting from one to the other, as if there were no overlap?

I definitely noticed how every time we went back to Europe over the summer, my whole body seemed to slow down. It felt like people weren't riding the same racing car I was strapped into, and not just because I was there on holiday.

I realised how much the crazy, fast-paced, highly pressurised environment that was Silicon Valley had chipped away at my resilience, and I felt even more strongly than before that I didn't want my kids to grow up with this. Amelie was now eleven, and definitely taking after me as far as her volatility and low tolerance for stress were concerned, was becoming increasingly sensitive to the high-pressure school and societal environment. Voicing her opinion and refusing to be forced into a particular mindset, she kept getting into arguments with one of her teachers, who kept ostracising her for 'disruptive behaviour'. My tween, who had always enjoyed her school environment, started to become morose and reluctant to even go to school. Her grades were dropping, which made her even more stressed.

So many of the children here were raised by parents at the absolute top of their profession, who expected their offspring to scale the same heights by choosing advanced placement classes in high school and achieving perfect SAT scores, sacrificing a social life and, most detrimental of all, sleep.

I couldn't detach myself from this; being surrounded by this mindset made me feel somewhat less than, as though I would always scramble just to hang on, sacrificing my sanity. I knew this wasn't just a Silicon Valley issue, but living in this area of the country certainly amplified it. And the teen suicide rate reflected this. Suicides were a pretty common occurrence in the Palo Alto school district; during the six years we lived there, there were often more than three or four in the space of four months. All this was happening in this shiny, smiley, beautiful state with perfect weather and interesting and educated people from all over the world who chose to come here. Something was utterly wrong. I didn't know how to live here without letting it affect me.

Of course, I wasn't the only one who was sick and tired of this mentality. One day, when the conversation once again turned to the insanity of Bay Area house prices, one of my fellow art docents, another expat, said something that has stayed with me ever since. I can still hear it in her Russian-accented husky voice: 'I don't think this is a time to strive for possessions. It is a time to create.'

And yet, even though Silicon Valley was full of start-up companies, and creative minds seemed to be all around us, creativity was never truly the focus at school. Academia over art. STEM but not STEAM*.

---

*STEM = science, technology, engineering & maths; STEAM = science, technology, engineering, art & maths.

Mavericks

L iving so close to the Pacific Coast and fascinated by surfing, even if I wasn't in the least bit tempted to get in the pretty cold and definitely shark-visited waters myself, I was always on high alert during the winter months. Late December, January and February were the months when the swells came to this part of the world, and a crowd of big wave surfers started to hover around the Northern California coast, waiting for the signal. Big waves meant one thing: Mavericks. This iconic, invitation-only surf competition, organised by the World Surf League, had taken place almost every winter since 1999, but you never knew if and when it was held until it was called a day before, and everybody rushed to the infamous surfing spot at Pillar Point Harbour, just north of Half Moon Bay. A mere forty-five-minute drive from our house.

One morning in January, we heard the news on the radio, and Amelie, who had just started to show an interest in learning to surf, got very excited. I secretly made a decision, and the next morning, instead of dropping her off at school, I turned the car towards I-280, and we headed to the coast.

During the first few years of the 'Titans of Mavericks' contest, as it was officially called, people had been able to walk right up to the cliff to watch the attending surfing legends tame those giant waves, but over the years, the crowds got too big and conditions too dangerous so that we actually had to stay within a fenced-off area watching the action on a big screen. We didn't mind; it was a windy but relatively mild winter day, the crowd was friendly and excitable, and there were plenty of food trucks and live music. Amelie was mesmerised by what she saw happening live on the giant screens, and I loved spending a day with my tween, knowing how soon the teenage hormones would kick in and make her want to spend her days with anybody but her mum. She had been so stressed about school and upset about her detested teacher that I was extra happy to have given her an extra day of peace.

We thoroughly enjoyed the atmosphere, people-watching and not-being-at-school, and when the larger-than-life winners of the competition took the stage at the end of the day, we whooped and cheered along with everybody else, trying to soak up some of the magic sparkle they seemed to spread as they talked about their experience in the ocean.

As we drove back home through the hills at dusk, the sun setting over the Pacific behind us, I felt almost at peace. California was about so much more than Silicon Valley; we just had to get out of our high-pressure bubble from time to time.

Decisions

Amelie started middle school, 'junior high', which brought new challenges and pressure. Socially, she was as bubbly and outgoing as ever and enjoyed making new friends beyond her old classmates. Academically, she did fine, however, keeping her schedule organised and staying on top of her tasks while absorbing the constant talk about college began to take a toll on her mental health.

Everything at school was geared towards college. As early as middle school, kids in the US start to accumulate credits for classes and plan extracurricular activities not just for fun, but also for the essential and profitable benefits they would prove to be when it was time to apply to the college or university of their dreams. It wasn't just the parents and teachers who kept talking about the importance of this; it was already a regular topic of conversation among the seventh and eighth-graders.

Scott's work underwent some significant changes, and he was getting increasingly frustrated with the new management and his changing role in the company. They had already moved location a few times, making his commute very challenging. We sat down to discuss our options. The extremely high cost of living in this part of the world meant we needed to decide fast what our life was going to look like; we couldn't stay here in the Bay Area for even a month without a high-paying job. He decided to quit, taking some time to decide what the next step would be, while taking on various short-term contracts.

All of this affected my own mood and stress tolerance. I felt guilty for having quit my career and relying on my husband to be the sole provider in this pressure cooker of an environment, and I struggled to deal with Amelie's moodiness; absorbing her stress and worrying about the uncertainty of our life made me frazzled and short-fused. When, one day, on our way to the riding stables, she had forgotten to pack her gloves and helmet, I lost my temper. Shouting at her, I reversed the car back up our drive and then, as if in need of some physical release, I didn't stop. I crashed into our garage, the car jerking and shuddering, and the kids in the back-seat wide-eyed with terror. Jolted out of my rage and back to the reality of what I'd done, I profusely apologised to my children and to Scott, who seemed to be more shocked by my rage than angry about what had happened. I was truly terrified of myself and this total loss of control.

We needed to make some decisions. The question was, did we want to stay here in California, make our luck elsewhere in this huge country, or did we want to leave the US altogether and go back to England? Staying would mean putting up with the stresses and cost of the Silicon Valley lifestyle. Leaving would mean uprooting the children.

I felt so torn. I really didn't know at all where I belonged any-more; I just knew I was getting disenchanted with our current location, despite all the beauty around us. My perspective, so strongly focused on returning to Europe for such a long time, had started to come undone, without a solid alternative mindset in place. While I had always clung to the idea of making my way back there at some point to live closer to our families, I had to accept that I wasn't so sure any longer, and that the rest of my family didn't necessarily share my desire for a return to the UK.

Maya probably wouldn't mind moving; she was now in fourth grade, and generally enjoyed school, but seemed to struggle with staying focused on tasks, frequently forgetting to hand in her homework. She was a popular girl, but seemed to get drawn into girl drama wherever possible; it was like she was attracting the more manipulative kids who would invariably let her down. I would be grateful to leave this behind. Often, she would come home exhausted and eager to spend quiet time by herself.

Amelie was going to start high school the following autumn and would certainly prefer a familiar system rather than fight her way through a new country's school system; staying in the US made sense. Plus, if we left now, our children, now nine and thirteen, would still be able to forge new connections and settle in another environment before heading off to college.

Scott wasn't ready to leave the US. He had really thrived in this American environment and worked too hard to sacrifice the incredible network he had built for himself. He started to look for jobs all over the country, and over the summer, a couple of options seemed to materialise. He called me from Austin, Texas, while I was in Germany with the girls, enjoying our usual few weeks with family, and told me how much he liked it and how well the interview had gone. I couldn't believe what I was hearing and furiously shouted 'I'm not moving to fucking Texas!' down the line. Undeniably, though, some obscure part of myself felt a tiny bubble of excitement.

A few weeks later, I boarded a plane to Austin, having agreed to at least take a look at the place before I passed a final judgement. To my utter surprise, the quirky and colourful capital of the Lone Star State managed to wrap me in its welcoming Southern charm. The minute I got off the plane, admiring the several feet tall, brightly painted guitars that adorned the baggage carousels to make sure you knew you had landed in the music capital of the world, I felt a huge jolt of excitement. A new sense of adventure was surging through my veins. A very familiar feeling. Sabina's spirit. The restless heroine of Milan Kundera's book, my fictional soulmate, was back.

Here I was again, reluctant to leave the familiar, yet seemingly unable to resist a new adventure. I smiled, realising why this character came to mind at precisely this moment. I knew now why she resonated so much with me: just a couple of months ago, I had found a copy of *The Unbearable Lightness of Being* in a second-hand bookshop and, remembering how much the movie had impacted me, decided to read it, in an attempt to placate my inner eighteen-year-old intellectual. I really enjoyed discovering all the nuances that the filmmakers hadn't been able to convey, and almost dropped my reading glasses when I came across the following passage: '[...] Sabina knew she would leave Paris, move on, and on again, because were she to die here they would cover her up with a stone, and in the mind of a woman for whom no place is home the thought of an end to all flight is unbearable.' I had my answer. There she was, my kindred spirit, fictitious as she might be. Of course, *of course*, this character had resonated with me, even at an age when I couldn't yet grasp why.

I threw myself into researching areas and schools, just as I had done for California all those years earlier. I even arranged some house viewings, and when the realtor took me to a house high up on a hill in a very leafy, not-at-all urban neighbourhood called 'Cat Mountain', with an amazing view of Lake Austin, I felt a massive tug inside of me. Could this be it? Was what I was feeling a sign, or just the wow-effect of this place? I wasn't sure I trusted my instincts any longer; I had fallen so out of touch with what I wanted or even liked. For the time being, I managed to shove my confusion firmly to the back of my mind, determined to stay rational and weigh up the pros and cons.

Texas might just be a good transitional place that would help us decide where we wanted to be eventually; maybe we would love it and want to stay; maybe it would be the opposite, and we would gladly return to Europe. At least, I told myself, we would be two hours closer to Europe, which should make communication with our families a lot easier.

There was some self-delusion at play; there was no doubt in my mind. Were we trading unaffordable living for a gun-crazy, ultra-conservative mentality? I had been told repeatedly that Austin was nothing like the rest of Texas, and my visit had certainly been encouraging. People called the city 'the bluest dot in the reddest state' – blue for liberal, red for conservative – which didn't sound too bad. After all, I'd grown up in conservative Bavaria and thought I could handle a less liberal mindset. How bad could it be? Austin had a vibrant art scene and was full of creative minds, lots of great music and good food. All things we appreciated and that made us feel like we could have a really good time. At least for a while.

We spent a bittersweet Thanksgiving weekend in Santa Cruz,

breathing in the salty ocean air, taking long walks along the beach and watching the sun set over the Pacific from our favourite spot, Pleasure Point. Knowing I was going to leave all this behind and wasn't likely to return any time soon, I gave in to big, heaving sobs and didn't even try to put on a brave face for the kids. I recognised the feelings of grief from all those years ago when it was time to leave England. Amelie was in turmoil, too, and my heart broke for her. What were we doing, contemplating another move, another puzzle piece in the big jigsaw of our life? 'Can't we just go back to England instead?' she pleaded. 'Is that what you want?' I asked, and she shrugged her shoulders. 'Not really. But we're going back there eventually, aren't we, so why not be done with it? We're just making it harder by adding another place.'

In the end, we were all swayed by a sense of adventure. The girls, sceptical at first about how my attitude about Texas had changed, came along on another trip to Austin for a few days, and we threw ourselves into all the fun things the city had to offer. Taking them to see a few small bands did the trick. Our children had definitely inherited their dad's affinity for music. Scott had always been passionate about making and listening to music, and the kids had grown up with music playing in our house or car all day long, and with mum and dad heading off to concerts. As expected, they fell hard for the appeal of a live performance.

We also looked at some houses to get an idea of what Texas living might look like, and I excitedly showed them around the house on the hill that I had earmarked during my last visit; it was still available, which I took as a sign. My family shared my enthusiasm, and tucking into delicious tacos, chips and guacamole that evening, we came to the conclusion that we were all ready for a new home. Amelie asked to move as soon as possible, wanting to rip the band-aid off the wound in one go rather than facing several months of slowly saying goodbye. We made an offer on the house, a milestone in our American lives. We would be homeowners rather than renters.

I wasn't looking forward to the unsettling experience of the actual move. Part of me felt calm because, after all, I had done this more than once and knew how to deal with all sorts of situations. But the other part of me was terrified, precisely because I had done it all before and knew what to expect in terms of emotional turmoil and loss of sanity.

I guess it was my dark side that came through again, the impulsive side that craved this: that delicious, terrifying, stomach-churning sense of encountering the unknown. Sad and scared to see the familiar go, leaving my comfort zone, yet all geared up for new things. Ready to jump.

PART 2: TEXAS

'The life you have led doesn't need to be the only life you have.'

—Anna Quindlen, *Short Guide to a Happy Life*

SF -> ATX

It was Super Bowl Sunday when the kids, Snowy and I boarded our flight to Austin. Scott was due to leave California the next day, making the two-day drive across half the country in our trusty Subaru, packed to the rafters with essentials that hadn't made it onto the moving truck. When we arrived in Austin, the airport was eerily quiet, which suited us just fine, wide-eyed and exhausted as we were, and carrying a cat that was very obviously furious about being stuck in a cage.

The flight was pretty turbulent, especially approaching Austin – something to get used to in this part of the country with unpredictable winds and no mountains to keep them in check – and when I tried to calm Snowy down, reaching into his crate that was half shoved under the seat in front of me, he buried his sharp teeth so deeply into the ball of my hand that I almost passed out from the pain. He'd also wet his crate, and the smell, along with my grubby T-shirt stained with blood and black cat hair, didn't exactly make me look glamorous. Waiting at the rental car desk, we hid the snarling crate behind our suitcases, and the girls managed to shush him long enough for me to secure a car without anybody threatening to charge us extra.

Once safely installed in our rental car, we found the roads to be deserted – the whole of Austin seemed to be glued to the TV to watch the Super Bowl – which made our drive quick and easy. The sun was about to set, bathing the city in a pink, almost magical glow. By the time we reached our new home, high up in the Northwest Hills part of town, the light had turned purple, and we quickly raced to the top-floor balcony to catch the last rays of the sun, amazed at how massive the sky looked in this part of the country.

The girls were fading quickly, so I looked at Google Maps to find the nearest supermarket, got in the car and hunted down some pizza and salads at Randalls, which turned out to be a Safeway, just with a different name. Another piece in the US culture puzzle solved. We ate, showered – luckily I'd packed a few towels in our bags – and collapsed in a big heap on the airbeds we had wisely ordered, Snowy happily purring in amidst the pile of sleeping bags and pillows, calm and relaxed without any trace of the ferocious beast he had pretended to be earlier. My thumb was still throbbing with pain.

The next morning, we went to register the girls at their respective schools. Moving mid-year meant no grace period or break of any kind. You had to attend school immediately. First, we headed to Maya's new school, Highland Park Elementary. After a very brief introduction and confirmation of vaccinations and address, and a visit to her future classroom, the teacher asked Maya if she wanted to stay right away. Being the curious little adventurer that she was, she immediately agreed, and Amelie and I were left to our own devices.

Not quite as keen to start school as her sister, Amelie had asked for a day off and wasn't supposed to start until the following day. It was hard for her, being new and knowing middle school was only going to be in session for another three and a half months until graduation. We were hoping that by joining school mid-year, she would at least get to know a few other kids who were going to attend high school with her in the coming autumn. But now that she was facing reality, the idea of joining a school where everybody had known each other for at least three years and probably all the way through elementary school was quite daunting. I cursed myself for putting my teen through this ordeal.

When I picked Maya up in the afternoon, waiting with a few other parents, I spotted her smiling face from across the courtyard; she was surrounded by several beaming girls, her hair braided in an elaborate style by one of her new classmates, who was still adding some finishing touches as they spilled out the door. I didn't need to ask if her day had been a good one, but did so anyway, and her resounding 'Yes, ma'am!' made my heart soar. I breathed a sigh of relief. Her Texas welcome was going well.

Scott arrived that evening in a very dusty car, shattered from his long drive from California, but ready for the first of many orders of Torchy's Tacos, a local chain with a branch not too far from our house.

Our first week passed in a blur of activity, getting used to new school drop-off and pick-up situations – no pick-up lanes here – scouting dance schools, grocery stores, doctors' surgeries, etc. I felt like an old hand at it all and was quite happy pottering around my house, creating our new nest. From time to time, I would even sit down at my desk, which we'd placed in prime position on the top floor, right next to our bedroom, with an amazing view of Austin's greenbelt, the wooded hills in this area and glistening Lake Austin in the distance. This 'lake' was actually part of the Colorado River, but no self-respecting Austinite would call it that.

The girls were adjusting to their new routines; we had found a welcoming little dance school not too far from our house, and Maya threw herself into her classes and made friends wherever she went. Amelie was less enthusiastic and was counting down the days until middle school was over, much like she would have done in California. The weather was beautiful, and I adored my new house. It was an unusual construction in greyish blue with a huge red door; one of a few houses in a row designed by an architect in the 1970s, it sat on four levels, with a basement that was accessible from the outside and the girls' bedrooms above it, each with their own bathroom and balcony, also accessible from outside. The main level consisted of a large American kitchen, dining and living area, and a spacious balcony; our bedroom, office, and bathroom were located on the top floor. A teenager's dream set-up. I could read the girls' minds when we first viewed the house, planning secret parties in the basement, with clueless mum and dad all the way on the top floor, oblivious to what was going on down there. Our bathroom was huge, with a giant tub in old-fashioned blue mosaic tiles and brass handles and taps in the middle, giving the whole place a definite James Bond ambience. I loved it, and didn't want to change a thing, even though the realtor insisted we needed to consider updating it.

We didn't have a garden, but the house looked out onto a lot of green; I was looking forward to not having to deal with Texan wildlife, but Snowy was not impressed by his new surroundings, finding the balconies more than confusing. He ventured out one night only to be ambushed by a massive thunderstorm and, no doubt, an array of snakes and coyotes, and became an indoor cat literally overnight. It made me sad to see him hiding under the bed, dreaming of his wild and free days in California, but I hoped he would get used to everything soon.

Trying to lure him outside, I spent a lot of time decorating the main balcony and attempting to plant herbs and tomatoes, none of which could withstand the elements for very long. Fierce winds and scorching heat meant that nothing stood a chance, and what was more, my fear of collapsing floors had returned. Some days, the wind was so strong that you could feel the balcony's beams moving even inside the house. I managed to ignore my phobia for the most part and stayed indoors more.

Lonely

A few weeks later, I began to crumble. I'd worked so hard at getting everything unpacked, hung up and organised that I had pulled a muscle and couldn't walk very well, let alone climb up and down our many stairs. As soon as the option to be physically active was taken away from me and I was forced to sit still, it hit me: I was lonely. There is no more profound sense of loneliness than when you move to a new place and don't know a soul. You feel displaced, like you've lost part of yourself, and all you crave is familiarity and friends to be there alongside you, someone who pats you on the back and squeezes your hand from time to time, even if just virtually. The problem is that nobody knows what it feels like to be catapulted out of your everyday life unless they've done it themselves. People can't guess; you have to tell them how hard it is and be explicit in how much you need their support. Something I, Miss I-don't-need-help-thank-you-very-much, am absolutely terrible at.

I had expected to take this move in my stride since I felt like a total expert, and it took me by surprise how much I missed having support. I hated feeling so helpless, but instead of just calling a friend for some kind words, I chose resentment. I was angry with all the people who didn't reach out to enquire how I was doing. During my first three weeks in Texas, I received a total of one email, one text message and one phone call from friends checking in. It was hard, especially because the kids were constantly on whatever electronic devices that connected them to their old friends. I felt utterly left out.

I could understand why my German and UK friends didn't reach out; after all, to them, it didn't make much of a difference that I had moved; I was still far away in the US, and a few time zones here and there didn't change anything. They were blissfully unaware of the fact that I had just added a whole new dimension to my being. But my Californian friends? *Nothing.* I began to question all the relationships I thought I had built during my six years in California. Was it me? Was I really this unlikeable, this forgettable? All my life, I had felt insecure about my friendships, always at the fringes of friendship groups, never feeling I truly belonged anywhere. Here was the proof that I was not friend material.

I was so exhausted and resentful during those initial weeks in Austin that it didn't even occur to me that people might be missing me, too, and weren't sure how to reach out. Instead of just picking up the phone and sending a few messages myself, I stewed in my own misery and self-pity, and ultimately, self-loathing. There were a few days when, after dropping the kids at school, I came straight back home and crawled under the duvet to cry, although I would always admonish myself for it. Instead of just letting it all out, I told myself I was behaving like a spoilt child. This was ridiculous! I had been all for the move; I had a gorgeous house, a whole new city to explore! I had no right to be so self-centred. After a while, a few sweet messages started to trickle in, and I slowly came out of hiding.

I had learned from my early days in California that the only real way out of loneliness was actually physically going out and meeting people. New friends didn't just knock on the door; you had to actively hunt for them. As an introvert, this was always daunting. Yes, I could switch on the outgoing, chatty persona when I needed to; I could don my smiley, outgoing, effervescent mask and lock up the witchy one that wanted to crawl back home and hide under a blanket. On some days, I managed to do this, but on others, there simply wasn't enough energy available.

I did what I could in those early days, but it took a few months until I made some connections. Since we had arrived in the middle of the school year, there weren't many volunteering options at either of the schools, something I realised I had relied on to happen. I missed teaching art and feeling a sense of purpose, but I didn't even have the energy to think about an actual job.

I felt different here. In California, we had been one of many international families; people were used to a variety of accents and backgrounds, and we always felt welcome and never like the odd ones out. Texas, however, was a different beast. The Austinites were extremely friendly in general, but definitely seemed a little wary of us newcomers. I was worried that we would have trouble understanding the drawly Texan accent, but it turned out that it was actually the other way around – we had a hard time being understood by the locals, our English accents unfamiliar and exotic, and I regularly found myself adopting a horrendous mishmash of US and British English to make myself understood. But I felt like I was constantly saying the wrong thing anyway, accent or not. Somehow, I wasn't hitting the right tone; I couldn't find my footing. I still think it takes a Texan to understand Texas – everybody else is tolerated at best. I was acutely reminded of my own roots; this character trait is definitely shared by the Bavarians I grew up with.

Big Weather

Austin's location in central Texas, right in the heart of what is called the 'Hill Country', means that it is a lot greener than most people imagine Texas to be. Unlike the huge green flatlands to the east or the vast dry desert to the west and, of course, one of the most remote National Parks in the United States, Big Bend, the Texas capital is set amidst lush, green hills with wooded areas. The Greenbelt runs all the way through it, with Lake Austin sitting right in the middle as well as several other waterways. St. Edwards Park, Walnut Creek Metropolitan Park, Onion Creek, Turkey Creek – all of those are within easy reach and make you feel like you're in plain wilderness rather than in the centre of or right next to a big urban hub.

When we arrived in early February, we were pleasantly surprised by the sunny weather and almost summer temperatures, and thoroughly enjoyed wearing sandals and t-shirts while the rest of the northern Hemisphere seemed to be wrapped up in winter coats. As soon as we crossed into March, and spring was well and truly in the air, Texas presented its full colour spectrum. In addition to the amazing murals that adorned many city buildings, bridges, and other structures, rendering ugly urban concrete into art, everything turned fifty shades of green, with gorgeous, colourful wildflowers dotting the landscape. It was bluebonnet season – the Texas state flower is the equivalent of the orange California poppy – and I fell head over heels in love with this beautiful lupine, whose gorgeous shades of purplish blue tinged every meadow and even grew in tiny cracks in the road. Taking photos amidst fields of bluebonnets is a Texas family spring pastime, and it's not rare to see haphazardly parked trucks alongside the motorways and little people posing in a field somewhere nearby. I learned that Ladybird Johnson, former First Lady and wife of President L.B. Johnson, a nature lover and environmental activist in her day, had ordered wildflowers to be sown along the major roads all around Texas, and now vast swathes of colourful Indian blankets, paintbrush flowers, bluebonnets and brown-eyed Susans adorn even the ugliest concrete jungle.

In April, real Texas weather hit. First came the rain, and with it the most almighty thunderstorms I had ever experienced. Some nights, the four of us huddled in our bedroom on the top floor of our house and watched the dazzling blasts of lightning create a performance across the sky, as if it were all a movie.

It was also extremely windy on a regular basis, and sometimes, the temperatures dropped from summer to winter overnight, and then rose back up again. We realised that we'd landed in a climate that was completely vulnerable to whatever weather was happening up north in Canada, since the wind simply blew everything southwards, without any mountain ranges along the way to soften the blow.

The rain didn't seem to stop at all throughout May, which meant that our first visitors, our Finnish friends from California, experienced a rather wet welcome and wished they'd brought their all-weather gear from Europe. As soon as the rain stopped in June, the temperature immediately climbed to high summer levels, and due to the overall wetness, humidity levels went through the roof. It was shocking how humid the air became when it was overcast or raining. The air-conditioning was running constantly just to keep the house dry, and I silently thanked the previous owner of the house for leaving a couple of dehumidifiers behind. I could barely keep up with emptying them each day.

I had started running again, back in March when I thought how lovely it was to be able to exercise without warm clothes at that time of year, but when June arrived, it felt like entering a rainforest the minute I left the house, and it was hard to tell whether I was sweating from exertion or simply from being outside. I felt like I was living in a golden cage: locked up in my big house on the hill, looking out onto blue skies and beautiful scenery, but unable to step outside or even open a window for fear of the sludgy soup-like air disturbing the bearable temperature indoors. I felt trapped. It was almost the reverse of being locked inside your house in England during the winter months, when it's too dreary and miserable to step outside, except it was summer and looked beautiful outside. My brain struggled to compute this new order.

Our New Normal

Friendly as they were, Austinites had a real problem with Californians. It was obvious that Silicon Valley was beginning to hold Austin in its clutches, which only intensified over the years, with lots of tech companies moving to the Texas capital, and Austin's residents lamenting the decline of their city's culture. The influx of prosperous Californians meant house prices increased at an alarming rate, and the city's streets and highways were permanently clogged. It seemed like as much as we'd hoped to escape this movement, it followed us here.

We learned pretty quickly that the correct answer to the question 'Where're y'all from?' was not 'San Francisco'. I started saying things like 'I'm German, but lived in the UK', omitting the California part, and found that people responded positively and were actually interested in my background. Texas has a lot of German heritage and a huge German community, and it tickled me to discover German-sounding towns on the map, such as New Braunfels, Gruene and Fredericksburg with its Haupstraße, Bierkeller and Ausländer restaurant. I even found a Weimar and a Heidelberg on the map, and decided to plan a tour around the German towns of the state at some point.

One of the things I was really keen to discover, and contrast and compare with my observations from California, was the famous Texan charm and hospitality. I guess it's fair to say that it's a Southern thing, and not just a Texas one, but after California and what I'd perceived as simply 'American', I was quite blown away by the way people interacted with each other in this part of the country. Texans definitely like their manners and take great pride in being courteous. Thirteen-year-olds introduced themselves to me by handshake without any parental prompting, making actual eye contact, which sometimes led me to stare back at them slack-jawed, completely forgetting my own manners. Good manners were a big part of the school agenda, too, and I was amazed to see that a lot of parents signed their children up for so-called 'Cotillion' classes. Those are essentially boot camp for manners, including etiquette and ballroom dancing – hence the name cotillion, originally a French dance – ensuring that the Texas offspring are taught to be respectful, polite members of their communities, who can look someone in the eye when speaking to them, hold the door open for the person walking in behind them and generally behave in a well-mannered, gracious way. I would learn later that just because someone attended cotillion lessons didn't mean they were more gentle or kind individuals, but it made for a nice initial impression.

I was definitely getting used to my daily dose of 'Yes, ma'am', which sounded so antiquated to me at first, but which I would come to truly miss the minute I left Texas. The courteousness of our new surroundings definitely suited my British socialisation.

I also totally and unexpectedly fell for the Texan drawl. Unlike the California drawl, which was just drawly with a fair amount of vocal fry, especially among the younger population, people here spoke with a much softer, slower and more melodious accent. Texan slang also had me hooked; the first time someone said 'howdy' as they were passing me on a walk, I almost fainted. Somehow, I hadn't believed this greeting to be real. My favourite expression, however, became 'y'all'. Of course, I'd known about its existence, but I hadn't had any idea it was so ubiquitous. And I certainly didn't expect to adore it so fiercely. 'Y'all' peppers literally every sentence and every interaction in this part of the world, and is used profusely in mind-boggling constructs such as 'what's y'alls' plan today?', 'so good to see all of y'all here', and 'all y'all's accents are so cute'. I knew I would never be able to live without it again.

My love of cowboy boots also reached a new high. On my first trip to Austin, I had discovered Allens Boots, a paradise for boot lovers, and the only reason I hadn't pounced on a pair there and then was the shocking price tag. I had been a fan since my teenage years, when I pleaded and begged until my exasperated mother gave in and bought me my very first pair of brown, synthetic leather cowboy boots. The teasing and laughter I had to endure when I wore them to school the next day, however, made me banish them to the back of my wardrobe, the confidence I felt wearing them torn into tiny shreds. None of my German peers seemed to recognise their appeal. And now here I was in Texas, and my inner teenager danced a little dance of joy. To my delight, I discovered that there were plenty of vintage alternatives to the pricey brands, and I started collecting pair after pair.

I found a pretty café where I could find refuge with my laptop for a couple of hours: Mozarts, right on the river, with shady benches and tables under big oak trees, and enough fans blasting cool air – the perfect spot for people watching and writing.

Both kids were doing amazingly well handling their feelings, but each of them had time off from school from time to time, simply because they were overwhelmed with being the new kid trying to make friends. One of Amelie's friends from California came to visit for a long weekend – flying by herself for the first time – and we took her around our new city, with Amelie eager to show off her new favourite spots and introducing her to a couple of girls from her new school. I saw again how healing it was to connect old friends with new places, weaving a few new strands firmly into the tapestry of our lives. But of course, we couldn't experience this with everybody. In an attempt to keep our connections alive, everybody spent hours online, which proved to be a truly double-edged sword: on the one hand, it was great to virtually spend time with friends and family and see what all the people we missed were up to, and to connect through little comments, pictures and sometimes even a chat. But on the other hand, it was a constant reminder of all the things we weren't part of any longer.

Watching a video of grey whales under the Golden Gate Bridge felt like a punch in the stomach; a picture of the Bavarian Alps gave me such pangs of homesickness that my eyes welled up. Listening to a BBC podcast made me yearn for England and the accents I missed so much. I felt so ungrateful – after all, it was such a privilege to have called all those places home. But I couldn't see it. My life had become so fragmented and disjointed, and now, I had added yet another location to the mix. I realised, for the first time, almost physically, that all those amazing experiences came at a price. To get to live somewhere else means you get to develop a connection to that place, and when you leave, you grieve for that place as if it were a person. Yet missing a place is different to missing a person. You can still reach out and talk to a person, but it's a completely different scenario with a place. This new life was going to take a while to run smoothly.

Maya led by example. This tough little cookie, who had seamlessly swapped her old school's grizzly bear for a Scotch terrier, the new mascot, started to throw herself into a variety of activities, from joining a dance team to mentoring new Kindergarten kids and volunteering as a traffic warden at school. She had come home from school one day with an application form for this highly prestigious position – the kids needed to write an essay and give reasons why they'd make a good warden – and when I asked her why she wanted to do this, she said: 'I want to help my school community.' A true little American.

Graduation

With May coming to an end, the final days of school were also fast approaching. We had three whole months of summer holidays ahead of us. The summer break in Texas was even longer than in California, and with the humidity and heat ruling out any outdoor activities, I was really grateful to be able to escape to Europe for a few weeks.

The end of school also meant the end of middle school for Amelie. Graduation day was just around the corner. I realised that she was approaching the point of having spent half her life in the US and half in the UK. But this sensitive little soul would never describe herself as American. She was a true transcontinental, with roots firmly planted in several places.

Having left California and joined 8th grade in the second half of the school year, she hadn't forged any deep connections with her peers so far. But being the bubbly, charming entertainer that she could be, Amelie had no trouble finding people to hang out with, and so there were at least two or three kids she knew a bit better to start high school with at the end of August.

Unsurprisingly, when we pulled the school's graduation invite from our postbox, Amelie was not excited in the least, and neither was I, although I tried my hardest to hide this and kept talking about what a great day it would be. I actually felt pretty sad when it was time to get dressed up for the event, finding it hard to smile at myself in the mirror while I adjusted the sleeves of the silky blue dress I had bought especially for this occasion, months earlier in California. The heavy rain and flood warnings Austin had decided to contribute to the day only exacerbated our gloomy mood, and the community hall that was the chosen venue for the event had a sterile atmosphere, with stadium-like seating and zero frills. I felt sad not because it was the end of an era, but because I wanted it to feel more like a rite of passage, a memorable occurrence in my child's life. But it wasn't, neither for me nor for her. This event would have felt so different had we stayed in California.

Like everyone around me, I expected to get emotional at the ceremony, but for me this wasn't caused by what was happening but because of what was not happening. As teenager after teenager was called up onto the stage to receive their diploma, a handshake and some words from the principal, or maybe even a special mention or medal for some achievement or other, I felt nothing. Or rather, I felt bereft, cheated out of the real thing, acutely aware of all the feelings I would have felt if we were doing this in California. I would be surrounded by other parents whom I'd known for several years, and most importantly, whose children I knew, and who knew Amelie. We would hold each other's hands, shed a few tears together, reminisce about our kids' earlier school years, and how far they had come. We would brace ourselves for the coming high school years, which we would spend together, or maybe get tearful as we parted ways with those who were heading to a different school. We would share both our joy and our sorrow. It would have meaning; there would be an emotional connection.

I could feel my daughter's pain while she was going through the same emotions. I knew that every second of this ceremony, she was thinking of who should be sitting next to her, who she should be pulling faces with. This graduation ceremony in Austin couldn't give her the closure she deserved. And while the logical part of myself was telling me that this was just a stage in life, a meaningless event that would soon be forgotten, the emotional part of me was grieving. So I cried not because it was the end of an era, but for the loss of an experience I felt we really needed.

It hit me hard that this wasn't the only time we felt or would feel like this. By moving around so much, we were robbing our children of a past that would give them stability, a sense of identity that had to do with location and long-term connections they would just accept, rather than an identity they had to create over and over again. The chance to be surrounded by people of all ages who'd known us and them from when they were little, and would provide a constant in their lives. Yes, we had long-term family friends whom we took great care to stay in touch with, but our daily lives happened without them. Watching the many grandparents around us hugging their newly graduated grandchildren, I also mourned for my and Scott's parents, who didn't have the opportunity to be part of this day. Everybody was missing out.

High School

After a few blissful weeks in Europe, which were especially blissful because of the beautifully cool weather, we came back to our new reality. To me, a new school year always felt so much more 'new' and 'fresh start-y' than an actual new calendar year, with all sorts of new resolutions. Of course, this was our first proper school year in Austin, and I was relieved not to be completely new to the system, with all its PTA groups, school supply lists, lunch order systems, etc.

Maya was starting her last year of elementary school before rising to middle school the following year, and Amelie was now a freshman in high school. Such milestones... I could so clearly remember each girl's first day at school here in the US, while memories of Amelie's time in the UK were fading at an alarming rate. They'd both grown up so much, and sometimes it was hard to reconcile the lanky, sarcastic and ferociously witty teenager who was now an inch taller than me, with the bubbly, high-energy little chatterbox who jumped right into second grade in California and made a ton of friends within her first few days.

Amelie had been so nervous about starting high school here, but she came home from her first day surprised that it hadn't been as bad as expected. Her school, McCallum High School, offered a fine arts academy for creative and musically minded kids, which had made it our first anchor point in our search for a home in Austin. After the dearth of art education in California, we were so excited and grateful for all that the school had to offer creative, artistic kids, and I knew she'd find her groove and her people eventually.

It felt a little bit strange sending them both off to school after eleven weeks of summer holidays, but at least I didn't have to return to a quiet house, as we had a brand new family member: we had finally done it and got ourselves a family dog, a five-month-old Irish Setter puppy. I had grown up with these red-haired bundles of energy and knew that if we ever actually got a dog, it had to be a Setter.

Idly googling 'Irish Setter puppy in Texas' a few days before the summer break ended, I couldn't believe my luck: just outside of Houston, someone was looking for a home for the last pup of a recent litter. My impulsive inner child felt instant validation, and within hours of deciding it was time for us to say yes to a dog and persuading my husband – the girls were already whooping with delight – I had arranged a 'meet and greet'. Just a few days later, 'Ziggy' joined us in Austin.

With the exception of Snowy, the whole family fell head over heels in love with this affectionate, long-legged goofball. Resisting any attempts of canine affection, our cat clearly took this new addition to the household as yet another sign that he hated Texas.

Our daily lives changed completely; I found that looking after our dog kept me so busy and distracted that I had no time to feel lonely. An active early morning dog walk – these dogs don't come with a 'slow' button – was a great way to kickstart my day, and I loved exploring my surroundings with my enthusiastic new friend. Our weekend routine was upended, too: instead of sleeping in, Scott and I got up early and took Ziggy to new places, discovering a whole new side of Austin in the process and spending valuable time together chatting, making plans, and laughing at Ziggy's antics. Austin also turned out to be the most dog-friendly place I'd ever known, and our boy was able to accompany us to numerous beer gardens, restaurants and even shops.

Foodies

O ur summer in Europe had been wonderful on so many levels, providing a sense of consistency and continuity for all of us. While I knew switching between all our worlds in the space of just a few weeks would feel discombobulating, I still hoped to slot quickly back into Texas life. Over the years, I'd developed a variety of 'how to survive coming back to reality' skills for California, anticipating how I'd feel and what I needed to do to get settled back in again. But here, things were different. I hadn't quite found my Austin groove yet. It still felt like a strange, liminal place, as though it hadn't quite worked its way into my reality.

One thing, however, definitely helped the settling back-in process: food. We actually realised how much we'd got used to our new surroundings when we started missing Texas food while in Europe. This might sound strange, especially as we always pounced on our favourite foods as fast as we could whenever we travelled to England and Germany, but we really missed the Austin food we'd come to love.

While we certainly couldn't complain about the quality of food in California, food culture was equally huge in Austin, albeit in a less aloof, fine dining sort of way, but rather a more relaxed and down-to-earth style, which suited us very much. We picked up tacos several days a week, whether for breakfast, lunch or dinner, accompanied by delicious salsa that made your tongue sweat, and with real, homemade soft corn or wheat tortillas, rather than the always-stale El Paso kits found in supermarkets across the globe. And we discovered *queso*, the gooiest, cheesiest, most perfect complement to tortilla chips.

I was delighted when I discovered that Whole Foods was actually an Austin-based company, and the flagship store on North Lamar Road was certainly something to behold. But then I found an even more impressive and maybe a tiny bit less expensive option: Central Market, the upmarket cousin of the beloved Texan supermarket chain H-E-B. While the acronym originally comes from its founder, Howard Edward Butt, we were usually given the Austin explanation: 'Here Everything is Better'. I always felt happy supporting this chain, knowing how much they did for the community, from supporting food banks to countless sporting and school events, including the *Excellence in Education Awards*, to contributing hugely to emergency relief efforts.

Missing our quick and dirty 'In-N-Out Burgers' from California, we were delighted to find that there were a few locations in Austin. However, complying with the overall 'don't California my Texas' attitude, we decided to give up our beloved 'double-double/ animal style/protein style' order in favour of the local burger chain 'P.Terry's'. While I don't want to take sides, I have to say that a stop or two at P.Terry's remains part of every trip back to the Texas capital.

Talking about food, I obviously can't leave out barbecue. As someone who doesn't eat meat very often, I didn't really care that much about the massive barbecue culture in the southern United

States, but after a few plates of melt-on-the-tongue beef brisket with all the trimmings, such as coleslaw, fried pickles and grits, a porridge-like sludge made of creamy, grainy, salty cornmeal and cheese, which is utter heaven if prepared properly, I was a convert. We sampled plenty of famous and less famous Barbecue hotspots in and around Austin, such as Micklethwait and the Salt Lick, which even has a location in the Austin airport, meaning that you always enter and leave Texas with a whiff of BBQ.

A Little Bit of Red With
Your Blue?

Moving to Austin in 2016, in the run-up to an election that was palpably more divisive and controversial than the last one, reminded us just how diverse this country really was. While we had witnessed Obama's reelection campaign in California, a blue, ie liberal, ie Democratic state, Texas offered us a very different experience.

However liberal Austin might appear compared to the rest of the state, it was still the capital of Texas. A deeply red, ie Republican, conservative state. When we arrived here at the beginning of the year, they had just passed the open-carry law, a law that allowed people to carry their guns publicly, in plain sight, even in places like the University of Texas, scene of the first mass shooting in the United States, back in 1966. To me, this was utter lunacy, and the fact that the people of Austin, the Democratic mayor, professors, dean and students hadn't been able to prevent this was deeply unsettling. It made me nervous about the city's future, and I began to wonder what it would look like in five or ten years' time.

Sometimes, it felt like living here in Austin, in our liberal, craft beer-brewing, Hipster bubble, you could almost forget that you were in the middle of a deeply red state. Austin – often described as the blue dot in a red sea, or, by more realistic observers, a purple island – could really fool you.

The city, historically a mecca for artists, musicians, and other creatives, had a huge LGBTQ community and generally seemed to foster an easy, down-to-earth lifestyle, with a dislike for megalomania and large corporations. This certainly seemed to be the general mood of the old Austin and was still palpable when we moved here in early 2016, but with the steady stream of affluent, tech-affine new residents, the tide was starting to turn. Still STEAM rather than STEM, but definitely different.

Texans are proud, and even though Austin might not be like the rest of the state, there is some fierce patriotism going on. This trait reminds me of the Bavarians or the Scots in relation to their fellow countrymen and women. For example, Bavarians would typically call themselves Bavarians first and Germans second, and Scottish people would probably never refer to themselves as British. As a Bavarian girl, I totally get this, and despite my misgivings about Texas, I have to admit that I felt an instant connection with some of the more patriotic traits I discovered in the Lone Star State.

Spotting the famous 'Don't mess with Texas' bumper sticker became a daily occurrence, with the occasional 'Come and take it' sign thrown in for good measure. Originally, this sign depicted the barrel of a cannon with a Lone Star above it, but more modern interpretations can include images of other weapons, such as assault rifles – a direct protest against changes to the Second Amendment. Nobody was to tell Texans to give up their guns. The words actually derive from Greek culture, a laconic reply supposedly given by the Spartan king Leonidas in response to the Persian king Xerxes' demand for the Spartans to surrender their weapons. They were famously quoted in the Battle of Gonzales, the first land battle of the Texas Revolution against Mexico in 1835. Once Texas declared independence from Mexico in 1839, it became the Republic of Texas, flying its famous red-white-and-blue flag with the lone star, as it still didn't exist under the Star-Spangled Banner of the United States. That same flag still represents Texas today, as a sign of its independence and existence as a republic, setting Texas apart.

State history is taught ad nauseam in American schools, so kids usually know a lot about local landmarks and events, but less about world history. In short, people here are proud to be Texan, proud of Texan values – above all, the love of freedom – and proud of their fellow famous Texans, from Willie Nelson to George W Bush.

One afternoon, as I was waiting for Maya's dance class to finish, a fellow waiting parent started chatting to me. This far into my time in the US, I was totally used to this – it is virtually impossible to share space with an American without striking up a conversation. As opposed to Britain or Germany, where you can get away with a mere nod and maybe something like 'Ah well, can't be long now till they finish' or maybe even 'Which one's your daughter?' There is no such thing as quietly waiting together in America. Everybody likes to chat. I've always appreciated those superficial conversations, as it's often interesting and eye-opening to hear people's opinions, especially when you don't know them and probably won't see them again either.

Obviously, I had to come clean and talk about moving here from California, and he indulged me and promptly burst into one of the typical 'Austin is overrun by Californians' chants, but in a jovial way. 'All we want is for people who move here to be nice,' he sighed. 'And unfortunately that's not always the case.' I could see his point and nodded in agreement. A Silicon Valley money-making mentality and an overinflated sense of self might rub an Austinite the wrong way. He went on to rant about house prices, In-N-Out Burger versus P.Terry's and, ultimately, cycling. I explained that my husband was a keen cyclist, but hadn't been out as much here in Texas as back in California. Partly, I told him, because he hadn't found any nice roads and tracks that felt as safe as what we were used to, because of big cars not taking too much notice of cyclists on the roads around Austin. 'That's because we have all those Mexicans here. They just—' he trailed off, rolling his eyes. Not wanting to start an argument, I bit my tongue; I had seen my fair share of dangerously fast pick-up trucks, driven by white men, as well as SUVs cutting corners near schools, big blonde Texan tresses at the wheel, but decided to keep my mouth shut. 'So, what's a good road then?' I asked him, trying to redirect the conversation.

'The one right at the back of this area,' he said. 'It was named after Lance Armstrong, as it used to be his training ground, but not anymore!' He snorted. Talking about Lance Armstrong, the controversial Texas-born cycling legend, was always a delicate topic in this town; I had already learned not to bring him up in conversation. There was even a bike path in downtown that still bore his name. 'Lance Armstrong, really?' I said, raising my eyebrows. 'That man, what a shame he turned out to be such a—' I paused, trying to find the right word, something that would accurately describe my disdain for the cyclist's morals. Texas dad cut in: 'Yeah, right? What a shame he had to get himself caught!' Biting my tongue yet again, I was glad that the dance class finished right at that moment, and hordes of smiling, chatty little dancers were filling the hallway.

Observing the American people in the run-up to the 2016 election was a whole new experience. During the last election, in 2012, we had been relatively new to the country, and couldn't believe the sheer amount of campaigns, rallies and debates, with which we were bombarded all year in the run-up to November. The noise and pandemonium created by the two opposing parties to push their candidates was certainly something to behold, which we observed from the sidelines, unable to cast our votes as non-US citizens.

To me, it seemed like a giant, nationwide circus, or rather, two rival circus families sending out their tightrope artists, contortionists, animal tamers, and above all, clowns, to entertain the masses. No truer words have been spoken than Frank Zappa's: 'Politics is the entertainment branch of industry.' If you could forget about the seriousness of the election and its consequences for the world, I would have given it a 10 out of 10 for entertainment.

Watching Obama and Romney's nomination acceptance speeches, I couldn't help but make comparisons to our European leaders and had a really hard time imagining Angela Merkel ardently proclaiming her love for her husband in front of millions of viewers, or Samantha Cameron making a passionate, tear-stained speech about David's accomplishments. And why did every speech have to end with 'God bless America'?

I wouldn't say California was very representative of the rest of the nation, but I could see how certain attitudes had evolved. There were a plethora of qualities to admire about the candidates' performances. Passion, enthusiasm and dedication to a cause were definitely amongst them, and putting issues into snappy sound bites. They all seemed to have gone to drama school. They were so good at the whole public speaking thing, with their booming voices that caught just in the right places... I was quite blown away by their acting skills.

California was certainly unique in being a state where politics wasn't talked about that much in day-to-day life, at least back in 2012. California's electoral college traditionally votes for the Democrats, not the Republicans. It was almost like nobody really wanted to get involved too much; the electoral college would take care of things. The socio-economic aspect of this was certainly a factor, at least in the area we lived in, and politics was something that happened whether you voted or not. I knew some people who volunteered on a local level, but nobody really talked about it very much, at least not in day-to-day interactions. I knew that, as a blue state, California had a generally positive attitude towards President Obama, which wasn't necessarily the case in the rest of the country. But California was also bankrupt, and it felt like people were very disillusioned with politics in general; this was definitely not a European prerogative. My impression was that this disenchantment made people more inclined to rely on their own resourcefulness and initiative rather than on help from Washington, D.C.

A political system that consisted of only two parties – the few little independents were barely worth mentioning – meant everything was incredibly polarised, which is why it seemed easier to avoid the topic of politics in your daily life altogether; professing any party affiliation might open a can of worms you weren't ready to deal with. Ironically, lawn signs bearing the name of the preferred candidate would adorn a lot of the houses in every neighbourhood in the run-up to the election, blatantly declaring people's party affiliation. I couldn't wrap my head around the logic of my new country.

At first glance, our liberal bubble in Austin in 2016 didn't feel all that different from election time in California four years earlier, except that there were a lot more lawn signs.

Things began to shift as we got closer to the big day in November. I spent a good two hours each day roaming the hills around our house with my dog and got a thorough view of how the mood changed. While our area was staunchly dotted with 'I'm with Her' lawn signs – some of which had been *Bernie* signs at some point – I noticed a definite increase in Trump signs and banners during those last couple of weeks before the election, and it gave me chills. It was like I was happily meandering through what I assumed to be a very Democratic area one day, only to realise there were Trump supporters all around me. We didn't get many MAGA trucks driving through our neighbourhood, but spotting the red hat at my local coffee shop was scary enough. I realised how innocent I had been after all those years in California. This was the real America.

The people we surrounded ourselves with, however, were mostly the same type we had always surrounded ourselves with, whether American, German or British, and there was the same degree of baffled disbelief and fear across the board. We heard horror stories about families torn apart, grandkids no longer allowed to see their grandparents because of the huge clash of opinions, parents denying their grown-up children access to their houses, and so on. It was clear that this was not your usual election.

We were all glued to the TV on election night, and at some point, a sort of dissociation set in. I had a massage booked for the next day, a belated birthday present, and found that it was an absolute waste of money, since there was no way I would be able to switch my brain off from our new reality.

Another American
Christmas

Perfectly timed to distract our minds from the whole election nightmare, the holidays arrived. I realised that Christmas was a much bigger deal here in Texas than in California. Never in my life had I seen that many garish decorations, and Christmas music was blaring from every corner of the city.

As much as I feared my usual homesickness at this time of year, I was also really looking forward to the Christmas period and happily heaved our big Christmas box up from the basement. I wanted the girls to have a Christmassy home to feel more settled. After all, they had lived in five different homes in the last seven years. This really struck me when, on the night of the 5th of December, it was time for them to put out their shoes to see if St. Nikolaus would fill them with goodies overnight. We were still doing it all, and German Christmas traditions could not be forgotten. As I looked at their boots, realising they were both a size larger than my own, I had flashbacks to previous St. Nikolaus days, remembering the assortment of shoes and boots over the years, all different styles and all in different houses. It made me feel rather nostalgic, and I had to swallow hard. Our kids had handled a lot of changes over the years, each in their own way.

Maya, who'd been very 'let's do this' from the start, seemed to be able to fully live in the moment, wherever we were, while never losing sight of her end goal, knowing exactly what she wanted: to study and work in fashion. Right now, she was preparing for a multitude of dance recitals, and we were racing from rehearsal to dance shop and back, adding to the ever-growing pile of pink and tan tights and ballet and jazz shoes.

Amelie, on the other hand, was very obviously my daughter and always seemed to miss what was past while being impatient for what was to come. As a consequence, she found it much harder to feel settled and happy in the moment.

I tried to compensate for any feelings of doom and gloom by baking our favourite German Christmas cookies. Baking was my way of distracting myself, and I put every ounce of goodwill into it, hoping the irresistible smell wafting through the house would make up for any emotional turmoil. Sometimes it worked, but since the girls were so much older now and not really into all the singing, baking and general festiveness anymore, I ended up feeling even more dejected as I was standing in my big Texan kitchen, covered in flour, German radio playing in the background and a tongue-wagging, appreciative canine dustbin next to me.

Austin Anniversary

I knew we weren't the only family to start 2017 with a sense of doom. Once inauguration day had passed, and Obama was firmly out of the White House, things quickly intensified.

We marched to the Austin Capitol in the Women's March in January, and Amelie turned into quite the activist, involving herself in school protests and generally becoming very passionate about politics. I could see it everywhere; political awareness was rising and galvanising the population, especially among the young adults. Their passion and despair were palpable, and provided a glimmer of hope amidst all the madness.

To escape Texas for a while, the girls and I boarded a flight to California to reconnect with old friends and get our little dose of Pacific Ocean air. We boarded the plane feeling a mix of excitement and trepidation. It had been over a year since we'd left, and I was particularly worried about Amelie and about how torn and unsettled she would feel seeing her friends again. We ended up having a beautiful time; listening to my girls' excited chatter and giggles with their friends in the backseat as we drove along Highway 17 to the coast healed my heart a little bit, but deep down, I felt torn. This was a great visit, a wonderful opportunity to see some people I'd missed, but no more than that. It didn't feel like *home*.

Sitting on a cliff above Pleasure Point in Santa Cruz, enjoying the light breeze and gentle spring sunshine and the sweeping view across Monterey Bay, I shed not just a few tears, wondering what on earth had possessed us to move to Texas. What had we lost by leaving California? What had this new random place we now lived in given us? I didn't belong in either.

I didn't want to live in California anymore, but neither did I feel like Texas was a good fit. It felt too insular, too isolated; I hated the fact that you had to get on a plane for a change of scenery. There had been so much to explore when we lived in California; we hadn't even been able to see it all. In Austin, on the other hand, it felt like we had explored all there was to explore.

As I was soaking in the view and the warmth of the California sun on my bare arms, a thought lodged itself firmly into my mind; I knew it had been trying to for a while, but I hadn't been brave enough to acknowledge it.

I wanted us to move back to England. After seven years of living far away from friends and family and our European roots, I was ready to say goodbye to the US. I was so tired of fighting the constant pangs of homesickness and missing my friends. I needed to stop living in limbo and start living a 'normal' life, with my own career, family nearby and familiar surroundings. I was sick of thinking that the place I lived in was only temporary; I craved a long-term solution. Texas was not where I wanted to stay.

I returned to Austin with a new sense of resolve, finally able to say what I had wanted to say for so long. But how was I going to tell my family?

Scott, the family realist, had felt this coming and started to discuss it as an option, in a very pragmatic way, just to get a feel for the girls' state of mind. I was under no illusion that moving with teenagers, or soon-to-be teenagers, was a monumental decision and required a unanimous vote, but everybody was remarkably matter-of-fact about it. Amelie, who hadn't been that keen to move to Texas in the first place, was on board immediately, and Maya seemed excited enough to live close to her beloved Nanny and Grandad. Scott was less enthusiastic, but I persevered. We were doing this.

We decided that the girls and I would leave Austin as soon as school finished in June and before the worst of the Texas heat descended on us, while Scott would stay in our house for the foreseeable future, gradually finishing the project he was involved in while working on a transition back into the UK job market. Until he found a new work opportunity in or around London, he'd commute every few weeks.

Our house in England, which had been rented out during our absence, was waiting for us; all we needed to do was give notice to the tenants. I didn't even know who was living there anymore, as an agency was dealing with it all, but we hoped that moving back into our old home would be the easiest way to return before making any further decisions on a suitable location. Maya didn't even remember the house at all, since we had left before her fourth birthday, but both girls were still familiar with the surroundings and seemed excited to reconnect with their English friends and their roots once more.

To say I had mixed feelings was more than an understatement. Seven years was a long time to spend in another country. Amelie had spent half her life in the US, and Maya more than half of hers.

We had changed, and no doubt the place had changed too. I acknowledged that it wouldn't be a case of just picking up where we left off. I just didn't really know what that meant.

Yes, we had always planned to return to Europe eventually, but that had been a rather vague notion and certainly didn't entail moving back into our old house. On the one hand, I couldn't wait to be back in an environment that I knew, with friends around the corner and easy access to places I loved, as well as my own parents. I was slightly worried about the winter after living in warmer climates for so long, but I would not miss the relentless Texas summer heat and humidity.

On the other hand, I worried how we'd feel being back, while all the people around us had been living their lives there and didn't know anything about this strange, amazing, parallel life we had experienced in the meantime.

Plus, moving from Trump America to Brexit Britain would most certainly not be the easier option. The process of the UK pulling out of the EU had only just begun, and I feared its toxicity, which had been palpable already in the run-up to the election. I was determined to bring back some of my positive, open and friendly 'American' attitude to fight the general doom and gloom and negativity that we might encounter.

Travelling with Pets

We had totally underestimated the complexities of moving pets across the globe, and I was glad that I started the process the moment we discussed moving back to England.

Having flown with our cat to Texas from California the previous year, I had at least some experience. Of course, that had been a very short trip, incomparable to the monumental task of flying long-haul internationally with all its pre- and post-flight intricacies. We knew Ziggy would have to travel in a crate in the cargo section, but we were hoping for Snowy to fly in the cabin with us in a carrier under the seat, just as we'd done before.

After a phone marathon involving various airlines, pet travel agents, veterinarians and customs agencies, we learned that we would neither be able to fly from Austin to London, nor in June as planned, since Austin didn't have adequate air-conditioned facilities to hold pets after check-in, British Airways – the only airline flying direct – didn't accept any pets on board, and the UK was tricky to fly to with pets. None of this information could be found online, and we had already booked our non-refundable flights.

I started to panic. Was this a sign that the move was a bad idea? We came up with a new plan: my parents, sensing my growing despair, offered to help. I would take Ziggy and Snowy to Germany in May, fly pet-accepting Lufthansa from Houston, thus avoiding any heat-related issues, and return to Austin to finalise the move, while they looked after our fur babies until we picked them up later that summer by car. Somewhat calmer and with the logistics seemingly handled, I set about organising the various vaccines, microchip updates and airport notifications, an intricately linked procedure that caused numerous sleepless nights.

Pets aren't allowed to be given any sedatives on an international flight; in fact, you need to sign a document to state that they are medication-free, as it interferes with their ability to cope with cabin pressure changes. My vet prescribed some herbal anti-anxiety drops for both pets, which she recommended to try out before we would actually travel. She had called my local pharmacy to fill a prescription for us, but when I went to pick it up, the pharmacist couldn't locate anything under my name. I tentatively asked for 'Ziggy Cook' and 'Snowy Cook', and *voilà*, he found them instantly. It occurred to me that, had I just asked for those names right away, he probably wouldn't have batted an eyelid – here in the US, those might just be perfectly acceptable kids' names, and the pharmacist probably didn't even realise that they were filling a prescription for non-humans.

I dusted off Snowy's fabric carrier from a year ago and found that it was too chewed and destroyed to weather another journey. A hard plastic carrier would be ideal; however, the carrier had to fit underneath a seat, and our long-legged panther was way too big for the small size that would. I purchased another fabric carrier that I knew could be squished enough to fit, praying Snowy wouldn't eat his way out during the flight. Ziggy's kennel was another matter. We had purchased one a few months before the flight, not taking into consideration that our dog was still a puppy, and not yet fully grown. When we showed up at the cargo gate in Houston, the check-in person took one look at our dog, another at the crate, and just pointed to the wall of crates behind him, all available for purchase at a nicely marked-up price. Defeated and with no time to drive to the nearest pet store, we had no choice but to dig into our pockets again. Already somewhat delayed, we bundled our dog into his very expensive new container, watched him being wheeled off and said our own goodbyes, Scott driving the three-and-a-half hours back to Austin, and me braving a long-haul flight with the cat.

Snowy and I headed to security; I was wearing a long-sleeved, sturdy top in anticipation of his claws, but he behaved like a routine traveller even when I had to yank him out of his carrier to step through the barrier and then lure him back in. Not a single person asked for the veterinary notes. I had put a harness and lead on him so that I could take him out of his crate and let him roam a little bit before we got on the plane without fearing his escape. In-cabin pets are supposed to stay in their carrier for the duration of the flight and under the seat for take-off and landing, but I pulled it out from under the seat as soon as the seatbelt signs came off and lifted Snowy on my lap a few times during the flight so he could look out of the window. Who knows what he thought, marvelling at those huge, pink, fluffy clouds outside; he probably thought he was in some kind of weird dream. Or maybe he knew that he was finally escaping Texas.

Arriving in Munich ten hours later, I wasn't sure how to proceed. If I'd brought somebody else's rabid, unvaccinated cat with me to Germany, nobody would have noticed. After all the procurement of certificates, fees and stress I had had to endure, nobody bothered to show even the slightest bit of interest in Snowy or any of his paperwork. Almost annoyed, I approached the customs officers in the 'items to declare' section, but they just shrugged their shoulders and asked whether my pets were pedigree breeds. I told them they weren't – they didn't check – and so Snowy and I set off to find the cargo section, where Ziggy would be waiting for us at the airport veterinarian's office.

Luckily, my parents were already waiting for me in the arrivals hall, waving excitedly, and we went on our way to locate my dog. After twenty minutes of driving around, we finally located the vet's office, only to be told that we needed to pay our customs bill and 'storage fee' at the main customs office before I would be able to claim my dog. At least I was able to find out he had safely made it to Germany and was doing well. We set off again, found the office, paid one of the bills and were promptly referred to the cargo gate desk at yet another location to pay the second one. After another little trek along various corridors and up and down various stairs, we eventually found the desk, marched back to the customs office, got our stamp, and drove back to the vet's office. At this point, not having slept for a good 24 hours and clearly unprepared for this amazing display of German bureaucracy, the whole experience started to feel very surreal.

Ziggy was already waiting for us, and when I called his name, he practically started doing somersaults in his crate, which made the trolley it was set on roll down the hallway towards us. He was beside himself with joy when I released him, and if I'd thought it odd that nobody had wanted to check my identity, it was probably unnecessary at that point.

As soon as we arrived at my parents' house, both pets seemed like they'd never been under any stress whatsoever.

Goodbye, America

When I returned to Texas, it was time for Maya's graduation from elementary school, a three-hour ordeal which looked essentially the same as Amelie's middle school graduation a year earlier. Each child got called up onto the stage to receive a certificate, and the principal and teachers presented special awards to those kids who had somehow elevated themselves from the crowd, be it through special athletic or musical prowess or some act of school-minded altruism. It was basically the same five kids who kept being called up and collecting praise and medals while the rest of us prayed for it all to be over quickly. What a horrendous display of favouritism; I hated every second of it. England would be nothing like this.

We began our tour of goodbyes, picked up Torchy's tacos for the last time, swam at Barton Springs once more, and had a farewell dinner with friends. It was much harder to say goodbye to Austin than I had expected it to be. It seemed that the city had crept into my heart while I wasn't looking. Now that it was real, I was doubting my decision. All of a sudden, I saw a multitude of beautiful things, frantically taking pictures of my beloved agaves, and tried to burn the view from my top floor balcony over the greenbelt and river below onto the hard drive of my brain. I knew I wouldn't miss the heat, the humidity, the giant cockroaches, the crazy gun laws and the insularity of liberal Austin in the middle of ultra-conservative Texas. But I was going to miss its open, down-to-earth vibe, non-judgmental, friendly people and its inherent quirkiness. I made a vow to take a bit of that spirit with me wherever I would go. I would miss bank employees with blue hair and school teachers covered in tattoos. I would miss the abundance of gorgeous food and great music on my doorstep. I hated the fact that California would soon be an expensive, ten-hour flight away instead of only four, and I couldn't imagine an existence without shopping for groceries at Trader Joe's. I would also miss the awesomeness of the Southern drawl, 'y'all', and 'yes, ma'am'. And how would I be able to live without looking up at that giant, overwhelming Texas sky, which was so truly amazing and bigger than anywhere I'd ever known? The last thing I threw into my suitcase was a big packet of bluebonnet seeds.

I was acutely aware that a huge chapter of my life was coming to an end, and I didn't feel so sure anymore that this was the right decision. But I forcefully shut down the alarm bells that were shrilling in the pit of my stomach, and kept my gaze straight ahead. I was hoping that returning to our old house would magically flip the switch and make us feel like we'd arrived.

PART 3:
INTERLUDE –
ENGLAND

'So, here you are, too foreign for home, too foreign for here.
Never enough for both.'

—Ijeoma Umebinyuo, *Questions for Ada*

Repatriation

By the time our plane touched down at Heathrow, I was totally wired. Running on so much adrenaline that I felt like I could do anything, I barely slept that first night back at my in-laws' home in Kent. Scott couldn't come with us because of work – he'd join us in a week's time. This 'commute' was going to be our new normal: him spending a week or two with us, then another two to four weeks in Austin, and so on, until we knew what his work situation would require.

I had a few extremely busy weeks ahead of me, during which I had to move back into our old house, supervise the moving crew and, most daunting of all, sort out the girls' schools for September.

We had already leased a car, which was waiting for me at my in-laws' place, and so early the next morning, I drove to our house to make sure everything was in order before the moving van arrived later that day. I had decided to do this by myself in order to gather my wits and not worry about my or the kids' emotions. My mother-in-law suggested dropping them off later, along with some lunch and some of our belongings that had been stored at their place for the last seven years. I didn't even know what they were anymore. I was buzzing with a mix of anticipation and dread, not sure how I'd feel entering a place I left more than seven years earlier.

It was a bright, sunny morning in late June, the temperature unusually high for this time of year, and when I turned the key in the back door, I smiled as my body remembered to wiggle the handle a certain way for the lock to loosen. I took a deep breath and stepped inside, bracing myself for an assault of memories. It was the most bizarre sensation; I felt a sweet sense of being reunited with my past, and yet I also somehow felt like a total stranger to this house. I climbed the stairs to the top floor, which were so much narrower and steeper than I remembered, and opened all the windows, as if the air could help breathe new energy into the house. I saw images of little Amelie and little Maya everywhere and couldn't quite picture them here in only a few hours, all grown up and out of place in this tiny old environment, which seemed so much smaller than my memory had had me believe. Then I hopped back downstairs, remembering that time Maya had slid down the stairs on her bottom, dragging her little suitcase, ready for her American adventure. Blinking back tears, I entered the kitchen and deposited the few items I had bought at the supermarket on my way over in the fridge and cupboards: a kettle, milk, tea, English strawberries, paper towels, toilet paper, sponges and cleaning supplies. I put on an audiobook I had started listening to in Austin and discovered that this simple act was extremely comforting. It felt like I was stitching together two timelines, providing a paper-thin link between my old life and my new one.

I headed out to the garage, which sat at the other end of the garden and sighed at the sight of this overgrown mess – nobody had cut the grass since the tenants moved out two months earlier, and when I opened the garage door, I recoiled from the vast amount of cobwebs that clearly hadn't been disturbed since the house was built ten years earlier. My phone rang; it was the removal company informing me that the crew had made good progress and was about to pull up outside. I wasn't ready at all, neither physically nor mentally, and I wished I hadn't been so insistent that I could handle it all myself. Why was it so hard for me to accept help? The task ahead of me, directing the movers and arranging our belongings, was gargantuan. I hadn't even hoovered and swept everything; I wanted it all to be perfect and ready for our belongings, but now it'd all be a mess. Furious with myself, I gritted my teeth and opened the door.

I loathe the physical act of moving, the thudding footsteps, groans, shouting, dirty marks on the floor, shoving and yanking, creaking of furniture scraping the walls, and general hectic energy created by a moving crew. Desperate to get them out as quickly as possible, yet grateful for their efficiency, I buckled down and didn't stop until they left, only a few hours later. I was just about to brew myself a cup of tea, surveying the boxes piled up in my kitchen with despair when, like an angel sent from the heavens, a smiling face appeared at my kitchen window: my friend Ali, a beaming smile on her face and her customary sunglasses stuck on top of her wild blond hair. She was clutching a bunch of flowers from her garden, and her sleeves were already rolled up to get stuck in whatever task awaited her. She must have remembered my arrival time and decided to come and lend a hand. I almost cried with relief, threw my arms around her, and we started opening the first few boxes together. By the time the kids and my in-laws arrived, the kitchen was filled with piles of packing paper, folded cardboard boxes and utter chaos.

Manic

I turned into a total maniac over the next few weeks, often working until the early hours of the morning. I simply couldn't stop until every single item was unpacked and put into its new place, as if an invisible force was driving me. After only a week of stepping over the threshold, our house looked like a home again. I smiled when I hung a picture in exactly the same spot as when we'd moved into this place ten years earlier, when Maya was a six-month-old baby; even the holes in the wall for the hooks were still there. It was almost like coming full circle.

We had left a few items in Texas, as they were either too old and shabby or simply wouldn't fit into our less Texan-sized house. I spent hours at IKEA, scouting for suitable replacements, and often enlisted the girls' help when dragging various items home or needed them to hold up a panel while I was hammering nails into it. They were enjoying their summer break, spending hours reading and watching TV, taking their time to readjust, and didn't quite share my enthusiasm for home improvements. In contrast, I didn't give myself any downtime. I was obsessed with the idea that everything had to be perfect, as though a perfectly styled, cosy home could make up for the fact that I had ripped them out of their lives in America. While I enjoyed my still familiar surroundings, this place was anything but familiar to them.

I knew I was driving everybody crazy and desperately needed a break. I was looking forward to our summer holiday; first, we would drive all the way to France to meet my sister and family, and then we would head up to Germany to see my parents and pick up our pets. But until then, nothing could stop me from slaving away at creating this perfect new life.

We also had a giant riddle to solve: slotting the girls back into the UK school system. With both of them bright and happy learners with a positive attitude, we didn't expect huge difficulties, but I cursed my naivete as soon as we started making inquiries. After a few failed attempts at testing for grammar schools, a process which required very specific preparations, something we clearly lacked, their confidence was severely dented. I was worried that this negative first impression of the UK school system had ruined their new start in this country, but luckily, we found an all-girls' secondary school with lots of creative options. Both Amelie and Maya seemed to be excited about their new school, the first time they would actually attend the same one, but they were a lot less enthusiastic about the prospect of having to wear a school uniform. With a lot of cajoling and promises of buying them 'normal' clothes too, I dragged them off to purchase a few sets of the required V-necks, skirts, dresses and shirts in wholesome red, navy and grey. We were back in England, after all.

Once all our tasks were accomplished, we packed the car and set off along the motorway and through the Channel Tunnel, a first for me, and the first time I was driving the whole way myself, usually letting my husband take charge. Suffused by a new sense of accomplishment and feeling fully in charge of my life, I thoroughly enjoyed the long drive south with my children. No doubt relieved that their crazy mother had finally stopped rushing around like a demon, Maya and Amelie were hesitant at first whether they could trust this happy and bubbly stranger behind the wheel. After a while, they both relaxed and we sang our favourite songs at the top of our lungs, enjoying a joint sense of adventure and freedom.

We spent two blissful weeks in the hills above Avignon. Scott joined us from the US about halfway through, and together we made the journey up to my parents' house in Bavaria, where we enjoyed our oh-so-familiar summer by the lake, feeling anchored in the continuity and familiar rituals that had been our backbone for the last seven years. After another week, Scott flew back to Austin from Munich, and the girls and I, this time with Ziggy and Snowy on board, set off on our long drive back 'home' to England.

Slotting Back In

It was early September, reluctantly donning their itchy, brand-new uniforms, set off on the bus to start their new school year. Eleven-year-old Maya slotted right into the British secondary school system, starting in Year 7, the equivalent of sixth grade in the US, and was thus just as new to the school as every other Year 7 pupil. She missed her friends back in Austin, but since she shared being new with a few other girls, some connections were forged quickly, which made this transition a lot smoother than her sister's. We had persuaded Amelie to repeat a year in order to give herself time to get used to the British system. The year she was supposed to join was the year in which English children were taking their GCSE exams, which was something that needed years of preparation – something she clearly lacked, coming from a completely different education system. Amelie, who had just turned fifteen, was not happy about the fact that she was now the oldest in her class, but she also welcomed the fact that she didn't have to deal with more pressure than necessary.

Things turned out to be tough enough. Amelie, who had always been an avid reader and excellent writer, struggled with English.

Her grades kept dropping, and it took me a while to get to the heart of the problem: essay writing was done in a totally different way than in the US, from planning and structuring it to writing it with a pen on paper rather than on a computer. Amelie started out full of enthusiasm but completely unprepared for the 'British' way, and rather than taking a deeper look at what was going on, her teachers simply graded her on what they thought was inadequate. We eventually managed to get to the bottom of it, and within a few months, Amelie brought her grades back up. But her confidence had been dealt a massive blow, and her mood was fluctuating along with her teenage hormones.

Not for the first time, I questioned the decision to force them back into this system, this country. I was doubting whether my attempt at raising my children as global citizens, able to think outside the box and feel a sense of home within themselves or wherever we were together as a family, was actually working. It didn't feel that way; worse, we weren't even really together as a family. While I felt a new sense of empowerment, working more or less full time and coping with the daily demands of life all by myself, including things like house and car repairs as well as banking matters – all things my husband had taken care of while we were in the US – the girls took a bit longer to get used to their new normal. I tried to paint a rose-tinted picture of our new life whenever I could, despite my doubts, constantly emphasising the positives of being back in England and pointing out how amazing it was that they were able to experience two countries and cultures at such a young age. They didn't buy it.

Making my house beautiful with all the things I liked, looking after the pets and working all kept me busy. With the girls leaving early each day on the school bus and returning pretty late in the day, I had more time to myself than I had had in a very long time.

I threw myself back into translation work, and for the first time since becoming a mother, I felt like an actual grown-up, in charge and earning my own money. I realised how much I needed this, and how much I had missed feeling this way, especially during my time in Texas.

The new routine suited me. I loved being able to work again, but I really appreciated that I could be there when the kids left the house and when they came home after school; I felt it was even more important now that they were older. It was so easy to miss the little changes in their moods that usually told a bigger story, especially with their dad not being around as much.

Maya was starting to settle in pretty well, had joined the after-school cheerleading team, and could already speak with a proper Kent accent. She loved being close to her grandma. We often drove over to my in-laws' house on the weekend, inviting ourselves to Sunday roast dinners and relaxing time in front of the fireplace.

Amelie, on the other hand, was having a slower start. Being the oldest in her class, on top of having a very different life experience than her peers, she was finding it hard to make real connections. Her old friends from before we had moved to the US were all going to different schools, with different people, and didn't have that much in common with her anymore. Her razor-chopped pixie cut, nose ring and androgynous look set her apart from the girls in the neighbourhood, and it broke my heart to see her spend so much time on her own.

Music, as always, was her saviour, and so was London. She slowly began to venture out to concerts and started meeting like-minded kids who took her under their wing, exploring London and finally reconnecting with her English roots.

Reverse Culture Shock

The days were getting shorter, and I was so excited to be back in England at this time of the year. Yes, I knew I would tire of how dark it got so early, much earlier than in Texas and California, but for now, I was indulging myself. Coming in from a long dog walk in the cold air, drinking gallons of tea and cosying up on the couch with a book and my cat, British shows on the television, I felt extremely content. The kitchen cupboards were filled with English chocolates, Marmite and squishy white bread, which the girls had always missed when we lived in America. We'd all slipped into our new routines, and while I missed sharing them with my husband, we kind of got used to being a three-women household.

Sooner than expected, however, we reached the end of November, and America crashed the party. It was time to think about Thanksgiving. I felt torn. I knew it wasn't really part of my life any longer, and I didn't think I cared that deeply about it, but somehow I couldn't ignore the day either; it had become part of our year. It was almost like now that I didn't live in America anymore, I finally needed it. A day to officially kick off the festive season, but in a non-religious way, unlike Advent, the four weeks running up to Christmas, which I had grown up with in Germany. For the first time in eight years, I was not on American soil. What was I supposed to do with this random Thursday, an ordinary day here in England? We weren't American, and I didn't have any American friends who lived nearby. Scott was in Austin and wouldn't join us until just before Christmas, trying to save up as much time as possible to spend more than just a week over here with us. The girls, both vegetarian and entirely uninterested in celebrating, ignored my lacklustre attempts to come up with a plan. 'Come on, you two, we need to show some patriotism!' I wheedled, trying to elicit a reaction. 'How about a Tofurkey?' Maya and Amelie exchanged a glance and rolled their eyes. In the end, I decided to forget about the whole sorry situation, but I couldn't ignore the feeling of desolation when I stirred the vegetarian pasta sauce that evening. As usual, I had waited too long to come up with a plan. It was too late to actually throw a Thanksgiving party, inviting my friends around for a proper American-style turkey dinner. I could have done it. I should have done it. They would have loved it. My girls might have felt a sense of pride, or at least, could have shared something new with old friends. Instead, the whole thing made me feel profoundly unsettled.

It seemed that all this moving had finally, irrevocably messed with my head. My poor middle-aged brain was working overtime to catch up with itself. As if the physical act of moving and all the planning it entailed weren't enough, I was also constantly confronted with situations that overwhelmed me in unexpected ways. I would go to the supermarket and couldn't work out why I was unable to locate the cereal Maya had asked me to buy, until I realised that it was a Trader Joe's special. Another time, I couldn't remember the British equivalent of the American 'parking lot'; all

I knew was that I couldn't use the American term and ended up saying 'where the cars wait'. Puzzled expressions ensued.

I also constantly saw people I expected to be elsewhere. A woman I could have sworn was a mum at our Austin elementary school was waiting in line at the local coffee shop, and one of my neighbours, who greeted me cheerfully one morning and even remembered me from eight years earlier, almost gave me a heart attack, as I was convinced he actually lived next door to us in California.

It was obvious: I had filled my brain with too many people, too many faces, too many names, too many places. I felt utterly discombobulated. It didn't help my general sense of isolation, but I was too knackered to socialise.

The question I dreaded the most, and one that I invariably got asked all the time, was, 'Do you feel settled now?' Or even worse, its more presumptuous relative: 'You must feel quite happy and settled now that you're back.' I didn't have the faintest idea how to respond. Yes, I did feel somewhat settled, in the sense that I wasn't a total stranger here. I knew people, places, and how things worked. It all felt more or less familiar. But no, I didn't feel settled at all because the familiarity was only on the surface. In fact, I felt like settling in would take much longer this time, longer than anybody could imagine. Of course, in true Brit style, I just gritted my teeth, plastered a smile on my face and said things like, 'Oh yes, I'm getting there. It's nice to be back.' And it was, at least on some days.

When it was one of those days, things *were* really good. I ventured out to a lot of places I'd never seen when I first lived here, feeling more like a tourist, exploring local vineyards that had surprisingly sprung up here in Kent, during our absence, visiting castles and heading to the coast on a gloriously sunny autumn day, camera at the ready. I found, much to my relief, that I still loved this country very much, even though I could feel that a chunk of that love was now reserved for a few other places.

Being back in, or rather, near Europe, was a good thing, and I was hopeful that everything else was going to fall into place eventually, even though I hadn't quite found the magic again that I had once felt for this country. After all, I knew from experience that feeling settled was a long process, and it definitely didn't help that my husband was still not fully back with us. Until he was, and we could close the door on our Texas chapter completely, we were still living what felt like parallel lives.

Long-distance relationships are never easy, whether you've just met or have been married for a while. There are so many moments in your daily life that can't be shared, funny incidents when you're thinking, 'I'll have to show him at dinner tonight', or pulling a face at a comment someone makes. Fleeting moments that arise, then disperse, forgotten. All you have to hold each other are words spoken into a screen. Not enough, especially on days when you're all out of words, and all you want is a hug or a hand on your lower back. Often, I would lie awake imagining Scott on the other side of the world, in our old house, so far away in a different time zone. The thought of him alone in a house that until recently had been filled with people, plus a dog and a cat – a family – tore me apart. I tried to reach through time and put a comforting hand on his shoulders as if I could magic away the sadness I was sure he must be feeling, too. Some nights, however, I tossed and turned and tortured myself with images of him with other women, now that he had this separate, almost secret, life. I couldn't talk to him about my obsessive thoughts; I was scared to show him how much I was suffering. I couldn't admit that I felt huge amounts of guilt for putting us through this. Moving back to England had been my idea, after all, so I needed to prove that it was the best option for us. What right did I have to be scared and jealous? When Scott came back to England on his short trips, it was almost like he was a guest rather than a member of the family, and I felt guilty for feeling like that, too.

But the more I felt like he was slipping away from me and the girls, the more I tried to avoid reality, and the more focused I became on creating my cocoon. I enthusiastically started painting the walls in different colours, exactly how I wanted, without another opinion clouding my newly found independence. I was in charge, or at least I played the role of someone in charge of her life.

I had filled the house with mementoes from our years in the US: a quirky collage depicting a woman in cowboy boots, 'Austin' spelled out behind her; our old fridge magnet from San Francisco; a piece of gnarled Pacific driftwood from the beach at Pescadero; some dried bluebonnets I'd slipped inside a book. I put pictures up the same way they had hung together in our homes in Los Altos and Austin; this was comforting and unsettling at the same time. I had even dragged our bedding back with us, sheets so faded that I should have just thrown them out, and yet I was unable to do so since they had moved all around the world with us. Why were all those objects so important to me? Was I trying to hold on to everything, pretending nothing in my life had changed?

I was well aware that I was experiencing what is commonly known as 'Reverse Culture Shock'. Basically, the shock of finding that coming home is difficult precisely because one didn't expect it to be difficult. There were plenty of articles about this phenomenon online, so I knew I wasn't the only one feeling the way I did. I read a description somewhere that said it felt like 'you are wearing contact lenses in the wrong eyes. Everything looks almost right.' That was *exactly* what it felt like. Everything looked almost right.

I fell into a decent routine and made sure every second of my day was dedicated to a task, with no idle time left to process this move, protecting myself from the overwhelming onslaught of doubts and guilt. Sometimes, when I was walking my dog through the many orchards and fields surrounding our small town and enjoying the fact that it wasn't hot and humid, I felt vindicated and came back with a renewed sense of righteousness. England was beautiful; with more time, we'd all feel more connected. When it was wet and windy, however, and I was lonely, I doubted everything, hating the fact that I felt so volatile. I tried to hide it all from the kids; they were only allowed to see my positive attitude.

The kitchen table, my office during the day, looked out onto a walkway, strictly for people and cyclists rather than cars, so it was the perfect spot to people watch: parents walking their young kids to the local primary school around the corner, people in work clothes on their way to their local office jobs, teenagers traipsing up to the bus stop and so many dog walkers. If they had looked over to my kitchen window, they would have glimpsed me with my laptop in front of me, but nobody ever did. So English of them not to ever breach someone's privacy. I spotted a friend of mine walking past and even raised my hand to wave at her, willing her to look over, but her gaze was firmly set on the path ahead of her. I thought to myself how differently people behaved in the US. I was certain that, given the same situation, a friend walking by my sunny home in California would definitely have tried to peek into the window to see whether I was home, waved enthusiastically, and probably even knocked on the door. My English friend, on the other hand, was clearly following English etiquette, thinking it rude to stare through the kitchen window, even if it was her friend's house.

I realised that I was getting extremely lonely again. Should I try to find a different job, one that got me out of the house? I had never truly loved being a translator, but this work was so perfectly suited to our life; I didn't have to go to a noisy office and deal with obnoxious colleagues, and I could do it from anywhere and at any time, finding slots of time that fit around my family. That's how it had worked for all those years, me moulding myself around everybody else's needs. Now was probably not the time to rock the boat.

Winter Blues

After nine months of being back in the UK, in the midst of a very dark and miserable winter, I realised that I'd been very wrong about my need to experience all the seasons again. I decided that I didn't need winter at all. However gorgeous summer was in this country – there is honestly nothing more beautiful than the English countryside in the summer sun – I had had enough of this prolonged greyness and rain.

I had barely got sick over the last eight years in the US, but during our first winter back in England, we were hit by one cold, cough, or flu virus after the other. The rain was relentless. When we last lived here, we didn't have a dog. I was wringing my hands every time we returned from a muddy walk, and Ziggy decided to shake not outside but as soon as we stepped into our narrow hallway. I knew already that I would need to repaint the walls once the weather got a bit drier, as they currently looked like some Jackson Pollock-inspired art project in every shade of grey and brown. Not even the expensive doggy raincoat I had purchased in desperation made any difference. I still get flashbacks to flying debris of mud.

Experiencing snow on the doorstep, however, was delightful. When you haven't had any for a while, there is nothing more magical than waking up to a landscape covered in white, and watching Ziggy fly across the snowy fields glistening in the morning sun made me fall in love with England all over again. Scott happened to be home when it snowed so heavily in February that school was cancelled; there were no buses and no trains, and we were forced to stay home. Everybody was outside walking and chatting and building snowmen; I could finally feel some community spirit. For the first time in months, it felt like we were a proper family again.

But even though it should have felt right, I couldn't ignore the doubts that were tugging at my insides. Some days, it was as if I were watching myself and my life from the outside, like someone watching a movie, rather than actually participating in it. It was that same sense of waiting for my real life to begin, just like all those years earlier. I felt more fragmented than ever and realised that a part of me had already started to wish herself somewhere else. Living here, living like this, didn't match what my mind had conjured up for us.

Once the snow had melted, we went on a short trip with friends. We came back home after a week to a bunch of flowers, along with milk, eggs and bread my friend Cat, who'd been watching our pets, had left for us, and I felt so grateful to her and so guilty for my dark thoughts. Life was good; I just needed to give it time to make it work. But when Scott left to head back to Austin again to attend to his job, which he was hesitant to leave, and which was progressing well while the job search in London was not, I realised that we probably needed to make some decisions.

If I were being completely honest with myself, I had assumed slotting back into my life in England would be easier. I had expected some hiccups, but I didn't expect to feel so different about living here. While I knew that I had changed quite a lot, I hadn't really thought it through; I hadn't really thought about how this new me would fare here.

I also had to admit that I was lonely. When I had first imagined myself back in England, I had assumed I'd be constantly going to the pub with friends or inviting my girlfriends round for drinks or dinner, reminiscing about our time as young mums. Somehow, none of this felt natural anymore. With the exception of Ali, who regularly joined me on dog walks and other outings, I couldn't reestablish my old connections. I knew I had to make more of an effort and invite people over; my experience told me this wasn't unlike being new in a place, eager to make friends. But I felt paralysed. I picked up the phone occasionally, but it didn't feel right. *I* didn't feel right. I didn't know how to find the right words, the right tone with my old crowd. When you move to a new place, you get so used to talking about yourself; in fact, you have to, it's expected, and people appreciate you sharing your story. As a sort of newbie after years of living your life elsewhere, however, this rule does not apply. I didn't know how to approach this. Downplaying or pretending the last seven years hadn't happened didn't work, but starting sentences with 'There was this taco place in Austin...', or 'When we went to Santa Cruz...' didn't either. It felt like showing off, as if I was trying to alienate people, which was the last thing I wanted to do. It was like I had to shut off parts of myself. I was caught in a spiral of overthinking everything and couldn't discern at all what I really wanted anymore. I continued to present the calm and collected front I had built up so elaborately, so that nobody could see the unravelling on the inside.

However, it wasn't only I who had changed. Britain had, too. Brexit wasn't a complete reality yet, but its looming spectre was definitely getting ready to take the stage. Almost two years after the vote, people didn't really talk about it that much, but you could feel a shift in attitude in many ways. After living in the US for so many years, I was used to speaking German with my children in public because it was never frowned upon there. In England, however, I had always avoided speaking it in public; I had always felt somewhat uncomfortable outing myself as a foreigner in that way and didn't like to draw attention to myself. I'd become very British. But now that we lived here again, I couldn't just go back to how things had been before the US. One day, I was at the supermarket with Amelie and didn't even notice that I was speaking German with her when I heard someone in line behind us mutter something to her companion. I turned my head slightly to catch what she was saying. 'I can't wait till they've all gone back to where they belong.' Amelie hadn't heard the woman, but to me, it felt like a door I didn't even know was there had been slammed in my face.

I found that Brexit was a topic that everybody avoided dealing with in a supremely British way. Most people, when asked about their thoughts on it, just shrugged their shoulders, rolled their eyes and changed the subject. Of course, this wasn't London, but the south-east, where a huge number of people had voted to leave the EU, and I honestly thought that nobody was very interested in this topic. Amelie came home from school one day, shaking her head in disbelief, and told me she had to explain Brexit to a fifteen-year-old classmate who didn't have a clue what it was all about.

This was in stark contrast to what had been going on in the US over the last few years. The election of Donald Trump had caused such a societal uproar, and the amount of political engagement, passion and willingness of people to go out there and become active in their protest and defence of human rights was remarkable. It was almost like they were trying to make up for the fact that they had made him their president by building resistance. British stoicism and phlegmatic disposition, on the other hand, seemed to be the opposite. The Churchill epic *The Darkest Hour* had just been released at the cinema, as well as *Dunkirk*, and the papers were full of raving reviews. While no doubt excellent films, I just wanted to scream. Why was this country so fixated on the past and just didn't seem to give a damn about the future or even the present?

I realised how my viewpoint had changed over the last few years. While all this behaviour, these typical British characteristics, weren't new to me, I saw them in a very different light now. When I first moved to England from Germany almost twenty years earlier, I just accepted them all, being a naive twenty-something college graduate. They became my 'normal'. After all, Germany wasn't all that different. But now I really questioned whether I actually wanted to live here. I was shocked at how much the tone had changed, for example, I had experienced more blatant rudeness in these last few months than in all my years of living in the US. Just the other day, I was driving to the station when a car was approaching very quickly from behind and flashed its lights, as though asking me to speed up. When I ignored this, the driver overtook me as soon as the road was clear, and, pulling up next to me, wound down his window and shouted expletives my way. At the coffeeshop one morning, when I asked politely whether I could have an extra packet of sugar, the barista rolled her eyes and muttered something along the lines of 'use your eyes' and 'get your own bloody sugar'. I thought back to my favourite Starbucks barista in Los Altos and sighed. The unthinkable was happening to my fervently anglophile soul: I missed America.

We decided to travel back to Austin over Easter, as the girls had two weeks off school, and we wanted to give Scott a break from the relentless commute. The girls hadn't been back to the US since last June, and we were in need of some Texan hospitality and warmth. And I wanted to see how we all felt when we returned to our former home. Would it be different to how we felt about California? I wanted to see the girls' reactions without my own judgement getting in the way.

It was like our shoulders collectively relaxed when we landed in Austin and breathed in the soft, warm spring air of the city that had been our home not that long ago. After stuffing our faces with tacos and queso, we collapsed into our old beds in our old bedrooms in our old house. I was amazed at how easy it felt to be here. Austin was still part of our lives; we all felt it.

Untethered

As much as our trip back to Austin had jolted me, I wasn't going to give up on England. May arrived and vigorously pushed away my wintery thoughts. England put on her most dazzling ball gown, with blossoming trees, lush green meadows, softly bleating lambs and whole carpets of bluebells – a worthy match for my beloved Texas bluebonnets.

The sun, gaining strength every day, did its best to keep my spirits up, but as much as I tried to put my pangs of longing for Austin out of my mind and focus on the here and now, I could feel, deep inside of me, that I was losing the battle. I had seen my children's faces light up when they were back with their Texan friends, and I had sensed the true 'us', our bond as a family, when we stepped back into our old house. It felt so natural. I recognised us, as a family, my family, again. Had I given up on making Austin a real home too soon?

I couldn't stop my rambling thoughts, and when I cried on the phone to Scott one night, trying to explain how torn I felt, he almost shouted at me. 'What the hell do you want?' His exasperated voice was shaking. 'You don't want to be in Austin, you don't want to be in England, so where the hell do you want to be? You don't even know what you want, do you?!' He was right. I didn't know. All I knew was that I didn't want *this*. I wanted my family to be a family.

In the end, it didn't really feel like a choice but more like a conclusion we came to: we decided to move back to Texas, and the narrative of my life was taking yet another turn. This made sense. Scott needed to stay in the US because of his work, we would be together as a family for the few years the girls were still living under our roof, the girls could finish school there and then had all the options open to them, and I would try to look at it all like a do-over, giving a place I had rejected another chance, making peace with my confused mind.

Maya, who hadn't even wanted to return to England after our trip, was all smiles. Amelie less so, but when we sat down to map out a few concrete steps, including the option to go to university in England in a few years' time, she seemed to be on board. She liked the connections she had made over the previous few months and, in some ways, reclaimed her English identity, but she also hated her suburban surroundings and had missed living in the middle of a quirky city.

I felt completely untethered. Inevitably, disappointingly, surprisingly, my original plan – family moves to the US for a few years, then returns to Europe and looks back fondly on that experience while feeling happy about being back home – had imploded. It was as though life was taking a good look at me, wagging a finger and whispering into my ear: 'Where is "home"? Are you really sure this is where you're supposed to be?' I could hear it, loud and clear, and thought with absolute certainty, 'No. This isn't it. There's more out there.'

They say that repatriation – the return to your country of origin, and in my case, returning from the US to the UK – is the hardest move, the biggest transition. On paper, you come full circle, tying a neat bow in your expat adventure and settling down. But the reality is nothing like it.

Seven years had passed since we had lived in this country; people had moved, got new jobs, had more babies, fallen out with each other, and some had got divorced. People who had been friends before had made new friends, their own horizons widening and changing. Our kids' old friends were seven years older, and essentially, we didn't really know them; we had missed too much time to keep the bond. The setup we had left behind when we moved to America no longer existed. I had been a firm part of that setup once, but in my absence, the gap I left had been closed, naturally, and I didn't know anymore where I was supposed to slot back in.

Over the last twelve months, I had felt a bit like a newcomer, except with an odd array of local knowledge. I had made some efforts to rekindle friendships but had to admit that I hadn't done enough; I simply didn't have the energy to really put myself out there. Fitting in but not belonging. I had counted on feeling 'like myself' again once we'd moved back here, but I didn't. Had I really believed I could recreate the magic of those early years of camaraderie and motherhood? A magic that was created by spending so much time with my mum friends and their children, getting to know each other through joint rituals and events and the daily grind. It had been disrupted, and I'm not even sure I really believed I could recreate it. I would have needed to start from scratch, just like when I first set foot in California.

The exception was Ali, who, along with her family, was so genuinely happy to have us back in the country and without whom I could not have survived. I didn't know how to tell her that we were moving back to America, but I think she knew it before I had even formulated it in my mind. She picked up on my mood while we were on a walk with Ziggy and called me out. 'You're moving back, aren't you?' she asked, her eyes so sad I could barely stand it. I nodded, feeling like a traitor.

PART 4: TEXAS, TAKE TWO

'You don't just move to Texas. It moves into you.'

—Manny Fernandez, "What Makes Texas Texas", *The New York Times*

The Return

We arrived back in Texas in the August heat, to the omnipresent screeching of the grackles, and dived straight back into our new old lives. It was almost like our year in England had just been a dream. Our house still felt like our house, and my first dog walk around the neighbourhood felt like I'd never been away. Ziggy definitely hadn't forgotten his old stomping ground either and happily trotted along, crossing the streets in all the same places he'd crossed before. The girls reclaimed their old bedrooms and got in touch with their old friends. Both were supremely disgruntled about the fact they'd had only four weeks of summer break, as school in England didn't finish until the middle of July, and here they were, packing their school bags already in early August. But the excitement of being back in Austin won, and helped them get over their sadness of leaving Snowy behind. Respecting his disdain for Texas and remembering his days spent under the bed, we had decided not to bring our black panther back to the US. I couldn't do it to him again and had decided he would be much better off in a home with a garden and temperate climate. My parents, who had already fallen in love with him, were happy to adopt him and sent numerous photos of him looking smug in his new European kingdom.

With only a few days left before the new school year started, we set off to buy supplies, American style. Of course, we went to Target. This mammoth one-stop shop with its iconic red-and-white bull's eye logo was definitely one of the things we didn't know we'd missed. Once we'd gorged ourselves at Target, it was time to find clothes for this new phase of life. The kids were desperate to get new outfits, finally rid of the confines of their stuffy English school uniforms, and eager to reclaim their identities with some new, or rather, very old, items. Austin definitely had a lot more to offer in terms of vintage and second-hand clothing than rural England.

We bought tickets for ACL, the annual Austin City Limits Music Festival, which the kids had loved when we first lived here, and which would become a fixture on our calendar for the next few years. Three days of spending time with friends and seeing live music in the sunshine – it was good to be back.

Once everybody was somewhat settled in their new routines, and our belongings had arrived from across the ocean and were carefully slotted back into place, I sat down to take stock: it was high time for me to come up with some sort of reinvention. I decided that I was going to put my translation work on hold for a while and focus on my own writing rather than someone else's. After seeing a book I had translated, or rather, ghost-translated for another translator, for sale with her name in the credits rather than mine, and having been given a really biting review by a very unpleasant client, who tore my confidence to shreds within minutes, I decided that I needed to shift gears.

I knew that his criticism wasn't in any way justified; I had delivered my translation in a professional manner, possibly less creatively or in tune with what he had in mind, but the way he unleashed his frustration was totally uncalled for. I found myself crumbling and couldn't stop thinking about what on earth I had done wrong. I couldn't let it go.

It occurred to me that it wasn't the first time someone's harsh words had led to me falling apart; in fact, I could recite a whole range of events where I had either made a mistake or been criticised for something. They all loomed like menacing ghosts from the past, whispering into my ears what a failure I was. Why was it that I could never stand up for myself, or if I did, maintain my position and stay calm and confident? How could I let this one silly translation controversy derail me? I decided to regard it as some sort of sign from the universe that it was time to focus on new tasks. I had enjoyed some of my translation work, especially the more creative projects, such as short stories and even a novel. But it had never really been my passion. Plus, I didn't want to continue working in front of a laptop from home every day, leaving me no time and inclination to spend any more time at my desk to actually write, which was something I actually did feel passionate about.

I knew that I needed to get out and mingle before I could fall back into my old patterns of retreating into myself. I went to an interview with *Anthropologie*, a fashion and design store I'd loved from the very first time I visited one of its locations in San Francisco all those years earlier. Being a sales associate would be the perfect part-time job for me; it required me to get dressed up and interact with people, offered a few hours a week of paid distraction while the kids were at school, and I still had plenty of time left to pursue my writing. I also joined a nearby yoga centre and promised myself to take regular classes again, in person and not at home, in my hidey-hole of a comfort zone. I was going to be proactive. I was going to get it right this time.

The wave of euphoria lasted a good couple of months. The weather was gorgeous, the food was delightful, I bought some more boots, we went to see a few bands, and the kids had more or less adjusted to their new and old environments. Amelie returned to her old high school, while Maya rejoined her old classmates, now in middle school. We also made a big effort to explore our surroundings more and realised we had never really appreciated the beauty of the Texas Hill Country. When one of Scott's oldest friends from England came to visit with his teenage son for a few days, we seized the opportunity to be tourists and ventured out on a day trip to *Enchanted Rock*, a giant pink granite boulder that sat in an otherwise flat landscape and looked like aliens had dropped it from above. On the way back, we finally stopped in Fredericksburg, the old German settlement town, which I had planned to visit much earlier but never managed to when we first lived here. While the German-inspired food at the *Ausländerkeller* failed to truly satisfy my German heart and stomach, it felt good to have ventured out, and I promised myself not to let myself feel trapped again.

Ironically, just as we were all beginning to relax into our second round of Texas living, Scott's work situation was turned upside down. We sat down to talk about other options. I couldn't believe it. Here we were, having established that it made more sense for the family to live in the US for the next few years, and now, things were up in the air again. He was approached by a company headquartered on the East Coast and accepted the position on the condition that he'd be able to establish an office in Austin within the next year or so. Initially, however, there would be plenty of travelling back and forth, and I feared that this would just be another version of a long-distance situation, echoing our time in England. Concerned about more separation and yet another gruelling travel schedule for Scott, I was appeased by the prospect of a Texas out-post.

We made it work. He started commuting to New Jersey every other week, making sure he was home every weekend, and I slipped back into my American mom life.

Unravelling

And then, things began to crumble. Maya, excited about re-claiming her old friends, had started the infamous American middle school. She had been looking forward to reconnecting with her American friends from elementary school, never having forged a very firm friendship in England. The bullying started almost im-mediately, but she managed to keep this from us for ages. Our sev-enth-grader seemed increasingly quiet, withdrawn, and generally overwhelmed by the size of the school, the new terminology, and the demands of homework, among other things. We found a new dance studio, which was the continuity she needed, as a way to de-compress and stay active after school, but it wasn't enough.

Several months after our return to Austin, her behaviour be-came increasingly erratic, and after my trust was broken when a few incidents at school got her a suspension, I broke my own parental rule number one and confiscated her phone. What I found made my stomach turn. We had to act fast. The horrendous bullying that Maya had tried to keep from us was right there, dis-played in her messages and on social media, and in the angry scars on her arms and legs, hidden under clothes. She was harming herself. 'They're telling me I'm faking my accent', she told us, which sounded like the stupidest reason to make fun of anybody, especially somebody who had clearly lived in another place. Maya wasn't sharing any further details. She was also exceptionally tall for her age, and I remembered how cruel teenagers, and especially girls, could be at that age. One day, she came home limping, as a classmate had tipped over his desk on purpose so it landed on her foot. I took her to see our old paediatrician, who confirmed that a couple of toes were broken. Maya begged me not to inform the school or the boy's parents. The doctor took me aside after our visit and asked if there was any possibility of changing schools.

In a desperate attempt to remove her from the destructive environment she was in, we looked for alternatives. Ignoring Maya's pleas to enrol her in online school, as we felt she needed the social interactions of a regular school day, we made an appointment at a Montessori-inspired school in central Austin, which advertised an alternative programme designed to rekindle the joy of learning. By that point, Maya was utterly miserable and despondent and didn't care about a new school because she couldn't convince us to let her do school online. She was also diagnosed with misophonia, a debilitating sensitivity to certain noises, and the loud and chaotic middle school environment destroyed her tolerance levels completely. We didn't know how to help her other than by asking the teachers to let her wear headphones when things were getting bad.

I arranged a 'shadow' day at this potential new school, a day when Maya would follow other students around, try various classes and talk to the teachers. She wasn't over the moon but agreed to go, and when I picked her up that afternoon, she was all smiles and said she'd had a really great day. I felt like I could breathe again. When the school principal called me a few days later to tell me they were unable to offer her a place, I was confused.

'Well, ma'am, Maya didn't seem to be that keen to become one of us,' she informed me, 'I missed any real enthusiasm.' I could feel anger bubbling up inside me. After all, they knew Maya's story and the fact that school had been such a miserable and oppressive place for her, so why on earth were they expecting a young teen to react 'with real enthusiasm' about going to school? The true reason for their decision, however, turned out to be a different one. When I dug deeper, dismissing the principal's vague notions, she told me that Maya had admitted something they simply couldn't accept. During one of the interviews she had to engage in during her shadow day, she was asked what her biggest mistake had been in life and what she'd learned from it. Maya had decided to do exactly that rather than make up a story. She told the teacher about how she had been caught vaping in the school bathroom a few months earlier when she was feeling extremely anxious, hiding in the girls' bathroom, and another girl had handed her a vape.

'Vaping,' the principal lectured me in an icy voice, 'is simply inexcusable'. I was speechless. Pointing out that it was pretty amazing for a not even thirteen-year-old to admit something like that, basically showing trust in a person and being completely honest, I asked her how she could make such a statement. But the door had been slammed in Maya's face, and when I asked the principal if she wanted me to tell my daughter that her honesty had been a mistake, which would clearly send the wrong message, she remained stony-faced. I was livid and told her in no uncertain terms that I would never send my child to a school like that, and slammed down the phone, vowing never to tell my daughter about this.

When I gave Maya the news that the school had turned down our application, telling her they had wanted to see more commitment and felt like Maya didn't show enough enthusiasm, she just shrugged. 'You know, mum, I didn't really feel like I belonged there anyway,' she consoled me. 'All the kids were talking about was getting out of there and going to other schools. I didn't like that.' I hugged her tightly and told her never to stop being herself, while silently crying inside.

For Amelie, coming back to Austin was hard on a different level. Junior Year in high school, the year before the last one, is arguably the most challenging in the entire US school system. It's when the focus, which is always directed towards college anyway, really shifts into gear, and when every single grade, volunteer time and extracurricular activity matters and takes up more space in a young person's life than it ever should. Sleep, the most important ingredient, is sorely neglected, and there's nothing you can do about it if you don't want to fall behind.

Amelie jumped right back in and was rejected at every level. Having left England after hard battles throughout the year, where she had to toss what she had learned in her years of American schooling and fought to wrap her head around the UK system, now found the opposite was happening. It was as if nobody at school wanted to accept that she had just spent a year being educated in another country, rather than being on holiday, not learning. The fact was that Amelie had learned more, and more intensively, during her year away from high school than she had in her previous three years at middle and high school combined. Nobody wanted to acknowledge that. No, she didn't have Biology 1, nor Chemistry 1, nor Geometry, nor English 2.

She had done it the UK way, with different names for different subjects, maths structured differently, and PE done the whole year, twice a week, but without a grade, because the school just issued a document of attendance but no grade, no points, just a detailed account of what was covered. 'Not enough!' said the school in Austin.

'We need grades and a transcript'. 'What's a transcript?' asked the school in England, and provided ever more detailed, ever more comprehensive accounts of what Amelie had achieved in her year over there. The American school baulked. Amelie had to fill her schedule with all the things she had already done, just not the American way.

The US high school system, as flexible and as wonderful as it is when it comes to deciding in what year to take which class or choosing interesting electives, is utterly rigid in its overall structure. You have four years to complete until graduation, and you need a certain number of credits to graduate. In addition to English and maths, which you take every year, you need to accumulate a certain number of credits. To turn up with a whole year of credits missing, and being unable to convert what Amelie had learned in the UK, turned out to be the most gigantic headache imaginable. I was in constant contact with our old school in the UK, trying to get ever more accurate teacher statements, then relay the information to the school counsellor in the US. Each high school student is assigned a 'counselor' during Freshman Year to help them along during their four-year sojourn at high school, establishing which subjects should be taken when, and ultimately, how and where to apply for college. It's a great system, provided your assigned counsellor actually cares.

The pressure, already intense and mind-boggling in that grade, spiralled out of control. And so did our precious child, her sparkling but equally scatty brain losing its grip.

It was the pasta bake. Amelie called me from school, sounding tired and despondent. She asked what we were having for dinner, and I told her I hadn't planned anything yet but was thinking about making a pasta bake. Mid-week cooking was the bane of my life; planning meals and shopping for ingredients was never high on my priority list. The silence at the other end of the line told me everything, and in that moment, I knew. I just knew. *Why has it taken me so long to see this?* I thought, and my stomach turned to knots even without her saying the words. Amelie had slowly, gradually, stopped eating. This started way back when we first moved to Austin, became more noticeable in England, and was now pretty obvious. But the unfathomable truth was that we hadn't really talked about it.

When it comes to teenagers, you take so many weird behaviours for granted and having been a teenage girl myself with a very unhealthy dose of body loathing, who had gone through disordered eating myself at that age, I didn't want to make the issue even bigger. Amelie knew I was worried about her, but neither of us knew how to address it. Until that day when she broke down, and I dropped what I was doing, got in the car, picked her up from school and drove straight to an emergency psychiatric hospital. The following week, Amelie was in treatment for anorexia.

And thus began a cycle of therapy, treatment inside and outside of hospital, family therapy sessions, parent support groups, endless hours devoted to reading books and attending educational and therapy classes, both online and in person. I spent my days liaising between therapists, school administrators, teachers, doctors and nutritionists and going to work simply to have a break and be distracted for a few hours each day. Luckily, the majority of Amelie's teachers at school, while powerless regarding all the missing credits, fully supported our family and eased the workload so that Amelie managed to keep up with her grades and other requirements and didn't fall back another year, which she was determined to avoid. Her goal was to become healthy again, to spend the summer in Europe and go to a music festival with friends, which was all she'd been talking about for ages. It was a tough battle, but we achieved the goal together, utterly depleted and without any real sense of victory. We knew that it was far from over.

We also realised how alone we were; we hadn't established a robust support network in Austin yet and didn't know how to explain what was going on to our new acquaintances and colleagues. Neither did we feel capable of divulging it all to our friends and family back home, who we felt didn't really understand or asked irrelevant questions.

It was hard enough to make sense of it ourselves. As a mother, I felt like the proverbial rug had been pulled out from under my feet, and I was tumbling free-fall into an abyss of guilt, self-loathing and utter despair. How could I not have realised how serious this had become? I had always prided myself on being a good mum, my one achievement in life, when my work life had been such a mess. How had I missed this?

An eating disorder like anorexia is something people who have never dealt with this disease can't understand. It's such a gradual process; there are so many incidents that can be 'explained away', so many teenage issues that make not eating look like one of the lesser problems. Teenage girls all want to be skinny, after all, and peer pressure and moodiness are fully expected in that age group. Got up too late to eat breakfast before school? Totally understandable. I'm not a breakfast person, either. You press a cereal bar and a sandwich into her hands. 'I'll eat lunch at school today.' No problem. 'I don't want to eat cheese anymore, it gives me a tummy ache.' *Fine, let's see how long you last, I know you love cheese so much that you'll eat it again, tummy ache or not.* I was rolling my eyes so much back then, although there was always, always, a sense of unease at the back of my mind. Anorexia is such a sneaky bitch though, that even I hadn't seen it coming.

When you're dealing with this disorder, the first thing you learn is that an evil demon has taken possession of your child, and that there's no reasoning with a starved brain. Forget about parenting as you've known it. Someone burned the manual, and you're faced with the complete unknown, and the fact that this is a highly deadly disease.

There is a very strong genetic component to eating disorders, which is something we discovered during Amelie's treatment, but I didn't know that when I was a young mother, naively thinking I could outsmart this curse. When we learned about all the different components of anorexia in treatment, a whole barrage of memories of my own messed-up adolescent relationship with food rushed to the surface, ripping band-aid after band-aid from my carefully but inadequately bandaged wounds.

One of the things I had promised myself to achieve when I had my children was to do everything in my power to shield them from the methods of my parents' generation. Having been an adolescent in the eighties and nineties, I didn't know anybody immune to the way society demanded thinness. Everybody's parents were on whatever diet promised them a thin body; it wasn't just my family. From the age of twelve onwards, I was body-shamed too many times to count, and had developed an eating disorder that I managed to hide for a good ten years. I say hide, but I'm sure most people close to me knew; the fact that I never 'reached my goal' and got really skinny, however – in my teenage mind, getting thin would have meant I would finally become acceptable and likeable – meant that nobody was too alarmed or even saw it for what it was. I didn't even realise myself that it had been a full-blown eating disorder, a combination of anorexia and bulimia, until we learned about it all during Amelie's illness, and a therapist put it into words.

All I knew when the girls were born was that I had to prevent this from happening at all costs, and I thought I knew exactly what to do and not to do. Scott and I never talked about calories, or 'feeling stuffed', or in any way negatively about food, at least not in the kids' presence, and I never made disparaging comments about other people's bodies, and more importantly, about my own. Too jarring were the memories I had of people judging people's bodies on TV or in real life – 'she really shouldn't wear shorts with those legs' – commenting on how many slices of cake a relative was eating at a family gathering; of a family friend grabbing my wrist while I was reaching into a bag of almonds, warning me to eat 'no more than three! You don't want to get fat!'; of a boyfriend telling me, 'I thought you were thinner' upon seeing my naked body for the first time. Those memories had irreversibly burned themselves into my brain, and I wanted to keep them locked up and far away from my own children. Often, I would eat more than I actually wanted or needed just to set a good example for them, and I never stood in front of the mirror criticising what I saw when the girls were around. Whenever we heard other people make remarks about bodies, sizes, and food in that context, I would call them out on it or make a point of discussing it with the kids afterwards.

In essence, I felt that we had proofed ourselves against eating disorders and that I would recognise any warning signs early on. I couldn't have been more deluded. Family therapy opened my eyes to the fact that Amelie's disease was not my disease; during one of our first sessions with the therapist, I felt very defensive, and somehow desperate to prove that I had done everything in my power to avoid this, almost like I was trying to prove that I had been a good parent in case the therapist was going to attack me. She interrupted my defensive laments: 'This is not about you! It is not about what you did or didn't do. We're here because of your child, and how she feels.' I had been so fixated on my own experience, fearing history repeating itself in Amelie, that I hadn't even considered the fact that there might be other reasons to stop eating than wanting to be thin.

We were told that Amelie was a 'superfeeler'. During one of the many presentations we attended as a family, we learned everything about this personality type, which totally resonated. Another, more technical term for this is 'highly sensitive person', or 'HSP', and when the presenter talked us through the many aspects of it, Scott and I exchanged glances and mouthed 'Maya' to each other. I silently added *and me, too.* It was obvious that we all fell into this category.

Meanwhile, it was a struggle to keep Maya's head above water. Witnessing her sister's mental health decline while dealing with her own, as yet unlabelled issues, plus recognising the horrendous stress everything put on us parents and not wanting to contribute even more, she descended further into a dark tunnel of self-destructive behaviours. We were dealing with a whole other beast here, one that resisted our parental efforts on every level.

Those long weeks when Amelie was in the middle of treatment and Maya was suffering silently through her bullying ordeal were hell for us parents. My traumatised mind actually refuses to remember what happened when; all I know is that it almost broke us. It is etched on our minds and bodies.

There were so many sleepless nights in which I would get up several times just to check that my children were still breathing.

Night after night, we would check on missing items, frantically hiding any sharp objects in the house, stopping short of removing glass-framed pictures from walls. Waiting outside a bathroom, my ear pressed to the door to listen to the sounds of vomiting. Discovering yet more disturbing messages and social media posts. The absolute terror of finding an empty bed that hadn't been slept in because Maya had sneaked out during the night, and calling the police to report her missing. Imagining the worst.

Pandora's Box

Working at Anthropologie was my perfect refuge from the horror of home life. I was surprised to find that I could truly relax in this busy yet unaggressive environment. Most of my previous jobs had been office-based; harsh overhead lighting and a constant barrage of noises from shrilling telephones to voices in every corner always made it hard for me to concentrate. Anthropologie, on the other hand, had soft lighting and gentle music, and instead of sitting still at a desk, I could move around and change tasks every hour.

Besides, nobody in my team knew much about my background, and I was doing all I could to keep it that way. I was acting from the moment I entered the store. It became my stage: on the outside, I was the stylish, helpful and always smiling sales associate, embodying the Anthropologie brand to a T, and distracting myself and everybody else from the fact that I was unravelling fast on the inside. It was like I was fulfilling a version of my childhood dream: to be an actress. I could dress in a flamboyant, bohemian way I wouldn't dare to adopt on the outside, creating outfits with the many clothes I already owned and rarely wore. They were carefully hung up in my giant American walk-in wardrobe, which became my princess cave each morning when I got ready for work. I added to my collection each month with my very generous employee discount, which I used to full effect. Searching for dopamine, at least temporarily. Perfect escapism.

I don't know how I managed to summon the strength to show up like this every day, but I guess decades of practicing being 'the good girl' had prepared me well. Instead of working on my inner balance, I used all my energy to present myself like the capable employee the customers – and I – needed to see.

One day, however, my carefully constructed facade was threatening to crack open. We had been assigned a new store manager, who turned up one morning and handed out personality tests to the whole team. The idea was to build better connections with each team member, knowing our own and everybody else's strengths and weaknesses, which would ultimately result in a better customer experience. I had always loved personality tests, even as a teenager, and had delighted in the fact that I could manipulate them pretty easily, basically deciding on what outcome I wanted and then matching my answers to the questions accordingly. With this test, I decided that I was going to be completely honest and really listen to my true self. Amelie had just finished her last round of daily treatments at the eating disorder clinic, but we were still attending regular psychotherapy sessions as a family, and I had already learned so much about myself and my patterns of behaviour that I knew I needed to be less self-manipulatory and embrace even my darkest shadows.

During my lunch break, I sat down and stared at the test sheet in my lap. The questions were pretty straightforward, neither superficial nor complicated, and upon completion, you were assigned one or maybe two of four personality types, depending on the points you scored in each category. As humans, we all have different, even opposing, characteristics, so it's certainly not rare to score high on more than one 'type'. I ended up with the exact same number of points in all four categories; the ultimate contradiction. Apparently, I was a good team player, yet thrived when working by myself; I seemed to be best suited to interacting directly with customers, yet was actually the ideal person behind the scenes. And so on.

It really hit me that this wasn't normal. I took the test again, and then one more time, slightly altering some answers, aware that I was starting to manipulate the whole thing. I also started to panic. Clearly, it was time to face some facts: I was trying too hard to please everybody. This test was just a tiny portion of a bigger problem. Yes, I was frazzled. The many moves over the last few years and the subsequent mental health struggles had taken their toll, plus, I was getting closer to 'a certain age' as a woman clearly in perimenopause. But who was I kidding? When and why had I turned into someone who so obviously tried to please everybody and couldn't even be honest with herself? Who had I become, at my deepest core?

Could it be that moving so much and starting from scratch each time had exacerbated this tendency to blend in, to adapt to whatever was required in each new life situation? When all that time I had thought that I was actually finding out so much more about myself and becoming very resilient, had I unwittingly become an impostor? I felt so certain that I had learned to live in the moment, to set boundaries while also being more adventurous. Surprisingly, it seemed possible that I was doing all of this simultaneously: I was inching closer to who I actually was, deep inside, while at the same time actively honing my masking skills. No wonder I was so exhausted.

The truth was that moving to England and then returning to Austin had not been the solution to finding a way out of my confusion. There was no such thing as 'just' going back to a place. People always say this when someone moves. 'Oh, if you don't like it, you can always come back!' I honestly think that this is one of the biggest misconceptions you can imagine when talking about being an expat. Even if you physically go back to a location, you cannot go back to who you were when you first lived there. You've changed, the place has changed, life has changed. There's nothing simple or 'just' about this. We had done it twice now, back to the UK, and then back to Austin. Neither was it simple nor easy. Neither felt like going or coming 'home'.

Meeting a couple of friends for coffee one day and unable to let my phone out of sight, for fear of missing a call from school, I realised how miserable my life had become. I didn't have what my friends had anymore. Days when I could drop my kids off at school, knowing I had a few peaceful, uninterrupted hours to do the things I wanted or needed to do. My life had turned into waiting for a phone call from the school counsellor or from Maya herself, hiding in a school bathroom, pleading with me to come and pick her up.

As one friend was talking about her daughter getting ready an hour before school because she couldn't wait to see her friends, and another about how her son had just auditioned for the annual school play, I had to fight back tears. That same morning, when I dropped Maya at the usual corner near school, her face had been a frozen mask, utter desolation etched into her features. I had begged her to tell me what was going on, but she remained silent.

I was no longer free; my child, no longer safe. More than once, I would get in my car and start driving, only to pull over after a few minutes, dropping my head in my hands. Sometimes I drove screaming. What had happened to my life, my family? I loved them all so fiercely, but somehow my love wasn't enough. Everything was out of kilter. Nobody was able to communicate what was going on; home had become a disharmonious mess.

Had I failed as a parent? Had I messed up the one thing I thought I was good at? I had hoped to raise my family as resilient global citizens, at home in many places and adaptable and resting in themselves, but I realised that I hadn't been successful; I was falling apart alongside my children. Pandora's box had been opened; there was no going back.

They say it takes a village to raise a child, and I had repeatedly taken them away from ours. Parents can't be the only safe space for their children; it doesn't work. You need others around you who know your child and can see when something is wrong – FaceTime is not enough.

Fighting

We did manage to go to Europe the summer after Amelie's hospital stay, as unlikely as it had seemed earlier that year. We were still treading very carefully, but also trying to simply focus on how positive this trip would be for all of us. Amelie made it to her music festival, and I even squeezed in a three-day trip to Vienna, a much-needed escape for the girls and me, filled with art, music and even food. A little bit of light was creeping back in again.

I came back to Austin with a glimmer of hope that this year, Amelie's final year of high school, would be a better one. She was doing really well, mentally and physically, and the thought of leaving school with all its pressures behind was appearing like a bright ray of sunshine on the horizon. Amelie was making some tentative plans; she was applying to university in England and wanted to spend time travelling and working in Europe.

Maya, who had finally been diagnosed with ADHD, after my repeated insistence to our doctor that her troubles at school and her sensitivity to noises weren't just teenage issues, seemed to cope a little bit better with the help of some medication, at least as far as focus and homework were concerned. Maybe things would be okay if I could create a cocoon for her at home to calm down enough to cope with the final year of middle school.

I was also determined not to let myself fall back into a hole. I had learned during family therapy how important it was to look after my own mental health and to practice plenty of self-care. I was going to be a mama lion, but I was also going to move my own needs higher up on the priority list. I was more attuned to the fact that I needed to preserve my own energy at all costs.

Being outside always helped. I had started to explore Austin's green spaces when we first lived here, but now I made it my mission to spend as much time as I could in nature. I let myself fall deeply in love with Austin's greenbelt. Walnut Creek Metropolitan Park became my refuge. We had discovered this park, a beautiful chunk of nature in the northern part of the city, during our first year in Austin, when Scott came here to ride his mountain bike, and I started bringing Ziggy as soon as we began off-lead training. The park was a 15-minute drive from our house, and Ziggy always started pacing excitedly in anticipation in the back seat once he realised where we were heading. In the summer months, when it was too hot to venture outside for most of the day, we would arrive here early in the morning, Ziggy always leaping out of the car, happily bouncing ahead, tongue lolling. Often, I longed for my friend Ali from England to come and walk with me here; she would have adored the untouched beauty of this urban Texan landscape.

I had missed this enormous maze of trails and creeks when we moved back to England, and the first time I brought Ziggy back for a walk there, I was glad to be wearing big sunglasses to hide my tears of gratitude. It was like meeting an old friend again whom I hadn't seen in ages and wasn't sure I'd ever see again. I let the green jungle pull me back inside as if I were a puppet on a string.

I came to walk here at least twice a week, a ritual that kept me sane throughout my years in Austin. The park absorbed the absolute worst pain I experienced, on those days when my children were so ill that I wasn't sure if we'd make it through the week; it bore witness to so many tears and heard me mutter and rant and rail against life, and above all, my own lack of direction, and work through my pain. I felt like I could pour all my pain into its trees, shaded trails, chalky hills and peaceful creeks. But it also saw me smile and heard me sing and laugh out loud, and listened to my imaginary conversations, as I began to heal myself. Here, I felt complete, my own person; here, I could forget about everything for an hour or two.

I've absorbed those trails so well into my core that even now, all I have to do is close my eyes and I'm right there. When I can't sleep, I travel to that park in my mind and walk along its pathways until I fall asleep, soothed by its reassuring beauty. Out of all the places I've lived, that park is where I feel most like myself.

When I wasn't heading to my park, I was roaming the hills around our house with my dog, engrossed in a podcast or audiobook, whether fictional or factual. As I had discovered before, I loved the continuity of a story that connected various places, for example, starting a book while on holiday in Germany and then finishing it weeks after returning to Texas. I found it soothing, as if listening to the same story in different places could somehow stitch the fragmented pieces of my life together. I really loved podcasts and was delighted to find an increasing number of them covering everything from health and well-being to crime and parenting. I had a few favourites that had been my steady companions all the way from my days in California through our year in England, and now back here in Texas.

It was no surprise that I turned to podcasts when I was at my lowest, and it was expat podcasts that helped me begin my slow journey back to the surface. I had discovered the universe of expat social media and had avidly followed various expat accounts on Instagram and YouTube for quite some time. What I found was a community that told me I wasn't the only one experiencing loneliness, disconnect and confusion. I found an expat coaching programme and met a group of women just like myself, who had left their home countries or returned after a stint abroad, and who felt stuck in a rut and wanted to achieve something, whether it was a book, a business, or simply find a way back to themselves. With my coach's help, I started digging my way back out of my hole and eventually created my own podcast.

Being part of an expat community was priceless. Exchanging our stories, we found validation and confirmation of so many issues. Expat grief and burnout didn't only happen to me, and disguising how we truly felt deep inside in order to not upset those back home was an exercise we were all familiar with.

As expats, we learn to wear a mask when we move, first to appear capable in our new surroundings, and later to show people back home that things are fine even when they're not. There seems to be an unspoken need to present a version of our lives that is positive and exciting, to show that we made a good decision in moving, and that things are exhausting but manageable. It's easily done; you just stick some pretty pictures on social media, smile brightly on FaceTime, and if people don't see you in person on a regular basis, you can keep all sorts of things conveniently hidden.

There are numerous reasons why we do this, including the need to protect others from feeling bad for us or getting tainted by our sadness. There's often a huge amount of guilt we feel for having moved away in the first place, and for doing so and not being happy. Very often, all we crave is someone who simply says, 'Oh that sounds awful, it must be so hard for you', which is basically the verbal equivalent of a physical hug. What we often get, however, is advice; I think people in our high-achieving Western societies automatically feel the need to offer suggestions and solutions. The thing is, once you've braved a few moves, you know what you need to do and what to avoid. We don't need advice; we need to know that we're loved and supported and that we still matter, regardless of how far away we've moved.

Expats also have to deal with a barrage of invalidating comments, both from other people and, even more frequently, from the relentless inner critic deep inside. 'You're so lucky you get to experience all those things and live in all those different places', or maybe, 'Well, it was your decision to move, so if you struggle so much, it's your own fault, and you shouldn't complain now!' I have heard all of these over the years, and every time, I either felt even more shame for being unhappy, or I decided not to share my struggles with that person again. My worst experience was with someone from Germany – oh, blessed German bluntness! I broke down in tears on FaceTime, sobbing that I didn't know how to shake off my sadness. The face at the other end was blank, possibly even annoyed. 'Well, I don't know what to say,' was the reply, and that was it. At least they were honest. And while all I needed at the time was some kindness, a part of me understood: they really didn't know what to say, not having experienced moving in this way themselves. Communicating what it feels like to be so uprooted can be impossible. It becomes easier to slip on the mask and to pretend things are hunky-dory. Until we run out of energy.

Feeling the Overload

As much as I kept trying to create a stress-free environment at home, I knew deep down that I couldn't keep the influence of the outside world, and in particular, US society, at bay. While I still couldn't see beyond our many moves as the source of my kids' mental health struggles, I knew there was more to blame. I recognised that we had never actually truly escaped the rat race that we thought we'd left behind in Silicon Valley. That sort of zeitgeist was everywhere – our times had become about 'being the best you can be at all times'. This wasn't just a California thing or a US thing; it was visible everywhere.

What was worse, I noticed in myself how I had fallen more and more into the 'I'm so busy, gotta go, no time' trap that so many people around me were caught up in. I didn't like it one bit. There's such a fine balance between being busy and fulfilled and being busy and overwhelmed. I didn't like feeling like I was constantly too busy to do anything properly and take care of myself and others effectively.

What had happened to me? Where was the mother who made sure that her kids had enough downtime, didn't have days filled to the brim with activities, and were able to sleep in, read books and simply exist? Who made time to sit on the sofa with a cup of tea and a magazine? I felt like I used to know where my limits were and when it was time to slow down and create little pockets of 'me time', but lately, life had been sucking me into this giant vortex of frenetic activity. On the outside, this looked very well managed, as I was able to present myself as a very organised person, and I knew I was excellent at juggling appointments, work, dog walks, school pick-ups, etc., without wasting time in between. I was never idle, which I realised was exactly the problem. My brain couldn't keep pace with it all; on the inside, my head was a scrambled mess.

One day, I was waiting in line for my to-go coffee in one of my favourite cafés in Austin, as I was in a rush and too busy to actually stay and sit down for half an hour. I watched a girl in her twenties, curled up on a comfy armchair, alternately sipping her latte and knitting. I could see that she was knitting in the American/British style, which is a little bit slower than the European style I had been taught by my mum. I was itching to jump in and teach her the more efficient way, but luckily my inner introvert prevented me from doing it; and I didn't want to lose my spot in the queue. I also realised that she looked absolutely relaxed and cosy, clearly in no need to be more efficient. She was fine, just the way she was. She didn't even have headphones on and was clearly immersed in her activity. The one who wasn't fine was me. It occurred to me that I really wanted to be her, sitting in a café and knitting and sipping my coffee slowly and feeling calm instead of feeling like I should be heading off somewhere else. Why did I always feel like this, always in a rush, always thinking I should be doing something else? Yes, there were always errands and chores and appointments to get to, but that was life, and everybody had to deal with that stuff. Why was it all so overwhelming for me, and why couldn't I just slow down and find my inner calm again? I decided to dig out my knitting bag as soon as I got home.

All this mental overload we were expected to carry with us added to the increasing amount of health issues apparent in our Western societies. Words such as burnout, overwhelm, fatigue, anxiety and depression had become such commonplace descriptions of what so many people were experiencing that they didn't even register as unusual anymore. Recent studies suggested that the average high school student these days had the same anxiety level as a psychiatric patient did in the 1950s. No wonder everybody was suffering. It all seemed to be particularly true here in the United States, where people weren't even able to take a lot of time off work. Why was it such a sign of weakness to take time off? Why was it not normal to have four or five weeks every year to travel, or to just relax at home and recharge your batteries, as it was in Europe? I was beginning to question our move back to the US all over again.

It was obvious to me that this country's obsession with self-optimisation was steadily undermining the health of its people. The concept of constantly striving for more, to go bigger, higher, further, was being drilled into everybody from a young age. For those who were willing and able to work hard and aim high and had the drive to push through their own boundaries, it was ideal. And there were plenty of people around me to prove this, including children and teenagers, who were genuinely thriving. But for those who didn't fit that mould, or rather, who couldn't quite keep up with this constant forwards-and-upwards motion, it was a different story.

I could observe in my own behaviour how I was undermining myself with these outside expectations. Constantly being asked to aim for more but feeling incapable of doing so was a disastrous set-up for someone with perfectionist tendencies. Sometimes, when my mind was in 'optimisation mode', I got a sense of overwhelm just by seeing others complete assignments or even just manage simple tasks. For example, when I was sitting in the car driving from school to work and saw somebody out running, I instantly felt guilty that I wasn't out on a run myself. I knew deep down that this didn't make any sense, but when I was in that mode, it was hard to snap out of it. I felt more and more like I had missed some vital part that other humans seemed to possess.

This attitude was visible everywhere, first in California and now here; it was hiding in plain sight in the many little details of everyday life. When we received an email asking us to order Amelie's senior school photos for the high school yearbook, for example, I saw that for an extra fifteen dollars, we could opt to have certain things photoshopped: blemishes erased, teeth whitened, stray hairs, tan lines and moles removed. All for the sake of having the perfect school photo. The message was clear: you're not good enough as you are. The status quo was never enough.

To me, it simply didn't seem to be a sustainable way to live, and I could see it in the breakdown my kids were experiencing. But what was the solution for those of us who struggled, those of us who were too sensitive for this system? Was mental exhaustion the price of innovation?

The main problem, as I could see it, was that nobody was taught how to handle negative emotions. In this society, negativity was extremely frowned upon. The message was to be happy, and if you weren't, to strive for happiness. To smile more, and if our smile wasn't quite white or straight enough, there were ways to sort that out. The status quo was never enough. Telling our children that we want them to work hard to achieve happiness is insane pressure in itself. Nobody can be happy all the time, and instead of reinforcing the message that happiness is the ultimate goal, shouldn't we teach everybody ways to handle negative emotions such as sadness, anger and disappointment? To learn that it is normal and okay to feel overwhelmed and unhappy sometimes? We were so afraid of those feelings that we learned to suppress them by staying busy, focusing on other, 'happier' things. As a consequence, those undigested emotions will make themselves known at some point, and often when we're not prepared for them.

Sharing these insights with my family, I was met with doubtful looks. The kids scoffed that I had lost touch with reality, and my husband just looked at me with a 'yeah and how do you expect to be able to slow down *and* keep the bills paid?' look. I knew it wasn't down to me to change the world, but I also knew that we all desperately needed to change pace in order to fight this crushing system, even if it was through tiny acts of rebellion, carving out little pockets of slow time every day.

Parallel Universes

After our *annus horribilis*, we didn't think things could get much worse and tried to approach 2020 with a positive mindset. We spent the transition period, the 'in-between days' after Christmas, with a quick one-week trip to England, which included a couple of days with friends, a few days in London where we caught up with both my parents and my in-laws, and finally meeting my new niece and nephew, who had been born just over three months earlier and whom I had only met via my laptop screen.

We'd ventured on a few of those mini trips before, and they usually caused some emotional turmoil for me, simply because they were so short I could never process the back-and-forth quickly enough. It was almost like travelling in parallel universes, and my brain could never keep the mental me and the physical me in the same place. Jet lag didn't help either, but I was so used to the woolly, disjointed mush my jet-lagged brain turned into every time that it was usually the least of my worries.

When we packed our bags for this trip, I felt tired, but I didn't anticipate any more than the usual emotional wobbles. Something inside me, however, had other ideas, and when I plunged deeply into a full-blown panic attack at the airport, just before boarding the plane to London, I realised something was really not okay, and I needed to take stock. I just felt an unavoidable wave of sadness engulf me, the sense that everything in my life was too much, too exhausting, and that I just didn't want to be where I was right at that moment. I didn't want to be living this very life, disjointed, always travelling, always in flux, never truly at home. I couldn't stop shaking and crying and gulping for air, slouched in my seat at the departure gate, and my poor family didn't know what to do with me. I had never experienced such a complete loss of control; I had always been so capable of reigning myself in. Luckily, I managed to calm down enough to board the plane and then slept during most of the flight. I was still unsure what precisely had set me off, but with hindsight, it all made sense: I was completely burnt out. It was like my body had already understood that I couldn't sustain this duality, but my brain still tried to make sense of it. My body had spoken when my mind couldn't.

In addition to the expected mental overload, my subconscious was already starting to say goodbye to England, the country that had once been my home. When we landed in London and queued up for immigration, I realised it would be the last time the four of us entered Britain together like this before Brexit was complete by the end of the following month. After that, I would be treated differently from the rest of my family, my German passport separating me from my British husband and children. On the surface, rationally and sensibly, this wasn't a big deal and shouldn't matter, but emotionally, it was hitting me hard. It was like a door I hadn't even noticed was closing on me.

Scott, who by now was half-American and had by and large disengaged from his country of birth, just shook his head at my dramatics. He couldn't wait to get home to Austin and away from the UK. The way he felt about the US was different; America had different emotional connotations for him than for me. It was the country he had chosen to live in, the country he had left his home country for. Just like the UK was the country I once chose to live in, and that I had left my home country for, almost twenty-two years earlier. The US was only second on my expat list, and while I enjoyed living there and considered it my current home, England had got there first and would always hold that special place in my heart. Brexit felt like a betrayal.

After a lovely week with friends and family, and plenty of time walking through the wintry countryside, we got picked up from our friends' house in the early morning. The English cabbie flew through the narrow winding lanes of Hertfordshire, disregarding both speed limits and the extreme lack of visibility due to January fog, and dropped us at Heathrow. We were dispatched with a hearty 'Cheers mate, safe trip!', crossed worlds and landed in Houston to be greeted by a warm, drawly 'Welcome home, y'all', and I couldn't help smiling. I had already missed the warmth of the Southern twang, so familiar to my ears and so welcoming. I chastised myself for creating so much drama for myself and my family. I could totally do this; it wasn't so bad. Texas was home, just as England had been home all those years earlier, but was no longer. How crazy, yet how wonderful, to be able to experience all these nuances in the space of less than 24 hours and know that this was my normal. It was, indeed, like living in parallel worlds.

We went back to California for Presidents Day weekend in February, the first time we managed to go together as a whole family since we had left more than three years earlier. I was desperate for this trip; Amelie's upcoming high school graduation and plans to move abroad were weighing heavily on me. She was doing so well now, and I couldn't have asked for a better outcome, still in disbelief that we had even reached this point, unimaginable just a year earlier. But I was still on guard, still afraid of a relapse. She had been accepted at an arts college in England but planned to defer her place while spending a gap year in Europe, working her way through as many countries as she could. I wasn't totally sure how I felt about it all, but her enthusiasm and positive attitude were infectious. It was like our bubbly, energetic little girl from years ago had come back to us.

For now, before school ended for good, I wanted us all to reconnect with California, the place that had once welcomed us with open arms, by visiting all our favourite spots, rekindling old memories and soaking it all up. I wanted Maya, who had completely retreated into herself and who wasn't sharing any of her pain with us, to feel something again, anything, and I hoped that revisiting the places of her childhood might trigger some happy memories and lure her out of her shell. I felt an almost animalistic desire to grab both my kids' faces and rub them into the sights, sounds and smells of their childhood, as if I could brand it all onto them. And I wanted to touch and smell everything and listen to the sounds of the Pacific Ocean, as though I could make it part of me and keep those feelings with me forever, to whip out whenever I needed them in future.

We had been through so much those last few years, and I rarely felt truly happy, but when I stood on the cliffs of Santa Cruz, overlooking the glistening waters of Monterey Bay, my children and husband by my side, I felt a huge rush of serenity.

Bullies

A few weeks after we got back, however, things took a turn for the worse. Towards the end of the previous year, Maya, who was now thirteen, had befriended some kids I had very mixed feelings about. They were friendly and polite at first glance, but Maya turned into a different person around them; I didn't like it at all. She also started reconnecting with a few girls from school who had treated her very badly the year before, falling back into an old friendship pattern we'd seen again and again: she was attracting people who weren't good for her and then tried to do everything in her power to please them. The wall she had built around herself was now totally closed off; neither Scott nor I nor even Amelie were able to get through to her. On the one hand, I was happy to see that she was socially engaged again rather than barricading herself in her room. But on the other hand, I felt extremely sceptical about the kids she chose to hang out with.

Brushing my fears aside – what parent doesn't go through a million stages of distrust and opposing opinions with their teen? – I tried to show my willingness to be open-minded. In an attempt to at least have some idea of what the kids were up to, I told Maya to invite them over to our house, so they'd hang out under my roof instead of god-knows-where, and I could keep an eye on things. Plus, I had grown up myself in a house that was always open to friends, and I wanted to demonstrate to Maya that I wasn't going to stop her from socialising. I made sure I had most of the parents' details and felt I'd done as much as I could. It wasn't until later that I knew how much these kids had taken advantage of my definitely more European openness. These American teenagers, however charming and polite they seemed at first glance, were nothing like the friends I had when I was a young teen in Germany. I had underestimated the fact that a lot of teenagers in the US don't experience a lot of independence when they're young – parental supervision is much more extreme. And I had underestimated the dismal level of sex education, especially in Texas.

When a few incidents of online bullying got so severe that we had to involve the school and other parents, things turned ugly very quickly. We felt Maya's safety was at risk. Even though I had kept screenshots of the worst threats, along with the perpetrators' names, the school point-blank refused to help or even get involved. The principal shrugged, claiming that 'threats and incidents had happened outside school premises', and we decided to pull Maya out for the remainder of the school year, aiming to have her complete her school work independently. High school would provide a fresh start later that year.

COVID

And then the world as we knew it came to a halt. It was March 2020, and COVID became a tangible threat. The Austin Independent School District decided to close all schools prematurely, a day earlier than planned before spring break, with the idea that this break could possibly be extended by another week in case the COVID situation required it. The message was sent by email in the middle of the night, and so we woke up on Friday morning and learned that spring break had already started. We didn't know, then, that the previous Thursday had been Amelie's very last day of school, ever. Our calendar was full of senior year events such as senior prom, senior pranks – a nationwide high school tradition – and eventually graduation at the end of May, but everything ended up being cancelled, and the kids never went back to school in person after that initial spring break closure.

To spend this period of your life locked at home with your parents instead of spending time with friends and relishing the last few weeks of freedom before heading off into the real world was a pretty hard pill to swallow. It couldn't have come at a worse time for our oldest, who had literally fought for her life just a year earlier and worked so hard to get through junior year in order to graduate as planned. Since she had already made the decision to defer college, she wasn't about to start her higher education remotely, like so many of her peers, but any dreams of travelling and living in another country for a while were shattered by the pandemic.

For Maya, COVID initially provided exactly the break from school she needed, and I was so glad to be able to keep her safe and supervised – little did I realise then how the stress of the pandemic would add to her already traumatised mind.

Scott could no longer commute to the East Coast but the Austin office still hadn't been set up, which meant he was now working from home full-time. Anthropologie closed its doors for the time being, and I made it my number one goal to build the cosiest nest ever for my little family. Time with both kids under the same roof was slipping through my fingers at an alarming rate, and I wanted to smother them with happy, peaceful memories amidst all the chaos of the outside world. I absolutely relished having them close and the hamster wheel of life grinding to a halt. I realised just how much I had needed things to slow down.

I also loved the fact that everybody seemed to have woken up to the power of online connectivity. While FaceTime and Skype had been our lifelines for so many years, I had always struggled with those friends who just didn't want to use them as extensively as we did. All of a sudden, there were countless WhatsApp groups and frequent Zoom meetings with people I hadn't been able to connect with on a regular basis. I even joined a virtual yoga class that a friend of mine in England was teaching and looked forward to it every week. I remember thinking how wonderful it was that people had realised this and couldn't imagine things ever going back to the way things were before COVID.

I knew I was well practiced at being home alone, with no friends nearby I could simply meet up with. As an expat and an introvert, I didn't mind being at home and pottering around the house by myself, a distinct advantage over people whose lives were very much about always being around other people. It was a constant battle of feeling happy for myself and guilty because my teenage kids were slowly losing their minds as they were prohibited from physically being with their friends. My heart was breaking for them every day. The only thing cheering them up was our latest addition to the family: Milo and Max, two rescue kittens from the Austin Siamese Rescue. We had missed having a cat ever since we left Snowy behind in Germany, and our two cuddly new felines more than made up for his absence.

Another thing I was used to as an expat and that I didn't find too difficult, was adapting to all those new rules and regulations. When you move countries, you automatically accept that what you're used to and what was the norm before is no longer the case; other countries have other customs, and adjusting to a new set of social guidelines comes with the territory. So when the restaurants shut and we weren't allowed to meet in groups larger than four any longer, and only outside, I didn't find it that hard to accept and was able to move on without instantly despairing. I noticed that a lot of people around me really struggled to come to terms with the ever-changing, ever more rigorous guidelines, and even openly rebelled against them. Witnessing this made me very grateful that I had been able to build some resilience over the years and had a whole armada of coping skills at my disposal.

Despite all the positive thoughts I had during that time, though, they ultimately gave way to waves of anxiety and guilt. People died every day, and I knew how incredibly fortunate we were that Scott was able to work from home and that we lived to-gether in a big house with plenty of rooms to get out of each other's hair when necessary. Nobody had to put themselves in danger, no-body in our close and extended family had got sick so far, and we didn't face financial hardship. It felt so wrong to be happily de-voting so much time to my hobbies and long-planned projects and having time to chat extensively with family and friends while all around us, despair grew.

May arrived, and all those important school dates kept popping up on my calendar, dates I had meticulously noted at the beginning of the school year, in a previous life. Now, they were evil reminders of all the things we were missing.

Maya, my quirky, beautiful middle schooler in the depths of teenage turmoil, was supposed to dance a happy dance, finally leaving her much-hated school and two years of bullying, girl drama, and general misery behind. Instead, she was hiding in her bedroom. As was Amelie, my senior, who was supposed to finally leave school and was full of ideas about what her future should look like. Amelie had always been somewhat cynical about senior prom, the big culmination of high school, feared and celebrated in numerous movies about American youth culture, but she had pur-chased a long, black velvet prom dress – in a thrift store, of course, in keeping with her principles – which had been hanging up on the door of her wardrobe, full of promises. One day, when I went down to her room to look for a pair of shoes I was missing, I no-ticed it was no longer there; it had quietly disappeared, and my heart broke all over again. School was ending online, and Amelie never got to say goodbye to her classmates and teachers properly, missing out on that essential rite of passage.

In an attempt to come up with something resembling graduation, McCallum held a drive-thru parade for the graduates, which
was beautiful and sad in equal measure. The kids turned up on the
last day of school with extensively decorated cars and drove a couple of circles around the school and its neighbourhood, with teachers, residents, friends and parents flanking the road, waving and
cheering their kids on with banners and chants. Nobody was allowed to leave their car and hug their favourite teachers, but the
sentiments were there on full display.

Road Tripping

With summer approaching, we knew we couldn't escape to Europe this year and needed to find alternatives. We had made the decision not to book flights very early on. At first, I felt desperation. If this was going to be the new normal, our lifestyle was not sustainable. Up to this point, going on an annual trip back to Europe had been an unbreakable rule; I had told Scott early on during our years in California that skipping a year wasn't an option. If this COVID situation led to a change of circumstances, however, making travel more complicated in future, we would have to seriously rethink our expat life. It wasn't just that we missed loved ones – should something happen to my parents, for example, I had to be certain that I could get on a plane at a moment's notice.

While I was extremely sad not to be able to see our friends and family in Germany and England, I didn't think my anxiety could handle the many tests, quarantines, potential flight cancellations, and above all, the risk of infecting an older family member. My brain felt like it was exploding, and I felt palpable relief at not having to stress about booking flights, finding convenient dates for everybody, and planning get-togethers. The agony we had experienced each year of making decisions on where to go first and how long for, was simply taken away. I could literally watch my shoulders drop and relax. COVID had made the decision for me.

But what else were we going to do? Spending the whole summer in Austin with its habitual temperatures of around 40°C/100°F was out of the question. Amelie was still at home, and so this would be the last summer of all of us together under the same roof. The only way to travel was by car. We perused the map of the US and decided to go on a road trip through New Mexico and Colorado to explore some of the places we had always wanted to visit.

After almost four months of being stuck at home, we were desperate for a change of scenery and an escape from the relentless heat. Armed with an annual National Park pass and a massive, comfortable Chevy Tahoe we had hired for the trip, we left the cats in the care of a sitter, packed the dog and teenagers into the car and set off for the endless drive through the fracking and oil-drilling landscape of West Texas, past roadrunners and tumbleweeds, through the dusty, sandy desert, towards our first destination: Carlsbad Caverns, New Mexico.

Not the best at dealing with enclosed spaces, especially underground, I was very nervous on our descent, but all fears vanished when I glimpsed the first cave's beauty. I would have been over the moon to just see a few bizarre sulfuric rock formations, stalagmites and stalactites, but there were over a hundred of them. It was a two-and-a-half-mile hike through the darkness, descending several hundred metres below the earth, through various 'rooms' that reminded us of *Lord of the Rings*, and I swear were still populated by gnomes and fairies. The contrast between the dry, sparse landscape above and this awe-inspiring, otherworldly scenery was phenomenal.

From the depths of the caverns, we drove on to Santa Fe, which, surprisingly, sits at an altitude of almost 2200 m, which meant none of us was prepared, and we all got head colds in various shapes and forms within our first day. I adored Santa Fe with its warm, earthy colours and quirky, charming atmosphere, and earmarked it as the perfect location for a girls' weekend, once we'd be able to travel freely and enjoy all the beautiful museums and attractions, most of which were currently closed. The city was small and cute, with a lovely, earthy, artistic flair and beautiful scenery around it.

Ziggy, who had been extremely happy to be accompanying us on this trip, clearly needed to stretch his legs properly after those first few days of driving and being a good boy, and so Scott and I perused the hiking maps around town and found Dale Ball Trails, a gorgeous tangle of trails through the hills above the city. Up, up, up we went through peaceful fields and fragrant woods and enjoyed amazing views of Santa Fe and its surroundings. We realised how much we had missed this throughout our time in Austin – being active outside, with views over beautiful mountain scenery, able to breathe and not be hidden away in air-conditioned surroundings. For the first time since coming back from England, we seriously talked about leaving Austin.

Our next stop, Mesa Verde National Park, a UNESCO World Heritage Site in Colorado, deep in the rocky heart of the country, was very different to the National Parks we'd experienced so far, and surprisingly not busy at all. We couldn't get enough of admiring the numerous ancestral cliff dwellings and ancient gathering sites, which gave us a whole new perspective on how far back life in this country actually went. As Europeans, we are brought up to regard the United States as a very young nation, and American tourists in Europe always fuss over how old our cities are. Looking at ancient pueblos carved into the rocks made us think of all that was lost in the history of this fascinating country.

Bringing our dog to a National Park meant that one of us had to stay behind with him in the car, as dogs were only allowed on limited paved areas, but not on any trails. I would have loved to go on extended hikes, but it was extremely hot, and the kids were more than happy to stay within the air-conditioned confines of the car, to venture out only briefly to walk to viewpoints and special landmarks. At one of those points, we encountered a group of motorcyclists who had adorned one of their bikes with a giant Star-Spangled Banner emblazoned with the words 'Trump 2020'. Another election was looming. Amelie and Maya were not impressed. While Scott and I walked down to the viewpoint, they stayed behind with Ziggy, and when we got back, the flag had a few noticeable slashes, making it droop like a wet rag. Amelie flashed me a triumphant grin and briefly opened her fist to reveal a pocket knife. Quickly, we climbed back into our car and fled the scene, back to the tiny cottage we had rented for a few days.

Having never spent a single 4th of July in the US as a family – some of us would usually be in Europe at that time – we didn't have a blueprint for any special proceedings that should happen on this day. A cosy fire in the little backyard fire pit of our Airbnb seemed appropriate, and Scott and I sat outside chatting for hours while the sun went down until we almost fell asleep. It was exactly the break we needed; we were together but not cooped up at home, feeling trapped.

Scott had to stay home and work for a couple of days, which suited us all, and we spent the days lazing in the hammock, sorting through photos, reading books and recovering from our colds. I discovered that while I adored sleeping in a hammock, my back did not, and the sharp pain that woke me the next morning reminded me that I wasn't twenty anymore. I could barely move, much to the girls' delight, since I was unable to drag them off on hikes, bike rides or even walks with the dog. At least, I managed to climb into the passenger seat of our car and we set off to explore the National Park around the corner, the beautiful Colorado National Monument, by driving through it, in true American style. We did the same at Arches National Park and Moab the following day, adding a few short walks this time. We were blown away by the beauty of the nature surrounding us, the giant red arches and imposing rock formations boldly staring at us, set in scene magnificently by the bright blue sky. Road trips are a wonderful way to see a country, and the scale, changing scenery and vastness of the American landscape is something that can only be fully appreciated when driving through it.

Our next stop was Telluride, a place I'd only ever associated with skiing and seen covered in snow on TV. I was really looking forward to experiencing it during the summer time. We decided to visit another National Park on the way up there, the Black Canyon of the Gunnison, which we had never even heard of before. The pictures we had googled looked nice, but nothing prepared us for the jaw-droppingly dramatic scenery of this unsung hero of a National Park, which would have made a fine setting for *Game of Thrones*.

We arrived in Mountain Village, a true little slice of paradise, a 20-minute gondola ride from Telluride Village, surrounded by snow-capped mountains and shimmering aspen forests. Ziggy, by now totally accustomed to living a nomadic life, happily entered and exited the elevator up to our room on the seventh floor, and I was certain I would have been able to teach him to push the button with his nose had we stayed longer. I took him on long walks through the silvery, shimmery aspens early each morning before the kids woke up, and soaked up the profoundly healing energy this mountainous landscape had on me. The last eighteen months had been such a strain on my mental and physical health, and I badly needed the embrace of nature around me.

A day before we had to leave our mountain retreat to start the journey back down to Texas, we decided to hike to a secluded spot called 'Little Hawaii', just off Bear Creek trail. A rare sense of happiness and togetherness accompanied us as we traipsed through meadows and woodlands and climbed down to the crystal clear creek, laughing at our blissfully happy dog splashing through the ice-cold water and collecting logs to carry along. It was like a little escape to paradise, away from the lunacy that was the real world.

There was no escaping it, though. That night, I was woken by retching noises and found Maya slumped on the floor in the bathroom, white as a sheet and almost non-verbal, her arms crisscrossed by angry red cuts and scratches. I sank down to the floor, cradling my child, and she even let me hug her. I knew I had put my head in the sand again. Keeping her seemingly out of harm's way at home and running away on a family road trip hadn't solved anything. We needed to get her help, and soon.

So we packed up the car and started the long trek back home, fifteen hours along straight dusty roads, past oil fields and dreary agricultural towns – the first town after crossing the border into Texas from New Mexico was called 'Progress' and proudly displayed a giant Confederate flag. My mind a mess of anxiety and fear of what was going to happen with my child and my family, knowing another change was inevitable, I stared out of the car window, mesmerised by the many oil pumps vying with windmills as far as the eye could see. A perfect example of the dichotomy of Texas, caught between staunch conservatism and innovative spirit.

A New Reality

We got back home just before the new school year started. Texas being Texas, Governor Greg Abbott had decided to loosen any COVID restrictions for retail and gastronomy, and Amelie found herself a job in retail, to earn some money in case travelling became an option again. She was hoping to move into a house with some friends soon.

Meanwhile, Maya was attempting to muddle her way through the weirdness of her first year of high school, which happened mostly at home, via Zoom, with the odd in-person event. It was still almost impossible to get through to her, but she had accepted that she needed a therapist. Trying to find someone suitable and available, however, proved incredibly difficult; COVID meant that everybody was booked up, with long waiting lists.

Miraculously, we got an appointment, and the relief was palpable; Maya seemed to soften instantly, and we felt like we had saved her just in time. After a couple of sessions, however, the therapist called Scott and me in and told us that Maya had something she needed to tell us both. We learned that months earlier, at the beginning of the year, after I had dropped her at a friend's house – a boy I knew, who had been to our home a few times – where she was planning to spend the afternoon with a few more friends, and after I had exchanged pleasantries with the boy's mother, who assured me she would be around the whole time, after I'd told Maya to call me immediately when she wanted to come home, the boy had sexually assaulted her. It was like the world around me came crashing down; I felt numb, trying to listen and process at the same time, understanding only that my child had been hurt and I hadn't been able to protect her. I think I even blurted out something like, 'But I told you not to be alone in a room with him!' something insanely inappropriate in any case, and the therapist cut me off. 'This is not about what you said or didn't say!' Here we were again, me trying to defend my capacity as a mother. Just as I had done with Amelie. I still hadn't learned my lesson.

The fact was that the assault had happened, and I realised that just telling your kid to stay safe didn't actually have any practical meaning. And that I hadn't even thought to ask further questions when she became more and more withdrawn. Had she tried to tell me, but I hadn't heard her? Had I been so wrapped up in creating a cosy home bubble that I had missed the signs? I guess I was remembering my own reticence and lack of communication with my parents when I was that age myself and had simply shrugged it off as teenage moodiness. Although now that I was thinking about that period in my life, I wasn't so sure it had been normal behaviour. Memories of the horse-riding accident I had when I was twelve flared up.

I had fallen off my horse on a trail ride with friends and hurt my leg so badly I couldn't stand, but I managed to ride back to the stable, put my horse away and even cycled home. I was trying with all my might to pretend everything was just fine. As I was cycling – god knows how I even managed to cycle – my mother drove past, and I waved at her as if nothing had happened, wondering only if she would see the dirt and the holes in my clothes, and how I could hide this. Once I got home, however, there was no pretending, as I clearly couldn't walk. It turned out I had ruptured several ligaments in my knee. I knew that, had I been less severely injured, I wouldn't have told anybody what had happened; the shame I felt at that moment was simply too great. Maya's behaviour after her infinitely greater trauma of assault reminded me of myself. It was clear that I wasn't the only one in the family who was keen to hide her troubles from the outside world.

The aftermath of Maya's revelations is a blur; I vaguely remember trying to talk to the boy's mother, who told me that if Maya had called for help she would have come into the room – they weren't even in his bedroom but the living room – and since she hadn't done so what had happened must have been consensual. Turns out that no amount of Southern charm and manners, nor the proximity of a parent in the room next door, will stop somebody from inflicting harm.

We filed a police report and spent a long day at Austin's Child Protective Services office to record mine and Maya's statements. The counsellors talking to us were wonderful, but we kept hearing the same thing: they couldn't do much because the boy was a minor, and Maya hadn't been vocal enough, hadn't fought back. When the police turned up at his door, his parents refused to let them talk to him, denying everything. 'He'll have a file though,' one of the officers tried to reassure us, 'If he ever does anything again when he is older, we will be able to see previous reports.' And indeed, a few years later, we learned that he was taken into custody for assaulting somebody with a knife, although I don't know how it all went down eventually; I doubt anything serious would have happened to this popular high school football prodigy. There were simply too many Brock Turners in the world.

After we'd reported him, Maya tentatively shared her ordeal with others and found that she wasn't the only one who'd been a victim. Nobody, however, wanted to come forward, terrified mostly of what their parents would say. I heard further horror stories of assault and felt sick. With Maya opening up about the things that went on amongst middle and high school teenagers, I got a shocking glimpse into the dark side of a deeply conservative, religious and inherently misogynistic state. Sex education was very rudimentary here in Texas, and parents were actually given the option to keep their children away from it completely if they chose to do so. I cursed myself for underestimating the gravity of this. Somehow, even though I knew sex was a highly controversial topic in this country and many people had a much more buttoned-up attitude to it than I was used to from Europe, I had assumed things would be okay for my own children, who had been brought up differently than many of their peers.

I knew what I really needed to address besides personal safety was the fact that my teen had gone through an ordeal like this and kept it to herself for so long. I sat down with her and listened, apologising for not questioning her behaviour more, and for not talking more explicitly about how to avoid dangerous situations, rather than just saying things like 'don't be alone with a boy if you feel unsafe'. Empty phrases in the face of a real threat. 'I didn't know what to do when the others left,' Maya had told me and the police about that afternoon. 'And he's such a strong guy, I couldn't have fought him off.' I closed my eyes, her words ripping the cover off of some long-suppressed memories of my own. I knew what it was like to freeze and dissociate from what was going on, in a strange self-protective mechanism; any thought of screaming or drawing attention abandoned, the relentless 'it's my fault' playing in your head. And the profound sense of shame that followed, making it impossible to tell anyone about it, only to find, much later, that so many others shared similar experiences.

It seemed things hadn't changed much since my own adolescence. In the age of #MeToo, we were hearing plenty of conversations about assault and aggression towards women; in reality, however, the story was still the same: girls were assaulted and too afraid to talk about it, blaming themselves or fearing being blamed rather than listened to, being told they'd been wearing the wrong clothes or shouldn't have been in that location at that time, etc. No wonder nobody felt like they could share their stories.

It was a real blow to my parental ego, however, that Maya had felt unable to come and talk to me, her mother. I had assumed that I'd had enough conversations with my children for them to feel safe in knowing they could tell me anything. If I had thought I'd done things differently from the way I had been parented myself, I now realised how mistaken I was. My constant efforts to gloss over negative words and emotions, whether we were moving or whether it was about issues at school or with friends, had sent the message that I wasn't really listening. There was no room for vulnerability. They probably felt just as unheard as I had as a teenager. While I knew that, of course, some of this was down to typical teenage angst and undeveloped frontal lobe issues, I knew I hadn't truly validated their feelings either. And here we were, history repeating itself. I hadn't made a big enough effort to become the safe space I had hoped to be.

Brain Freeze

S cott was still working from home, and it seemed like he was keeping even longer hours than before COVID. Any anxiety he might have felt was drowned out by the demands of his schedule. Working as the sole provider and looking after Maya and me took every ounce of his time and energy. Amelie had moved into a small house in the middle of the city with two friends, all keen to escape the clutches of their parents after being cooped up at home for so long; we barely saw or heard from her.

I returned to work at Anthropologie a couple of times a week, grateful to leave the house but stressed with customers not adhering to the health and safety guidelines and my hours still severely cut because of the pandemic. This meant I had a lot of time on my hands to fret and run circles around my mind. I barely slept, my anxiety spiralling in ever faster circles.

I kept finding myself in a weird state of brain freeze. Unlike at the beginning of the pandemic the previous March, when I was almost excited to be given so much free time to do things that I'd always wanted to do, I now found myself stressing over the tiniest issues. One morning, I almost started crying when I couldn't rip a piece of paper towel clean off the roll; another time, I stepped into a wet patch on the floor wearing socks and felt such intense anger well up inside of me that I was worried I'd lose control and smash something. I could barely make simple decisions; it was like my brain was incapable of holding on to any thoughts, and I was perpetually paralysed and promptly angry with myself for feeling so foggy.

Simple, irrelevant things, such as 'do I take a yoga class on Zoom now, or should I spend an hour writing, or do I clean the bathroom?' turned my brain upside down with stress, but I was unable to calm it down and found myself creating new, bigger decisions, including whether we should move to a smaller house, or renovate our current one, or leave the city altogether. Maya seemed to get better – the combination of therapy and school via Zoom made a difference – but I felt like I wanted to airlift her out of this town into a new, safer environment. But was another move wise? I had lost any sense of intuition, trusting my gut, and going with the flow. I was scared of myself and my brain.

I booked an online appointment with a psychiatric doctor and tentatively asked whether there might be a possibility that I had ADHD, just like my daughter. I had been reading so much about neurodivergence in order to be able to help Maya, and had recognised a huge number of symptoms in myself. I tried to tell all this to the doctor, but he brushed me off: 'Ma'am, you're approaching menopause. And you have a Master's degree. You cannot have ADHD.' I tried to argue, repeating what had happened with Maya, but he was clearly eager to end the call and told me he'd call in a prescription for antidepressants to my pharmacy. I had tried antidepressants in the past, but they always made me feel sick and didn't make anything better; out of desperation, I tried again, but the same thing happened. I also hated that they made me feel numb, as if I were wrapped in a layer of cotton wool, which caused even more frustration. I knew it wasn't the right approach, and I knew there was more to it, but I had no idea what to do. Nor did I have the energy to trawl through endless lists of therapists again. There were barely any who accepted new patients anyway; COVID made sure of that.

I felt utterly helpless. I knew that my game was up, and I could no longer function based on what I'd been clinging to my whole life: my perfect facade. No more 'The Show Must Go On'. The show had to end; it wasn't serving anybody, not myself, not my family, not my life. But how was I supposed to dismantle a construct that I'd been building for so long?

Snowpocalypse

The warmth of January gave way to some freezing winds blasting down on us from the north. A few mornings brought ice on the roads, and even snow flurries, but we still brushed it all off as normal occurrences during this time of year. It was our fourth winter in Texas; we were used to its capriciousness.

And then, real snow arrived. It started snowing one evening and never stopped. The next morning, we woke up to our whole neighbourhood covered in gorgeous, glistening, knee-deep powder and bright blue skies.

Completely perplexed but mostly excited about this fun, novel experience, we located our snow gear in the storage box in the basement and took Ziggy out for a walk – he was deliriously happy, frolicking without his lead and barking loudly at us as we joined others in sledging down hills on plastic bags. We tired ourselves out, returned home for some hot drinks and a warm shower and were just about to turn on the TV when the power went out and didn't come back on, not within the next few hours, nor the next few days.

The city had announced they were doing 'rolling blackouts', turning every household's power off for an hour here or there, in order to preserve enough energy to keep Austin going. As it turned out, the plan failed abysmally.

It got cold really quickly. At first, inspired by some 'when life gives you lemons' ideas, I thought I'd keep warm by doing some exercise, a few yoga stretches and push-ups, to stay warm, until the heating came back on. But my body, wiser and clearly following some survival instinct, just wouldn't comply. Grateful for our thermal underwear and multitude of hats, scarves and gloves, we tried not to panic. Maya practically stayed in bed all day, covered by several duvets and even an emergency foil blanket, and with the occasional cat burrowing somewhere by her side. Ziggy was wearing his winter coat from England, which I'd miraculously found in a box that was still unpacked from our move back, and barely left his spot in front of the fireplace on the top floor. We had never used it before, but we had a couple of logs left over from making pizza a few days earlier, in the sunshine on our main balcony outside, and decided even a small fire was better than no heat.

At its lowest point, the temperature inside our house dropped to 4°C/39°F, and only the fact that we had a gas stove in the kitchen saved us from total despair. At least we were able to make hot tea and cook the food from the freezer that was unaffected at first, but definitely started to slowly melt. In my pioneer-woman resourcefulness, I surveyed what needed using up, and we enjoyed some adventurous dinners, huddled by candlelight and surrounded by the pets in front of our bijou fireplace.

Three days in, we still had running water, albeit very cold, and felt luckier than a lot of people in the vicinity, but the cold was starting to really seep into our bones. Once the last log was used up, I decided to summon the neighbourhood community spirit by asking on our online forum if anyone close by had any firewood to spare. Someone replied, and I grabbed a backpack and a couple of carrier bags, pulled on my snow boots and set off on a crunchy, slippery three-mile trek through ice and snow to retrieve the promised logs.

I caught myself whistling as I was trudging through the snow and smiled in exasperation with myself. What was wrong with me? Just like during the early days of the pandemic, when I excelled at making the most of this time by pursuing things I'd always wanted to do, my crazy resilience was coming to the surface again, and I rolled up my proverbial sleeves and found some weird strength in this dire time. I found that I was exceedingly capable of dealing with this misfortune. But why did I feel like this? Why was it easier for me to walk up an icy hill, frozen to the core, than to pick up the phone and make a doctor's appointment? Why did I feel like I could handle a true crisis like this, but I continually struggled with basic life skills, such as knowing how much money was in my bank account?

Still shaking my head at myself, I turned the corner onto the firewood people's drive and loaded up my bags, feeling very heroic. Unfortunately, I returned home to a burst water pipe above the garage, and my hopes of being celebrated as the heroine of the day were squashed amidst gushing icy water and the rising panic that the ceiling would cave in and crash down onto our car, which we weren't able to move, since our other car was frozen onto the drive in front of the garage. Luckily, we were able to locate the turn-off for the water by digging through snow and mud somewhere under a nearby bush, and catastrophe was averted. Having no more running water didn't even seem that bad after such a shock. We still had some bottled water to drink and wash our faces.

By day four, we were so cold and miserable that we spent most of the day in the car to warm up, charging our phones while we still had gas in the tank. Scott, who received zero sympathy for this laughable little snow extravaganza down south from his East Coast colleagues, who had weathered several severe winter storms already, spent most of the day working in the car and came back into the freezing house for cups of tea, which by now were made on the stove with melted snow. We still couldn't get out of our drive and up the hill to the nearest road, which was more than frustrating, as the main roads were slowly looking a bit clearer, and the prospect of a friend's house and some heat, electricity and hot water within tantalising reach. Maya, who never once complained about the cold or lack of electricity, took herself off to shower at a classmate's house nearby and returned with a big smile on her face.

Day five started very slowly. We were so cold and felt so disgusting; any sense of stoicism and ability to see the humorous side had dissipated. Luckily, we finally managed to move our car off the drive and escaped for some blissful hot showers, and as we drove back home at dusk, we saw lights popping up in various neighbourhood windows. And indeed, as we turned the corner into our drive, our house was illuminated, and we were greeted by warmth and very happy pets. Miraculously, a friend of a friend found an available plumber, who was able to put a temporary cap on our pipe, and so we had running water again, too. We were almost back to normal.

During the whole ordeal, I was blown away by the strong sense of community spirit – Americans doing what they do best. The online neighbourhood forums were awash with requests and offers of help: there was a woman stuck in her house on top of a hill who was about to go into labour, and a kind soul with a 4×4 braved the roads and took her to hospital, only to spend the rest of the day running errands, picking up food, and carting elderly residents to safety. Police were walking the icy roads, knocking on people's doors to check whether they were alright, and a huge number of people who had their power come back on early opened their homes to those still without. No questions asked. Volunteers rescued frozen turtles from the lakes, and motels were turned into emergency shelters for Austin's huge homeless population. People completely unaffected by the cold started cooking meals for those in need; neighbours helping neighbours fix pipes, lending power tools and muscle power to remove fallen trees, and the general sense of 'we can do this together' was palpable. It was obvious how much Americans were used to the authorities failing them.

Once the snow and ice had disappeared, spring returned to Texas in full force. Literally a week after wearing our warmest winter coats, we were in T-shirts and shorts. My brain fog was subsiding. It was like once the snow and ice had melted from the palm trees and cacti around me, so had the paralysis of my mind. A long and arduous cycle had been broken.

It had been over a year since I left this country and almost a year since I'd been outside of Texas. But I had to admit that something had shifted during that time: I had made peace with being in Austin. I hadn't been able to run away to Europe for a while now, and driving along the city's streets, I now felt a sense of deep connection and appreciation, maybe even love. It was like Austin was winking at me, saying, 'See, I knew you could do it.' This city that had asked so much of me and my family, a place I never felt had opened itself up to me fully, had finally chuckled, pulled me into a headlock, ruffled my hair and put a big smacker on the top of my head. It had become home.

I even made a new friend, another international German, who had just moved to Austin from Vietnam. Through her, I met another couple of German women and relished the opportunity to meet up with them and speak my mother tongue for hours. It felt like a new beginning for me; I had missed the shared context of being with other Germans and enjoyed our small circle for the welcoming, no-questions-asked cocoon that it was.

We found a volunteer opportunity, which meant we were able to get our COVID vaccines early, and with that, a sense of normality flooded back into my life. It was like my brain had needed this fresh start, after a year of pandemic, trauma and then the snowpocalypse, to regroup, and now I could even feel creativity pouring back in; I was brimming with ideas and plans, and none of it had anything to do with other places and a 'the grass is greener elsewhere' mindset. I still felt raw and unsure of our future, but I was starting to get a sense of how I belonged here, in the capital of Texas, at least for now.

Decision Time, Again

Meanwhile, Maya's bullying hell had continued and was, in fact, escalating in ever scarier ways. As if someone had stuck a giant magnet onto her back, she kept being drawn into ugly new scenarios where people relentlessly mocked and harassed her. This even followed us to Europe that summer, where some new horrific messages trundled in, contaminating this place, up to now her safe haven, seemingly so far away from her daily hell, with the ugliness of cyberbullying.

We knew things would get even harder when we returned to Austin after the summer. Maya, now a fifteen-year-old sophomore, in her second year of high school, was returning to high school in person for the first time in eighteen months, making her even more vulnerable. We began to build a case to take to school, determined not to let them get away without taking action; we were now dealing with high school, another principal, and another team of student support staff. I saved screenshots of all the worst messages, from those telling Maya to kill herself, to those inciting others to harm her, as well as an array of the nastiest rumours and videos imaginable. The school baulked and failed to discipline the perpetrators, even after I had provided them with all the names I could find. At one point, we involved the parents of one of the bullies, which made things even worse for Maya.

We knew we needed external support; after yet another argument with the school police officer, Scott could barely keep himself from starting a physical fight. He threw himself into researching legal pathways and came across David's Legacy, a foundation that had established 'David's Law', an anti-bullying law that was created after sixteen-year-old David Bartlett Molak from San Antonio killed himself in 2016, after being relentlessly bullied and harassed by a group of students through text messages and social media.

For the first time, someone truly listened and showed empathy for our situation. They warned us, however, that while we could try to fight our case based on this law, it would be a long and arduous process. 'I would strongly suggest you take your child out of that school and environment,' the woman we spoke to implored us. 'You won't have the energy to fight and keep her safe at the same time. Your focus should be on her mental well-being.' At that point, Maya's anxiety, combined with not feeling safe without any COVID regulations in place – this was Texas – had spiralled out of control.

One morning – it must have been after a rare night when I didn't get up to check on her – I found Maya's bed pristine, clearly not slept in, and her phone on the bedside table. It was as though an icy fist was clutching my heart, squeezing it until I could barely breathe. I wanted to scream but couldn't; all I could think was that Maya had gone to end her life. I felt numb. And then I did what I always did each morning: I grabbed the lead and took Ziggy out for his morning walk. There were some woods near our house that I knew Maya ran to from time to time; I thought, *at least my dog will find her if she's in here.* My heart constricting, barely beating, a sob caught in my throat and my limbs shaking, I combed the bushes for a body. And then, my phone rang. The mother of one of Maya's 'friends'. 'She's safe. She ran off with my kid last night. My husband is on his way to get them.' My legs gave way, and I crumpled to the ground, unable to speak, Ziggy licking the tears off my face, and I just wanted to stay there on the ground and close my eyes; I was so tired.

We knew we couldn't go on like this. Maya was barely able to attend classes, and the school finally told us to find an alternative solution, or they would fail her. When a child who loves to learn doesn't feel safe in a school environment and shuts down completely, you don't have many choices. We knew she couldn't stay, but we were scrambling to find alternatives, looking at online options and various private schools. Unfortunately, those we liked had horrendously long waiting lists – a lot of people had opted to go down that route in the aftermath of COVID – and the rest were so academically demanding that we feared Maya would shut down even more.

Scott, who had started travelling to New Jersey for work again, was the first to suggest a move. He was increasingly worried about my mental health and knew he needed to be around more. He started inquiring about areas to live and schools near his office in northern New Jersey and found a small private school that agreed to take Maya on as a remote student with the goal of having her attend in person once we'd made the move.

My memory is patchy; I'm still unsure how it all came together in the end. Maya accompanied Scott on a short trip to New Jersey and seemed relieved at the thought of a new place, and after that, the three of us went together to look at a few towns and houses.

I felt numb throughout the process, looking at new homes as if I were an extra in a film, and then starting to organise this next move, trying to stay positive. The thought of another transition terrified me, but rationally, moving to the East Coast made sense: we desperately needed to save our child and find a way for her to finish high school and leave the toxic environment that had almost destroyed her, and being in New Jersey meant Scott would be home every evening, and we would be able to take on this task together. We had never really abandoned the idea of moving back to Europe eventually, once the girls had finished school and university and Scott's work wasn't the number one driving force anymore, but we knew we weren't quite ready for another transatlantic move yet. The New York area felt as close to Europe as we could get, and it seemed like a perfect ending to our time in the US – a stint on the East Coast would mean the trilogy that had started on the West Coast and taken us to the southern middle of the country would culminate in the east.

Eventually, we decided on an area close enough to the airport, school and work and a direct train line to New York City. Once that decision was made, I mentally switched off and left the house-hunting and logistics to my husband. I was utterly paralysed by the thought of breaking up our family. As soon as we'd mentioned the idea of moving, Amelie made it clear that she would not come with us. After all those years of changing locations and continents, she was considering Austin to be the place she felt most at home; she was enjoying her independence, her music and her friends, and, understandably, wasn't the least bit interested in being uprooted again.

A Special Visit

It was six am on a late October morning when the doorbell jolted me from deep sleep. I was solo-parenting that week; Scott was away on business and already halfway through his day in another time zone. Maya was still sleeping, unperturbed by the shrilling of the doorbell and the persistent knocking.

I had stayed up late the previous night, unable to fall asleep as usual, and it took me a while to make sense of the noise. But Ziggy was already racing downstairs, barking ferociously at whoever was outside our front door. A quick glance at our Ring doorbell camera revealed two men in dark clothing and what looked like body armour, decorated with three white letters I had so far only seen on TV. Had something happened to Amelie or Scott? I jerked upright, pulled a sweatshirt over my pyjamas and rushed down the stairs to the door, my legs shaking.

'Hello?' I asked with a thin voice through the wooden safety of our big door, 'Who is this?' I quietly chastised myself. *As if they didn't already know that I'd seen them.* The ring camera was right there. Through the window pane next to the door, I glimpsed a gun and felt sick. 'FBI, ma'am!'

My head started spinning. Was this real? It felt like I was in a movie, digging in my brain for my character's lines as I slowly opened the door, trying to keep hold of Ziggy, who was snarling and clearly beside himself with the rage of a thwarted guard dog. 'Can I see your ID?' I asked in what I hoped was an actor's authoritative voice. *How stupid*, I thought, *as if I knew the difference between a real and a fake ID*. A badge was shoved in my face, but the letters blurred in front of my eyes. The two men looked at me with serious expressions.

'Ma'am, excuse the early visit, but we're looking for Amelie Cook.' My stomach dropped. 'Amelie is my daughter, but she doesn't live here. What is this about?' I croaked. The men exchanged a glance. 'Ma'am, we can't give you any details, we need to speak with your daughter. It's to do with social media, Twitter. Do you know her whereabouts?'

Reluctant to divulge any information, feeling exceedingly vulnerable and unsure of how to behave in this strange situation, I tried to press for more details. I really didn't want to fall prey to some elaborate fraud project or worse. This could all be a set-up, and these men might not be official at all. Shaking off the sense of hysteria that was building in my stomach and shushing the thoughts that started racing in my psycho-thriller-devotee brain, I remembered that Amelie had planned to come over later today, so I calmly asked the men to come back in a few hours. To my surprise, they agreed.

As soon as they left, I called Amelie's number. 'Are you on Twitter?' I screeched. Twitter was not my medium, and while I did have an account and checked it about once a year, I had no idea about the existence of my kid's account. Amelie, still sleepy and confused at seven am, mumbled she had been on it once or twice a while back, but couldn't figure out what this special visit was all

290 ~ STEPHANIE X COOK

about. She promised to get ready to come over. I made myself a cup of tea even though I definitely needed something stronger.

The officers returned as promised, and I was almost surprised; it all felt like a bad dream. This time, they arrived in plain clothing without any special equipment. I couldn't see any weapons. They must have decided that we didn't pose a threat to their safety, a dishevelled, middle-aged white mother and her wayward teen daughter in a nice-looking house in this leafy, upper-middle-class Austin neighbourhood.

We sat down at the dining table, and they introduced themselves; one of them worked for the Federal Bureau, the other for the Texas Department of Public Safety. They cut to the chase.

'Do you have a Twitter account?' Amelie slowly nodded.

'Can you remember what you posted back in March of this year?' Amelie frowned. 'Well, I remember being on it, but not sure what I posted?' she offered, her face a mask of defensiveness.

'Were you planning to instigate the assassination of Governor Abbott?'

Amelie's eyes widened, and she threw a nervous glance in my direction. My mouth fell open. It turned out that my little activist had posted some encouraging messages for those planning to take their protest a step further. I remembered the heated debates and passionate protests against Greg Abbott's abortion politics earlier that year, which were still ongoing. I felt sick. 'No?' she said with a mix of defiance and embarrassment.

'This is a substantial threat, and we take these matters very seriously,' one of the officers explained, a stern look on his face. Amelie lowered her gaze.

'But it's October?' I pointed out. 'This was months ago?'

'Ma'am, had we not been so short-staffed, and had someone picked this up in March, we would have taken your daughter into custody.' Amelie's face turned white.

'I take it you have to read a lot of social media posts like this?' I quipped and instantly worried that I had said the wrong thing.

He looked at me and sighed. 'You have no idea, ma'am,' he said, shaking his head. 'We don't have nearly enough people to work on this stuff.'

Amelie opened her mouth, but I gave her a death stare, silently willing her to keep her mouth shut. She had a belligerent look on her face, which worried me.

The men grumbled something more about the never-ending flood of direct and indirect threats they had to wade through all week, and then decided to call it a day. One of them looked straight at Amelie and asked: 'Okay, before we wrap this up, I need to ask you once more: do you still intend to assassinate the governor or instigate his assassination?'

Amelie quickly shook her head and said no, she did not. Then he turned to me. 'Ma'am, I need to ask you too, can you confirm that you don't fear your daughter has any plans to follow through with her threat?'

At this point, I'd become completely detached from what was going on here; I felt like a witness in a crime thriller. I switched back into actor mode and managed to declare, 'Yes, sir, I can absolutely confirm that I do not think that she has any such plans.' I think I even spoke with an American accent.

The cops scribbled a few more notes on their pads, and then one of them turned to Amelie and said: 'One more thing: please never, ever, stop being an activist. We need people like you. Just lay off the terrorist threats, okay?'

They rose, apologised for the inconvenience, and with a jovial 'Have a beautiful day, y'all', they left.

I shut the front door behind them, closed my eyes and took a deep breath, then walked back into the dining room where Amelie was still sitting at the table, a blank expression on her face. We locked eyes and just stared at each other for a few seconds before bursting out laughing, gasping for air, like a pair of hysterical banshees.

Later that day, I called my husband to tell him what an exciting morning he had missed. What I didn't tell him is that just a couple of days earlier, I had ordered a lawn sign that I'd seen proudly displayed in various front yards in our neighbourhood: 'Mothers against Greg Abbott'. I had a feeling that our day would have progressed somewhat differently if that sign had already been delivered.

Maybe it really was time to leave Texas.

Last Christmas in Texas

After celebrating the last three Christmases in Texas, just the four of us, we had hoped to spend this year's festivities with our families in England and Germany, meticulously planning the trip with potential COVID obstacles in mind. Planning travel to multiple foreign locations over the Christmas period is never without risk and stress, but we hadn't expected the restrictions the German government put in place the day before our flight, as a consequence of recent outbreaks.

We desperately tried to find a solution, but couldn't find one. One of us would most certainly be unable to enter one of the countries we were heading to. The girls would be okay in any case, but I didn't have a British passport, and Scott didn't have a European one. We didn't want to risk being split up.

An hour before we were due to leave for the airport, we broken-heartedly cancelled the whole trip. I waited until my tears had dissipated and drove off to pick Ziggy up from the dog sitter, where I'd dropped him off that morning. Scott and Maya went on a hunt for a tree and found one of the last spindly specimens just before the tree lot closed for the season. We were determined to celebrate, even if it was only the four of us. We would have a last Christmas in Texas. Amelie and I slumped off to the supermarket to find some last-minute Christmas ingredients, and the staff at Trader Joe's felt so sorry for us that they gifted us a big bouquet of flowers.

In lieu of our trip to Europe, we decided to do what our family does best: a road trip. We couldn't possibly leave Texas without visiting Big Bend National Park, a place we'd been meaning to see for years. Now was our chance.

A road trip was my panacea. I'd become such a terrible traveller over the past few years, with huge anxiety about packing, airports, taxi rides to and from airports and flying itself, pretty much anything to do with having to get to a place at a certain time and dealing with lots of people, queues, stress etc, so the thought of simply getting into a car and driving along straight, wide and mostly empty roads sounded marvellous to me. As someone who gets car sick when reading or looking at a screen too much, all I can do is gaze out of the window and let my mind wander, making me feel calm and creative – the opposite of my usual state of mind. Maybe it's because two things I like happen at the same time: I get to sit still while actually not sitting still.

We arrived at our beautiful little home for a few days, the Windmill House in Alpine, a cosy little gem of a place in the middle of nowhere, close enough to venture out to Big Bend one day and Marfa the next. Big Bend did not disappoint; named after a large bend in the Rio Grande, it sits right on the border with Mexico and offers the perfect mix of colourful desert vegetation, craggy alpine peaks and stunning views across the Rio Grande to Mexico. The weather was mild, and we spent the day driving along and getting out for short hikes whenever a new spectacular plant or view made us gasp and grab our phones to take pictures.

Marfa, our destination on day two, was easily one of the weirdest places I had ever been to, an odd assortment of run-down or abandoned shacks, hidden coffee shops, quirky art galleries and a general end-of-the-world vibe. Driving out to Prada, Marfa, a permanent art installation along US 90, through this incredibly desolate and yet stunningly beautiful, otherworldly desert landscape, I felt torn. I was blown away by the endless horizon and the vast Texas sky while at the same time experiencing serious 'get me out of here' feelings. A weird sense of claustrophobia was taking hold of me; it was like this wide-open landscape was closing in on me. Something I'd felt in this part of the world for a while, and which reflected my opposing feelings for Texas.

I had totally fallen in love with Austin, which I had never expected, but it happened in an intense, exhausting love/hate sort of way. The city with its lush greenery, hilly landscape, cute little neighbourhoods, romantic swimming holes and creeks and hiking trails all over certainly didn't make me feel caged in, but maybe it was the sense that everywhere around it was deepest, darkest Texas, and it would take a flight or a day's driving to get to another state. I got so used to that feeling that I only notice it now when I come back to Texas from another place. It feels like a hug on the one hand and a vice on the other. A feeling I'd never had in any of the other places I've lived in, and part of the reason why I knew I needed to get out, as much as my heart was already constricting in anticipation of the pain of leaving.

The main source of this pain, however, was the fact that we wouldn't move as a family of four. Of course, leaving a child behind meant that there would always be a reason beyond friends and music to come back to visit and get our little Austin fix whenever we wanted to; leaving didn't feel so final this time. It's hard to explain that I was glad that I had come back to live here and give this city another chance, even though those last few years in Texas had been the hardest of my life so far. Maybe it was the fact that it woke me up. When I was at my lowest, I finally began to see that I needed to address what was going on with me. I wasn't quite sure yet what it was I actually needed to do, but a seed had been planted and was growing. I knew that some of that growth absolutely needed to happen, not only to deal with the past but also to open myself up to the next chapter of my life.

Did this mean I was ready for our new destination? Probably not. But I knew it was time to leave, and we needed a fresh start for Maya. I decided to direct my gaze forward, to a home that would offer new opportunities, new weather, new places to explore and a shorter flight back to Europe.

Another Move

Before I knew it, we only had a few weeks left in Austin, and I was knee-deep in moving boxes. We had entered the 'yes, I know we're out of ketchup, but I'm not buying a new jar' stage. Realising around every corner that 'this might be the last time we drive along this road' and 'Oh no, we'll miss the bluebonnets this year'. Trying to squeeze in dinners with friends, visits to favourite places, bulk buying salsas and mole and spices, and stuffing our faces with tacos at every opportunity. Saying goodbye to my agaves, big spiky succulents that I had planted myself, just a couple of years earlier, wishing I could uproot them and take them with me. Both of my largest ones had produced 'pups', tiny new baby agaves, and I dug them out and replanted them in big pots to pass on to a few friends as little good-bye presents.

I was doing most of the packing myself, as I found it helped me process the move. Everybody kept telling me I was crazy to do it all myself, but to me, going through the pain of wrapping, discarding, and sorting out boxes for donations or gifts to friends was somehow cathartic and a vital part of moving on to the next stage of my life. The only thing I needed to watch was my tendency to get lost in a packing trance and remind myself I needed time away from it, too. I knew I wasn't coping well with it all, knew that deep down I hadn't really committed to this new chapter and was seriously doubting whether I would like New Jersey. My gut feeling had tried to warn me when we were looking at places in the suburbs of New York back in October; I hadn't really felt much at the time, neither liked nor actively disliked any of it. Of course, my brain wrestled me into submission again: the move made sense. We had done and experienced all that Austin had to offer, Maya needed new surroundings, we hadn't been able to find her a school here, and the new school seemed like an amazing opportunity, and it would be much easier for Scott to live in the actual location of his work.

All of these conflicting feelings weighed heavily on my mind, and while all the packing kept me physically tired so that I would crash into my bed each night and fall asleep before I even hit the pillow, I was extremely stressed. At night, I would jolt upright from the weirdest dreams; during the day, I would forget where I was going while driving on the freeway.

On some days, I felt certain that we were doing the right thing; on others, I had absolute clarity about the insanity of this endeavour. We were leaving a child behind – yes, that child was a young adult now, but still. Wasn't it supposed to be the other way around, the child flying the nest, not the parents? Was a move really what we needed right now?

Hating myself and my dithering, indecisive brain, I ploughed on. The pathways of my brain were too warped to see clearly. I didn't know how to say no at this stage.

PART 5: NEW JERSEY

'When it is dark enough, you can see the stars.'

—Ralph Waldo Emerson

East Coast

We left Austin one early morning in February; I was sweating under several layers of clothing, anticipating the temperature drop at the end of our long journey to the northeast. Scott enjoyed the balmy 25°C/77°F in a T-shirt. As ever, he was living in the moment, unfazed by the fact that we were going to need our winter coats at the other end, while I was prepared for all eventualities. After all, we were spending three days on the road, crossing from Texas into Arkansas, passing Tennessee and Virginia, before reaching Maryland, Pennsylvania and, finally, New Jersey.

Maya was staying with a friend and looked after the cats while we were driving to New Jersey, since my husband very adamantly refused to share a car with any more pets than absolutely necessary. I had already booked a flight back to Austin for the day after our arrival to collect our teenager and the felines and travel back up by plane.

Our car was packed with only the bare essentials since we were racing the moving truck, which had only left a couple of days ahead of us. The back seats were folded flat, with Ziggy perched on top of it all in his big soft bed; that way, he could be as close to us as possible, and I could reach out to him for comfort if he needed it. I wasn't kidding myself, though; it was more likely me who would need the comfort of my warm, fluffy dog.

We didn't stop much along the way, except for a big helping of hot chicken at Hattie B's in Nashville, Tennessee, which we'd been really looking forward to. Exhausted and sad after the last few weeks of packing and saying goodbye, we found that it was exactly what we needed; the gooey, viciously spicy drumsticks felt like a slap in the face and lifted us straight out of our glumness. We swore and laughed and cried for a good hour, and I doubt it was just because of the spices.

We reached our new home in Madison at dusk, the most surreal arrival I had ever experienced, as I had only seen the house I was moving into via FaceTime. Ziggy ventured out for a quick tour of his as-yet unfenced backyard and barked into the New Jersey night before settling into his bed, which we'd pushed in front of the fireplace in our big, empty living room. We set up our airbeds, which we'd ordered in advance, picked up some delicious Thai takeaway from a local restaurant, and collapsed with a bottle of wine next to our dog.

I took him for a short walk around the neighbourhood the next morning, wondering whether there would be more snow, and how long it would be until spring turned all this grey and brown into green. There were lots of trees everywhere, bare and forlorn looking at present, but no doubt impressive when we got to May and June. I marvelled at how different the houses were, and how houses always varied so much in different parts of a country, whether it was the United States, Britain, or Germany. The houses here, in this small New Jersey town, clapboard structures in various colours and with small or large porches, looked like they had come straight from my childhood books. One house looked just like Pippi Long-stocking's *Villa Villekulla*; you could almost see Pippi waving from an upstairs window or sliding down a banister. I was surprised to see a lot more American flags displayed outside the homes here than in Texas. But then, Texans would rather fly the Lone Star than the Star-Spangled Banner.

'Oh my gosh, is that an Irish Setter?' I turned to the car that had pulled up next to me and Ziggy. 'I haven't seen one of those in a long time!' It's always easy to exchange words with strangers when you have a dog, especially a big red one like ours. I was grateful to be able to strike up a conversation with these locals; it broke the ice. We were really here now. When I turned back into our road, the moving truck with our belongings was just pulling up in front of our driveway. Scott and I threw ourselves into unpacking, which suited me perfectly as my chest was already tight with the looming sense of overwhelm. I didn't have time for emotions right now.

That very evening, I hopped on a plane back to Austin, promptly spending another two days cleaning and sorting stuff out at my old home, which brought me dangerously close to breaking point. I summoned all the strength I had left and powered through, driven by some relentless, masochistic interior demon. Of course, I could have simply opted to stay at a friend's house and hired a re-moval crew to sort through the remaining items at our old house, but I knew I had to do it this way. I needed to find closure by say-ing goodbye in my own way.

There's something gut-wrenching about the echoiness of a house that's been moved out of. It's a shell, a home no longer, aban-doned and almost ashamedly waiting for someone new to move in and give it life again. The bare walls, the ghosts of your furniture still hovering, anything you say out loud sounding hollow and un-real. Mentally, I had already left this place and moved into another, but here I still was, hanging onto my memories. The cats, some-what confused by the emptiness of the house and maybe sensing my sadness, stuck by my side the whole time. When it was time to manoeuvre them into their transport carriers for the journey to the airport, they didn't even complain. I'd given them some herbal anti-anxiety drops, and they appeared calm and patient, much to my and Maya's relief.

Our flight, however, ended up being two hours delayed, and by the time we finally boarded the plane and took off, Milo decided that he'd had enough of being confined in his cage. Our delicate little Siamese boy cranked up his super-feline powers and broke his carrier within minutes, gnawing holes into the mesh fabric and busting all the zips. We had to spend the remaining three-and-a-half hours of the flight clutching him to our laps with all our might while he shapeshifted from ferocious mini tiger into slippery eel, attempting to escape, digging his claws into anything that tried to stop him. He was panting and shaking so much that I started to worry, but after a couple of hours, he calmed down a bit. When we exited the plane, I tucked the shivering little guy deep into my thick coat, which I'd wisely left on during the flight. I could feel his heartbeat pounding against my chest. His brother Max, on the other hand, remained calm and stoic the entire time and just slept, a big Cheshire cat grin on his friendly orange-and-white face.

Ziggy was waiting in the car with Scott, and the moment Milo spotted his dog friend enthusiastically wagging his tail in the back-seat, he leapt out of my arms and into Ziggy's furry comfort. I swear I heard him whoop with joy.

When we reached our house in the early hours of the morning, Maya disappeared straight into her new room while both cats, now completely at ease, set off to explore their new surroundings, tails swishing curiously, before falling asleep on top of us.

New Surroundings

Ignoring all the warning signs my body was throwing at me, from sore throat to neck stiffness and twisting my ankle when getting out of the car one day, I carried on with my usual moving-in routine as if on autopilot, heaving boxes, hanging pictures and assigning furniture to new spots. Going through the motions of making a nest.

I felt stuck in a strange in-between world, where my head couldn't quite keep up with my physical body. Or maybe it was the other way around. Emotions such as an overwhelming sense of loneliness, missing my other child, longing for the familiar, and being bombarded by a flood of memories that kept pouring onto me, as well as physical sensations such as hunger or tiredness, felt surreal and unrecognisable. I knew this state of being so well, so while it wasn't a great way to spend my days, and admittedly it seemed to be worse than ever, I told myself it was only temporary. I knew that the only way out of it was to head straight through it.

At least I knew it in an intellectual sense. Actuating it was a completely different matter. I knew that what I was feeling was grief, and that I needed to sit with it. I needed to keep myself busy, but not too busy, allowing time to attend to my wandering thoughts and open myself up to all those new impressions. Scott didn't seem to have this problem. Maybe he had already assimilated enough, after years of adjusting to New Jersey on his frequent trips. This environment wasn't new to him.

I had to remind myself to eat, since my stomach was still in knots, and I was ready for bed by eight pm, which might also have had something to do with the fact that it was winter and the sun set really early, just like in Europe. I tried to squeeze some yoga practice into my day in order to feel a physical connection, anything to break through the numbness, and made a mental note to sign up for classes at a yoga studio I'd spotted in the neighbouring town. Looking after Maya preoccupied most of my time; I would look after myself more when I had got her settled into a new routine.

Strangely, the fact that we were the tiniest bit closer to Europe created a huge sense of proximity, even though it was really just an hour less than from Texas. It meant that finally, I was able to communicate with friends and family over there in the afternoon, and they were not asleep. I felt so much gratitude for this small feat, as making time for people during our busy mornings had never been easy.

But it was mainly our new surroundings that made us feel closer to Europe. Vegetation, street names, architecture – everything was much more European in style, completely different to both Texas and California. One day, driving through some smaller back roads in the countryside, I was briefly tempted to swerve into the left lane, momentarily confused about where I was, as everything looked just like the old village lanes I had got to know so well in England. Walking my dog one morning, I smiled at the snowdrops and crocuses popping out from the still wintery-brown grass, perfectly in sync with what was happening in England and Germany at this time of year.

So far, the people here had been extremely friendly. I'd been so worried about the famously brusque and straight-talking East Coasters, but after just a few days, some neighbours rang the door-bell to introduce themselves. We realised we might cause a bit of a stir in this sleepy New Jersey town, with our Texan licence plate, a big, loud, shaggy dog, a purple-haired teenager and a German woman clad in cowboy boots, speaking with a British accent.

Answering the question 'Where are you from?' for what felt like the hundredth time was getting tedious, but I gritted my teeth and smiled as hard as I could, appreciating people's friendliness and in-terest. It amused me how apologetic people were about New Jer-sey; we were told again and again how hard it must be for us to give up our southern surroundings. In fact, when I got some pre-scriptions sent through from our doctor in Austin, since we hadn't registered with a new one yet, the pharmacist asked what made us move up here and then said he hoped New Jersey had welcomed us kindly, even though he knew it obviously couldn't keep up with Texan hospitality.

I completed numerous tasks in record time, ranging from finding a new family doctor and dentist to getting my hair done. I knew I wasn't really okay, but on the surface, I managed to keep the demons at bay. I had become excellent at this charade and wasn't ready to surrender.

I even made a friend within just a few days – a friend of ours from our London days had relatives who lived right here, in Madi-son. I had already connected with them, asking questions about doctors, dance studios and other local points of interest, and they, in turn, had told another couple, British and German like ourselves, about our impending arrival. One bitterly cold and rainy morning, a few days after moving in, just as I returned from a walk with a very muddy Ziggy, cursing this new place and missing the sun, a car pulled up on the curb. A blonde woman jumped out, ran in my direction, yelling 'I'm Sybille, welcome to Madison!' in German, thrust a few carrier bags into my arms, invited us for dinner, and with a 'See you soon, got to go to work', she disappeared. I was too stunned to say much and just stood there clutching my homemade potato salad, German sausages and a bottle of wine.

Maybe things were going to be okay.

Exploring

J ust a couple of weeks after our move, my mother and niece arrived from Munich, and Amelie joined us from Austin a few days later, filling all four bedrooms of our house. We set off to wander the streets of New York City, let the chilly March wind blow through our hair on the ferry to Ellis Island, strolled around the Statue of Liberty and ventured over to Asbury Park on the Jersey Shore, where we posed for photos in front of the Stone Pony, New Jersey born-and-bred Bruce Springsteen's home venue.

We were excited to find that a lot of people expressed interest in visiting us in our new home, which was very different from when we lived in Texas. New York was significantly more accessible from Europe and seemed to draw a lot more interest than Austin ever did.

Sharing a new environment with people who've known you in other places at other times is a really special experience, and I felt so sad that so many important people in my life had never managed to see us in our Austin environment. I would have loved to share that city with others, shed some light on people's perception of Texas, and maybe shatter some preconceptions. Somehow, this fact felt like a giant piece was missing from my nomadic life puzzle, one that I knew I would never find. But I was learning to accept this missing piece, and I hoped that exploring New Jersey and New York with friends would make up for it in some way. I just needed to get myself in a better mood.

I knew I had to stop pining for Austin and embrace what this new part of the country had to offer. A big aspect of moving up here was, after all, the fact that we had a whole new landscape to explore. The US was such a huge and diverse country, and all of a sudden, we had so many new places on our doorstep. There was New York, the most diverse and flamboyant metropolis of them all; the Jersey Shore with its big dunes and wide sandy beaches; and plenty of rugged, hilly terrain and nature reserves within easy driving distance. Ziggy was always game for exploring, and often, when I felt the need to escape my house, I would get in the car to try and find a replacement for my beloved Walnut Creek park.

Nothing fit the bill. I would feel momentary relief, but couldn't push myself to feel more enthusiastic. I felt cranky all the time. When Scott suggested picking up bagels, I would just shrug. The bagels here were outstanding, big, fluffy and chewy at the same time, and came in a gazillion flavours. But I didn't want bagels; I wanted tacos. People would recommend Italian restaurants – New Jersey has a long history of Italian immigration, and the pasta and pasta sauce assortment in our local supermarkets is mind-blowing. I found it all too American, arrogantly claiming that I'd been to Italy too many times as a child to be able to accept this adapted style of cooking. I knew I was being petulant, but I just couldn't summon any positive energy.

Plus, I discovered that the local water was a nightmare for my hair. Somehow, it was hard and soft at the same time, and it felt like I could never rinse the shampoo out properly. My thick hair became dull; any dye or new style never stayed for long, and I was tempted to just cut it all off. To put it briefly, I couldn't find one good thing to say about New Jersey.

One weekend in May, when Scott and Maya were on a trip back to Austin for a few days, I drove up to the Catskills with my friend Claire to get away from it all. I had known her since our time in California, another expat from the UK, whose husband had worked with Scott for a while. They had moved to Austin shortly after we did, and then to New Jersey just before the pandemic. At times of feeling disorientated, there is no better company than another expat to share your woes, and the fact that she had experienced all the places I had, too, was comforting in itself. No need to explain my doubts, yearning for other places, and my exhaustion. We rented a little artist's cottage somewhere in the hills behind Woodstock, the perfect base from which to explore the area, and we did nothing but hike, eat in quirky little places in town, roll out our yoga mats each morning and relax with a glass of wine in the evenings. It was a blissful break from my still totally unsettled daily life, and I relished the healing atmosphere of the stunning mountain scenery and the lush green woodlands of upstate New York. I could always rely on nature to be my healer.

Now I just needed to find some spots on my doorstep that could help me settle in more quickly.

Breakdown

As I frantically tried to build scaffolding around her by creating a cosy new home, hanging pictures, and buying drapes, rugs and bookshelves, kidding myself that this was working, Maya plunged deeper and deeper into her darkness. As keen as she had been to move and leave her nightmarish surroundings behind, a shift had occurred just before we left Texas. This is a phenomenon that occurs often when you're about to leave a place. The few weeks just beforehand, when everything is already booked, signed and finalised, and your mind is made up, things seem to turn around. You start feeling lighter, and all of a sudden, the place you're about to leave appears perfectly okay.

Back in November, when we had already known we were moving in February, Maya had finally made a leap and connected with a couple of people she could be herself with. Her whole demeanour changed; she was smiling again.

And now, here we were in New Jersey, and Maya struggled to adjust to yet another home. This transition was coming down hard on us; we found that we were dealing with a whole new set of challenges. She had started at the New Jersey school remotely back in November and instantly formed a great rapport with her new teachers. The workload seemed a lot more manageable, and they put her through an intensive screening process, establishing her learning style and eliminating methods that didn't work for her neurodivergent brain. They fully accepted her ADHD diagnosis, and for the first time ever, Maya could simply enjoy learning without fear of exams.

When I took her for her first in-person class sometime in early March, she came home beaming and relaxed, and I almost fainted with gratitude. A couple of weeks later, however, we were back to square one. Maya's misophonia, her inability to tolerate certain noises, was back in full force, an irrefutable sign of overwhelm. Even though she was allowed to wear headphones for most of her day at school, she couldn't get through a whole day's schedule in person. We implemented a hybrid model, which meant that some classes could be taken from home via Zoom, while others were in person, in an attempt to increase her tolerance without falling behind academically. Looking at my withdrawn, stressed and absolutely miserable sixteen-year-old, I tried to detect some traces of the enthusiastic, positive little adventurer from years earlier, but there was nothing left.

I barely recognised myself. My days now revolved entirely around Maya's schedule, as I often had to take her to class, wait in the car and bring her home for lunch, sometimes heading back to school in the afternoon. There was no time or energy left to even think about part-time employment. I adjusted my day accordingly; on some days, I brought Ziggy with me and walked him around town while Maya was in class, one hand wrapped around my phone in case I received an emergency phone call from a school bathroom. I discovered that I could log on to the school WiFi from my car and started bringing my laptop with me. I took Zoom calls, prepared my podcast episodes and worked on my book from the driver's seat, staring at the back wall of the school and missing my gorgeous writing spot on the top floor of my house in Texas.

Meanwhile, Scott went to work each morning, never leaving his phone out of sight, fearing an emergency call from me. He never knew what state he'd find us in when he came home at the end of the day; some days he'd leave us smiling and full of plans, only to return to a sullen teenager in one room and her mother in tears in another.

We tried to find a new therapist, as Maya's old therapist from Austin was no longer allowed to help since we had moved states. We had a final session with her just so she could talk Maya through some tools to use in her new surroundings, but it wasn't enough. My teen was falling apart, her declining mental health starting to become visible on the outside. Her face became increasingly puffy, her once-luminous skin turned blotchy, and she began to gain weight. In desperate need of help, Scott and I combed the internet and called various practices, vetting more psychiatrists and therapists who would accept our insurance and seemed a good fit, telling our story over and over again. Maya couldn't connect with the therapist they recommended; she was crumbling in front of our eyes, only sleeping with the help of medication, and then struggling to get up in the mornings. Her eating habits became increasingly erratic, the old eating disorder clawing its way back into her life. Some new medication showed some initial improvements, but after a few months, I realised Maya just seemed numb and dissociated. I was terrified that she'd start self-harming again.

One day, as Scott and I were downstairs, having dinner with friends, she did. This time, her cuts were so deep and so extensive that she needed stitches, and we ended up spending the night at the ER. As we crawled into bed in the early hours of the morning, numb with pain and clinging to each other, we had no more tears left. We had reached rock bottom.

As any parent knows, *you're only ever as happy as your unhappiest child*. My body was throwing more and more warning signs at me: I found it increasingly difficult to get out of bed in the mornings, my shoulders screamed with pain and my neck was even more tense than usual, my legs tingled, and sometimes I couldn't even get up without feeling dizzy. I couldn't drink coffee anymore, not even my beloved Austin blend, which I'd bought in bulk before we left; it tasted weird to me, and I decided to skip my mid-morning ritual of brewing a cup. I felt almost hysterical without this anchor in my morning routine, but my brain couldn't come up with an alternative. Nothing felt like it should. I missed Amelie and my life as it used to be, a long time ago.

I went to see an osteopath because I could barely lift my arms; they hurt so badly. I told her I couldn't remember a time without shoulder and neck pain, and she asked about my lifestyle. 'Well, sounds like someone's tried to squeeze a lot of lives into one,' she said with a reprimanding smile. 'You're grieving. That's what your body is telling you. And please remember: you only have one body.' I shrugged, unsure of how and what I was supposed to change.

My old phobia of collapsing ceilings was making itself known again. At first, I pushed it away as usual, but its roar got louder and louder, and I had to accept that it had been there the very first time I set foot in this house. There was no denying it, and I needed to talk about it. Like most houses in this part of the country, our house was built on three levels: basement, ground floor, and top floor. The basement with its two big steel pillars felt oddly safe to me, safer than the one in my house in Texas. The ground floor – living room, dining area and kitchen – however, was open-plan, with high ceilings, which made everything look beautifully light and spacious. There were no additional walls or pillars on this level, which had to support the top floor with all our bedrooms and the laundry room, and I lost my mind.

While I had always been more or less able to suppress this phobia, or sometimes even laugh it off in a 'I know this is ridiculous, but hey, I'm just a crazy lady' sort of way, I was unable to do it this time. At first, I tried to fight it, as I had done so many times before, forcing myself to run a bath in our beautiful new bathtub, which was situated right above our dining table. I managed to sit in it for five minutes before my mind went into emergency mode and I clambered out, dripping water all over the floor in my haste to get to safety. I had no energy left to fight this. Some days, the only way I could get from my bed to the bathroom was by crawling on all fours along the edges of the room. My body warned me that if I crossed the room through the middle, walking over the area that was furthest from the walls, without any supporting wall in the living room underneath, the ceiling would cave in, and I would fall into the abyss. I had no power over my mind any longer. Any reasoning was in vain. I could rationally tell myself that this was a strong, solid house with strong, solid walls until I turned blue in the face; my body was telling me otherwise. It was worse when we had people staying with us; if I was sitting in the living room, hearing somebody walk across the floor above me, I often had to get up and leave the room or even the house. Occasionally, I managed to stay put, silently screaming inside.

Scott was losing his patience with me. He couldn't understand why I was unable to fight my phobia, explaining over and over again that the house was safe, that an inspector had given the whole structure the green light, and that I was overreacting. Why was this becoming such an issue, now, after all those years of being able to control it? I countered that he had known about this phobia all along, and that I could never forgive him for choosing a house he knew would trigger me. I knew, logically, it was irrational behaviour on my part. And I was so ashamed; how entitled was I? My husband had taken care of everything, fully acknowledging my exhaustion and my frantic state of mind, without complaint. But what I felt was real.

I realised that I was experiencing a breakdown. I could no longer pretend that I was a functioning adult who could handle things, knowing that everything would be okay if I only put my mind to it. For the first time, I truly accepted that I needed help. I started seeing a therapist.

As a typical 70s girl, brought up amidst a generation that considered intense self-analysis to be egocentric navel gazing that wasn't helping anyone, I really struggled to silence that dismissive voice in my head. The voice that talked to me in that chastising tone, barking at me to just pull myself together and stop wallowing in self-pity. For the first time, however, I understood that this 'navel gazing' wasn't some self-indulgent escapism but a necessity not only for myself but for my family. It was something I needed to do not only for myself, but *for them.*

All the time I'd been telling myself that I was doing everything for them, keeping myself so busy to ensure everybody else's wellbeing and putting their needs ahead of my own, I was actually a million miles away from it. It was finally sinking in, that phrase you keep hearing: 'Make sure you put your own life vest on first before putting it on anybody else'. Thinking you were doing it wasn't actually doing it. Going to yoga classes and booking the occasional massage wasn't quite what it took.

With the help of my therapist, I slowly began to unravel my mind. My children's suffering had ripped open this whole Pandora's box of medical and mental health issues that I had carefully stashed away in the far recesses of my mind, crumbling the armour I'd built up around myself over the last few decades.

Once I started talking, I surprised myself by how easy I found it. It was like I'd been waiting to spill the beans my whole life. When she told me my floor-collapsing phobia was a manifestation of OCD, obsessive-compulsive disorder, I was not surprised. When she gently introduced the idea to me that I, like my children, might have a neurodivergent brain, all I felt was relief. Amelie had received her own ADHD diagnosis too, just a few months earlier, when a new psychiatrist noted down her mental health history and found that things didn't add up.

I learned that neurodivergence has a large genetic component, and to this day, I am stunned that I was oblivious to this fact for so long, and that at no point during our many appointments and family sessions with and without the children had any psychiatrist or therapist mentioned the possibility that this might have been something that had been passed on through generations.

The many challenges of moving had brought all my symptoms to the surface. On the one hand, the chaos in my brain that I was experiencing, from doubting my decisions to feeling horrendously lonely, from always missing places whenever I was somewhere else to feeling immense guilt for upending my children's lives, was all part of the normal reality of life as an expat. There isn't a single person moving to another country who doesn't feel one or all or even more of those things at some point.

But on the other hand, my intense, neurodivergent brain had added a few extra spins to the whole experience, until I couldn't handle any more changes. While ADHD was clearly part of this insatiable appetite for new things and places, it also meant that I had some extra challenges when it came to managing the huge amounts of stress a move entails.

My therapist painted a picture for me: what I had tried to do all along was to plant my roots in one single pot so that I could carry them with me. Because of my restless mind, however, I could never just 'be' in or simply 'enjoy' a new place; I felt a strong urge to grow roots wherever I went, and those roots wanted to grow further with each new place I moved to. Ultimately, though, they were far too strong and too big for one single pot; they demanded soil, land, *earth*, otherwise they'd crush me with their weight. *But how can I stop this?* I wailed, *What do I do?*

'You need to let go of that pot,' she told me. I knew what she meant, but I had no idea how I was going to do this. I needed to find a way to plant my roots firmly into the earth without the need to have them all close to me at all times. I realised that I had tried to hold on to everything throughout my life, literally and figuratively. I had dragged all my physical belongings with me, pictures, furniture, mementoes, as broken and faded as they were after a while, and I had tried to keep all my relationships going, even the ones that were slipping away and ready to be let go of. I had amassed so much baggage that I was crumbling under its weight. Not feeling rooted at all. I needed to find a way to feel my roots, my connections with both places and people, in a way that didn't overwhelm me. I needed to set the pot down.

I understood that I had approached it all wrong. How could I give my children a sense of being rooted when I wasn't rooted myself, carrying a pot that was way too heavy for me? Children see so much more than we think.

What I thought I was doing was raising my kids to not need physical roots, to be strong in themselves and have us, their family, as their roots. But how could I teach them that when I wasn't living it myself? All the excitement of going to new places, finding things to keep busy, the opportunity to reinvent yourself as much as you wanted to, and looking at all the shiny new distractions that a move entailed did not foster a sense of grounding.

They could see straight through me and slipped through all the gaps in this very brittle construct I had attempted to build. Until I fell through the cracks with them.

Revelations

I threw myself into learning everything I could about neurodivergence, both in children and in adults. My therapist guided me through various tests for ADHD and confirmed the diagnosis. She also gently suggested I should get an evaluation for autism, as my history and symptoms fit the 'AuDHD' pattern, but I decided to wait. I was overwhelmed as it was. Somehow, it felt a lot safer to tell people 'I have ADHD' than to say 'I'm autistic'. When I took the tests later, by myself, and, unsurprisingly, scored highly, I decided to just sit with this rather than pursue any further official testing or psychiatrist appointments.

I had been burnt so much during sessions with professionals over the last few years; I had sat in front of therapists who weren't listening or dismissing my and my children's concerns, and we had to go through every piece of medical history again and again, only to be prescribed another set of medications that didn't work. I didn't want to deal with any more of this. I knew I had learned enough to recognise which resources could be helpful tools to deal with my daily challenges, and which conversations to avoid in order to stop the gaslighting. Talking about neurodivergence wasn't easy. Nobody wanted to hear about it, and eye-rolling exclamations such as 'But everybody does this', 'It's a trend these days', 'Everybody is a little bit autistic' were more usual than not. For someone like me, who had never been good at standing up to criticism or confrontations, those reactions were debilitating. I decided that the only way to stay strong was to arm myself with information. I read voraciously, from both clinical studies and medical books to personal accounts, and listened to podcasts, wanting to scream with fury and sob with relief in equal measure. As much as these revelations shocked me, I felt calmer than I had ever felt before in my life. The more personal stories I heard and read, especially by women my own age, the more I recognised myself in them, their struggles and experiences mirroring and confirming my own

I finally understood why I'd felt the way I had for so long. It was like a giant veil had been lifted, and the jumbled puzzle pieces of my life were falling into place, one by one. There were explanations for my problems, words I could use to describe my feelings. I grieved for the little girl inside of me who had had to go through life feeling like something was wrong with her, but I was so happy for the woman I was now to discover ways to exist with, and in spite of, this differently wired brain.

I still wasn't sure who that woman really was, though. I knew she was there, but she was hidden under so many masks and layers of self-delusion, people-pleasing and self-contempt that I knew it would take time to lure her out of hiding.

The relief I felt when I started to put the puzzle pieces together was immense. Talking to my children felt different; it was as if our eyes were now wide open, and we had a new way to connect with one another. For the first time, I felt capable of truly helping them.

I wanted to crawl back in time and educate myself about neuro-divergence, to understand that the most debilitating, and much more dangerous thing about ADHD isn't having a chaotic brain that can't focus, but the inability to regulate your emotions, which so easily leads to low self esteem, depression and eating disorders. But that was then, and this was now, and I finally had an explanation for so many situations that had proved to be so difficult for me and for my girls. And I had words to explain it all to my husband, who was trying his best to keep up with my new insights. I learned that for a neurodivergent person, and depending on where you are on the spectrum, any kind of transition is decidedly more energy-consuming than it is for someone who is neurotypical. From tiny transitions, such as getting out of bed in the morning, taking a shower or leaving the house, to bigger ones like starting a new job or, at the top end of the list, moving to another country, it is all much more impactful and emotional for people like me. I wanted to scream.

Doing it several times, especially moving to a fast-paced, high-achieving society like the United States, had certainly added some extra spice I didn't know I needed to be more careful with when I sprinkled it so liberally on my and my family's lives.

I also understood that while all of this knowledge was a great starting point, I had to let go of the idea that it was all down to me to teach my children how to cope with their multifaceted lives. I couldn't control this process for them. Confronting my perfectionism in everything I did meant I had to let go of the idea that I had to be a perfect parent. There is no such thing, and part of parenting is precisely that: being imperfect. Yes, I could provide an anchor and hold their hands while helping them cope with transitions, but I couldn't provide resilience. They had to figure that out from within themselves. We, as parents, had driven the moves, which means it wasn't a choice for them to build resilience; it was a survival skill. All I could do was be there for them, both perfectly and imperfectly, and trust that they would. And that some day, when they'd be able to choose their own moves, those skills would reveal themselves.

Surrender

With all these revelations gradually coming to light, something really shifted about a year or so after our move to New Jersey. It was like the much-anticipated spring sunshine – late, just like in England – breathed new life into us.

Maya was managing to stay at school for most of her lessons and had even started making some friends, occasionally going out for lunch with classmates. Traces of the active, open little girl she once was were coming back, as was her determination to study fashion. With high school graduation just over a year away, she was laser-focused on building her portfolio for several art schools in Europe she planned to apply to. She joined various clubs at school and even some organisations in the city, where she would often venture at weekends.

I slowly began to tiptoe around the possibility of signing up for art classes and finding myself a café to sit and write in for a few hours with my phone on 'do not disturb'. I could feel lightness creeping back into my thoughts and my body. Scott and I started to go out for dinner from time to time, just the two of us, without fearing for our teen's safety. We began to *recognise* each other again.

I also decided that I needed to address my relationship with New Jersey. I was boring myself with all the negativity I had felt about this state. One day, when I was talking to a friend in California, complaining about how ugly and dilapidated the roads were and how boring and small-minded I found my new town, she just sighed and said: 'You're doing your thing again. Stop whining.' I gulped. She was right. What was I doing? Hating your surroundings wasn't a sustainable way to live; I should know this by now.

I recognised this old pattern of behaviour – I had done this when I was new in Austin, all those years earlier, and to an extent, even in our early days in California. It seemed like an automatic process that was set off whenever I was confronted with a new situation: my brain, wired to resist transitions and change and yet desperately craving the novelty factor of a new place, was overwhelmed, and the first thing to offer relief was rejection.

I knew it wasn't New Jersey's fault. It simply never captured my full attention and never had the benefit of the open eyes, curiosity, and eagerness to learn that I brought to California fourteen years earlier. My brain simply didn't have any more capacity for newness. I had run out of steam. I couldn't blame this on ADHD.

'Maybe I just need to go to IKEA,' I mused at breakfast one morning. Scott's eyes widened in horror. 'But you just got rid of so much stuff,' he reasoned. 'We don't really need anything, do we?' I just smiled at him. He hated shopping, and a trip to IKEA was his literal idea of hell. But for me, a trip to the ubiquitous Swedish furniture haven had always been part of moving to a new place. In all that time I had lived in New Jersey, I hadn't even bothered to look up the nearest store. Maybe I would feel more grounded once

I'd completed this ritual from my past. Scott was right, of course. We really didn't need anything, and so far, I just hadn't had the energy or ideas to change a single thing. However, a few new touches as a nod to prettifying my new home surely couldn't do any harm. I decided to look up the nearest location, but when I found out that it was in one of New Jersey's busiest and ugliest industrial areas, I decided to skip the journey.

Driving in the Garden State sometimes felt like a suicide mission; drivers here were more reckless and aggressive than anywhere I had experienced, including Germany, which is saying something. Besides, the roads with their crazy potholes were a disaster for car tyres, and I hadn't quite figured out the unpredictable on-ramps, which meant that cars often merged into the fast lane. I tried to avoid the busiest roads whenever possible. Honking aggressively was a normal part of everyday driving, and I quickly had to unlearn the behaviours I had picked up in the previous few years. In Texas, it's considered rude to honk, unless there's an absolute emergency that may excuse such an uncouth display of road rage. East Coast people were quick to shout, too, as I discovered several times when trying to cross a road at a zebra crossing and cars would just fly past, either ignoring my scowl or yelling at me to be more careful. I learned that you had to step into the road if you wanted a car to stop for you – something extremely ill-advised when you have a boisterous dog with you.

It really bothered me that I couldn't love New Jersey; it didn't fit into the neat narrative of my transcontinental trilogy. Somehow, I couldn't shift this attitude, even when we'd lived here longer than two years. I realised that I never missed New Jersey when we travelled elsewhere. I missed being 'at home', being in my own space, sleeping in my own bed, with my things and my pets, and ideally, people, but I never missed my house, let alone our town and surroundings. In the past, after a couple of weeks away, I would start craving little things in both California and Texas. For example, when we went to Europe during the summer holidays, there was always a point when I'd really look forward to going back 'home', smelling the eucalyptus and the jasmine that scented the air around my house in California, or sitting under the gnarly live oak trees in Texas and listen to the electric buzz of the cicadas. And when we returned from wherever we'd gone, I would start to feel excitement bubble up in the pit of my stomach even while still on the plane, and crane my neck to spot my current home from high above.

The descent into San Francisco was always spectacular; approaching from the north-east, you could spy the reddish hues of the Golden Gate Bridge against the blue of the Pacific Ocean from far away, and then the grid of the city's roads, until reaching the Silicon Valley towns and glimpses of the familiar landmarks of our neighbourhood.

Even with Austin, where the landscape wasn't as impressive as California, I would always strain my eyes to identify Cat Mountain and the area surrounding our house before landing, and feel my heart constrict in happy anticipation. And travelling in March and early April always meant descending over swathes of bluebonnets, which looked like someone had rolled out a purplish blue carpet especially for us.

Coming back to New Jersey never felt like that. Sure, flying over New York City into Newark is always impressive, simply because it's so iconic, and when the sun hits the Empire State Building and you spot the Statue of Liberty from far above, you can't help but smile. But I never felt my heart do its little dance of joy.

Was it because New Jersey felt simply too similar to the places I'd grown up in? Both California and Texas offered such exotic, distinctly different environments from the landscapes of my childhood and adolescence, but New Jersey, with its familiar flora and lifestyle, just didn't elicit the same sense of wonder.

It was a beautiful state, if you ignored the industrial hub around Newark, and much more picturesque than the media and general attitude of people would make you believe. The countryside offered everything from mountains to beaches and forests that turned into a breathtaking sea of colour every fall. And yet, I felt rather indifferent. I wondered if it was because, knowing that I needed to plant my new roots in a different way, I was incapable of letting this place into my heart as much as the others. A protective mechanism to shield myself from further heartache. 'I like it, I don't love it', was Scott's standard response whenever someone asked him what he thought of New Jersey. I wanted to feel the same way, but somehow, just 'liking' something wasn't something I seemed capable of.

I needed to find a way to live here and accept New Jersey for what it was, without making huge emotional demands. I needed to understand the meaning of the word 'temporary'. I had thought I knew what it meant, but never actually did; instead, I had stuffed everything into this pot I was carrying. I hadn't considered that anything that is of a temporary nature, including a place, also has a liminal quality, which makes it less linear and thus more complicated to handle. Loving a place isn't something you can grasp, and that's what I needed to accept. To open myself up and let the feelings in without needing to define them.

Scott, who had witnessed me fret too many times about not liking a place and heard me conjure up millions of reasons to initiate another move, came up with a solution. 'How about France?'

he casually asked one evening, when I was complaining for the hundredth time about my hair not getting on with New Jersey. Friends of ours from our London days, who had moved to south-west France during the pandemic, were selling their small home in the Basque country. We both loved the area and had spent some time there, both before our move to the US and later on.

'What do you think?' he asked, his mouth twitching as he could already see the answer written all over my face. 'Could you see yourself living there at some point?'

We sat down and made the decision to finally sell our house in England. A house that had become an anchor I didn't need anymore. We would have a new place, a place we knew, a place that was neither England nor Germany, a base that would wait for us at some point in the future when we were ready to leave the US. We didn't have to move right now; I didn't need to pack bags and think about moving containers just yet.

Gratitude

The moment I realised that New Jersey was a place where I wouldn't stay for very long, a pit-stop on my way somewhere else, a place I didn't need to plant roots in, I felt liberated. I knew what would come next. This new place in France, even if it didn't offer an imminent escape, was giving me a sense of certainty. I could just live in the present without having to think about our next step.

Looking around me, I began to allow myself to like New Jersey a bit more. The wall of resistance to this new place was crumbling anyway, whether I contributed to this consciously or not.

I admitted to myself that, as much as I loathed the cold winter, I actually really enjoyed having proper seasons. After living in such warm climates for so long, with no great distinctions between summer and winter except for the temperature, New Jersey gave me a whole range of weather. Deep snow in winter, with access to mountains, a lush, verdant spring with an abundance of flowers, followed by an occasionally very hot and humid summer with access to long sandy beaches, and finally a spectacular autumn, when the many trees started to compete with each other for the most vibrant shades of red, yellow and orange.

Often, when driving along tree-lined country roads, the landscape reminded me of the *Holly Hobbie* books from my childhood, or television shows like *Anne of Green Gables*, filled with village ponds, willow trees, flower-filled meadows, orchards and picturesque clapboard houses. Somehow, it all looked like a movie set, or maybe like a scene from one of those kitschy Thomas Kincaid Americana wall calendars.

There was also a lot of history. We walked Ziggy through several parks and woodlands that were marked with signs of the Revolutionary War; we found that the trail networks were so vast that they seemed mostly deserted, and it was easy to imagine Washington's troops hiding amongst the trees and undergrowth. Historical markers could be found everywhere, giving us another glimpse into the country's past, and completing a few more sections of this giant United States jigsaw puzzle.

I still had trouble with New York City, and finally allowed myself to say this out loud, no longer trying to be worldly or cool. I knew that being so close to one of the most exciting cities in the world drew the envy of most people, but for me, it was one giant sensory nightmare. I couldn't handle the crowds, the noise, the smells. With all its skyscrapers, tunnels, bridges and rickety subway system, the city was a non-stop trigger for my floor-collapsing phobia. I could appreciate its proximity and venture out from time to time to enjoy all the cultural and culinary offerings, but I would no longer try to pretend I loved it as much as everybody else seemed to.

The strongest emotion I feel when I think of New Jersey is gratitude. This unobtrusive location gave me the time and the final push to sit down and really make peace with myself. It was the place I didn't know I needed.

Austin is of such great significance to me because it peeled away all the layers, exposing my most vulnerable core, and then pressed its fingers into the wound, as though to tell me, 'Here! That's you, right here.' But I didn't understand, then. All I felt was pain. I didn't know yet that this was the beginning of the healing. Austin was the place where I ran out of energy to fight and keep up the old facade. I came home to myself, not because I wanted to, but because it was demanded of me. New Jersey was the place where I put the pieces together again, in a way that worked *for* me, in a healthy way.

When I leave New Jersey at some point, I might not miss it as viscerally as I miss Texas, California, Germany and England, but I will miss it nonetheless.

I'm actually smiling to myself while writing this. Who am I kidding? Knowing the way my brain works, I can guarantee that I'll be sitting down with a friend one day, in another country, describing a perfect rose-scented spring day in New Jersey, dotted with cherry blossoms, an abundance of tulips and every shade of green imaginable, and I'll feel a giant pang of longing.

PART 6: HOME

'I was born lost and take no pleasure in being found.'

—John Steinbeck, *Steinbeck: A Life in Letters*

Home

D id I have to move to the East Coast so that I could actually write this book? Probably. It was the piece that was missing when I started writing it in California and added to it while living in Texas. My story wasn't ready to be told then. Also, living on the East Coast provided a nice way for me to wrap up my American chapter, create this impressive US trilogy, put a pretty bow on it, and say, *hey, this is what it's like to live in different parts of the US.* I had to hang on to the most eastern edge of this continent to pay homage to it before packing my bags again to head back to Europe. Of course, calling anything 'overload' should probably have come with a warning.

My controversially minded brain also loves the fact that it was New Jersey that handed me this ending. Not hippie-dippie, in-touch-with-your-feelings, do-yoga-and-drink-green-juice California, nor reach-for-the-stars, buy-the-boots and just-listen-to-music Texas. But straight-tawking, no-nonsense, tough-as-nails New Jersey. Go figure.

It seems that this rather unassuming location, with its quiet beauty, provided exactly the blank canvas I needed.

'Would you do it all again?' my friend Sybille asked me the other day when we sat down for a coffee at a new café I'd discovered in a nearby town. Just as I'd given up on finding a comfy place here in New Jersey to find refuge in, another friend had mentioned this place, and something inside of me paid attention. It was quirky and cosy, books and whimsical art objects adorning the walls and repurposed coffee tables, and the coffee and cakes served in mismatched mugs and plates were delicious. *Finally*, I grinned to myself. I was telling Sybille about writing this book and had just started listing the many houses, cars, schools and doctors that had peppered my path for the last fifteen years. I stopped counting. 'Knowing what I know now? God, no!' She raised her eyebrows, and I had to laugh. 'Of course I would. I think I would.' And that's the truth. Not knowing what I know now meant that my anxiety didn't stop us. Pushing past and ignoring painful experiences can be a good thing, too.

While I wish I'd been better prepared to deal with the upheaval of each move, I would not have wanted to miss out on this amazing, multifaceted life experience that brought our family closer to several cultures and, ultimately, to each other. We know what it feels like to have each other's backs because, at some point, we didn't. I could never have felt the gratitude I feel now for the life I've been able to live and for the experiences that will be the building blocks of my and my family's story for the rest of our lives.

And here it is, the million-dollar question, the question I've been asked more than anything else over the course of my life: where is home for me? The term has evolved; it is not clearly defined for me. I can make 'a home' anywhere; I'm excellent at packing and unpacking and creating a space that feels homely and cosy and 'us' in a relatively short period of time. Even if it's on the surface. Even if it's sometimes a delusion. Practice makes perfect.

It definitely takes practice to create a home; it doesn't just happen. Familiarity helps, which is part of the reason why we've always dragged so much of our stuff with us, rather than selling or donating and buying new things for each new place. As much as these things can weigh you down, they provide a sense of continuity. Baking moulds, faded blankets, chipped mugs, dog-eared cookery books and so on have accompanied us along the way; I feel that while I couldn't give my kids that forever home they can regularly return to, I can damn well keep items that make them *feel* at home.

This has made moving more difficult at times, and not just physically, as I've found out. Moving on gets harder with all that baggage; you definitely need to set the pot down from time to time. But it's helped to create a much-needed sense of familiarity in new surroundings. I still remember the joy we all felt when our container arrived in California from England after a two-month journey, and we were able to fill our new house with our old things. Often, seeing your favourite painting on the wall can provide more comfort than a brand-new sofa.

These days, it makes me happy to know that a few of our belongings and sentimental heirlooms are adorning my children's current homes; an old clock on the wall of my oldest's living room in Austin; the special, much-fought-over children's cutlery with bunnies and kittens in my youngest's kitchen drawer in her student home in London. They're mementoes, much cherished and much needed, tiny anchors in their transient lives, but not a burden that weighs them down.

Having been an expat for over half of my life and visiting my country of birth only a couple of times a year, I feel a little bit more desperate for a break from all the running. Yes, living abroad has satisfied the hunger for adventure and change and has rescued me from constantly asking myself 'what if'. But it's an ongoing internal battle, balancing the adventures and delights of exploring new horizons and the sense of loss and disorientation that come to the surface. A constant dichotomy of wanting to be in two places at the same time, feeling free and trapped, happy and sad all at once – something we expats are oh so used to.

I want to be able to look at the homes I've lived in as decorative pillars of my life, some maybe a little bit more sturdy than others, but I know I must avoid relying on them to bear the full weight of my experience. I need to find a way to do the lifting myself without crumbling under the weight. Part of that is embracing where I am, in the moment, and enjoying the ride, however hard it gets. And know when it's necessary to move on. Sometimes, you need to move on physically in order to move on mentally. There is a difference between moving on because you need or want to, and running away from a situation you don't know how to handle.

I could have said no to any of our moves; the decision to go was always a joint one. It was never, or rarely, a case of caving in to my husband's ideas; rather, the suggestion of a move appeared like a tempting offer to run away and try my luck elsewhere. I didn't know that what I was doing was running away, looking for a solution to a problem I couldn't name. Not knowing for so long who I really was, deep down, I was constantly trying to tie my identity and sense of belonging to a place because I didn't have any other parameters.

England was an easy place to feel safe since I could hide how weak and insecure I felt without having to bare it all – the English are so good at their restraint in showing and demanding emotions, after all, and I could live there without unfurling the full extent of my chaotic interior. But it also kept me at a level of restraint that I needed to leave behind, and I don't think I would have got to that point had I stayed.

I thought I needed a place I could call home to feel like I existed, and with each move, my sense of self was being shattered again. Conversely, this sense of not belonging was always the driving force to move again; I must have subconsciously known this concept wasn't working; I didn't feel like I belonged, and so a new place sounded like the perfect way to search for a new sense of purpose and identity.

I've had to find a way to live in this fragmentation, always missing a piece while finding new and magical ones. The tricky part is not to fall apart but to stay in one piece, regardless, and you need a true motherfucker of a glue stick to do this. I've learned that the glue I need cannot be found in the places I've lived in, but deep inside of me. And I needed to learn that healing hurts. Much like you need to pierce a needle through fabric in order to repair the hole, you can't fix something without feeling pain.

Sometimes, I feel like a giant nesting doll, and maybe that's what we all are: we start out tiny and then grow new dolls around ourselves so that we become bigger and more complex while cocooning the other dolls from earlier times inside. I'm still four, thirteen, twenty-two years old, somewhere deep inside.

But these dolls are not silent, tucked away, never to rise again. When that tiny doll right at the centre is hurt or damaged or simply not *seen*, none of the next ones that form around it can really fit properly. There are dents and bruises, and the next doll won't be able to cover them up, however hard she might try. Instead of valiantly forming a neat new shield, she becomes deformed herself, bulging out here and there and sometimes allowing holes for the previous malignant growths that pierce the surface. The result is a mess that's never fully contained.

I don't believe that you can ever really heal your inner child; you can only heal the current version of yourself by holding space for your past ones and hugging them tightly, allowing for their pain to find a way out.

I've realised that my sense of never belonging and the unique wiring of my brain are not character flaws or deficits; they are my natural state of being, and they are a strength that adds resilience and open-mindedness to the mix. It's the very reason why I've always felt so strangely at home in other countries and cultures. Being foreign is the most legitimate way of saying 'I am different'. Not until I was allowed to be 'other', in other words, a foreigner, did I feel a sense of identity. It's taken a few decades to realise this, and I know I couldn't have done it in my home country, especially not as a young person who was so busy trying, and failing, to fit in.

I've come to accept that I might never find stillness or solace in settling in one place. There is too much of Sabina's essence in me, my fictitious soulmate, who panicked at the thought of a finite place to stay. My own restlessness might simply not allow me to do that, but rather propel me forward again and again; I'm a pawn in this constant game of push-and-pull, sometimes energised, sometimes exhausted. But it's who I am, and as long as I do it because I want to, not because I want to run away, I will be fine. I will explore new places and maybe even put some roots down. Maybe I will find a place that I actually want to stay in. Maybe one day, I'll feel like I no longer need to make myself fit in. Maybe I'll just belong.

My home is where I am. It has to be.

Epilogue

I suck the air in through my teeth. *Damn, this hurts.* I can't help flinching. The girl holding the tattoo needle looks up from my ankle, which she has just started to decorate, and raises an eyebrow. 'I'm good,' I reassure her. 'I didn't realise this spot is so sensitive, but it's ok!' And it is. It's a good pain, and it feels right that it hurts.

I can hear my daughters giggling and chatting as they approach my corner from the other end of the tattoo studio here in Morristown, where they've just been looking at jewellery for piercings. They have already received their own tattoos; the skin on their arms is still red and slightly swollen from the recent addition of a delicate Texas bluebonnet. We've planned to do this for so long, to create a shared symbol of our life in Austin as a token of a time that was both painful and incredibly important for us.

They've both flown in to celebrate Christmas here in New Jersey, and I have gone above and beyond my usual Christmas decorations, baked up a storm of *Plätzchen* and filled the pantry with all their favourite treats, trying to make this home, which Amelie has never lived in and Maya has never truly loved, as welcoming as it can be.

I haven't seen Maya since she moved to London for college at the beginning of September, and the four of us haven't been in the same room together for almost ten months. When it's time to pick Maya up from the airport, I find that I'm too fidgety to sit in the car, so I send Scott to go and get her by himself while I finish preparing the Mum-style Spaghetti Bolognese she has requested for her welcome-home dinner.

An hour later, my beautiful girl bursts through the door, her voice bubbling over with excitement. 'Mum, you'll never guess who I saw last week, there was this girl I met in Berlin when I was there this summer, and she was at this pub around the corner from uni, and so we were speaking in German, and then her friend looked at me and it turns out she knows Amelie's friend Bella from Austin!' I laugh delightedly, trying to process this onslaught of information and throw my arms around my beaming daughter, who seems to be humming and fizzing with energy. I point out that not many eighteen-year-olds are as well-connected as she is. 'I know, it's so crazy!' she agrees. 'And last month, I met these two friends who were travelling together, one was from Princeton and the other from San Mateo! How nuts is that?' Germany, England, Texas, New Jersey and California, all within a couple of sentences. Her life is so full. She grins. 'I am so glad that I grew up like this and know all these different places.' While I fight back my tears, shocked and delighted by this statement, Maya drops her bag and slumps to the floor, stretching her arms out to cuddle Ziggy, who is doing frantic circles around her, barking and yelping excitedly, followed by the cats, who've both come running to greet their long-lost mistress.

Amelie arrives a couple of days later, ready for Christmas with all her favourite home comforts. 'I can't wait to watch *Drei Haselnüsse für Aschenbrödel*!' she exclaims, ready for our annual tradition of watching this German-Czech adaptation of Cinderella together, which is mostly unknown outside of Central Europe. She has introduced numerous international friends to this gem of a tale over the years, and a tattoo of three hazelnuts adorns her shoulder, paying homage to this important part of her childhood.

I do not get homesick this year. As the four of us cuddle up on the sofa after our Christmas dinner, a cat on a lap here and there and our dog snoring on his bed by the fireplace, I'm struck by a profound sense of peace. We're watching the *Gavin & Stacey Christmas Special* on BBC iPlayer, all bound together by this whimsical show that we started watching long before we moved to the US and which is full of shared references and nostalgia. I feel completely at ease. This house has finally become a place for us to feel at home in, even if only for a fleeting few days. It might not be our kids' childhood home; it might only be temporary. We might not actually love it. But it feels like a home, and we've all created this together as a family.

And then it hits me: I don't feel at home. I *am* the home.

Acknowledgements

Writing a memoir is a tricky undertaking, as you can't write about your own life without simultaneously writing about others' lives, too. What I'm trying to say is there are other people in this book, not all of whom know they've become characters in a story. In any case, I've changed almost every person's (and animal's) name.

I would like to thank the following people (as the obsessive overthinker that I am, I couldn't decide who needed to come first or last or in the middle, so here they all are, as they came to mind):

The many writers, artists and other personalities who have shaped my journey and made me want to write, helped me understand myself, made me feel seen. A few of them: Milan Kundera, Jilly Cooper (I bet you never expected these two in the same sentence), Fiona Walker, Lisa Genova, Lisa Jewell, Matt Haig, Clover Stroud, Stephen Fry, Gabor Maté, Trevor Noah, Hannah Gadsby, Anthony Bourdain.

Fran Lebowitz, my editor, for taking on 'the book before the book'. You saw the essence and helped me shape my story, and your stern, surprising and encouraging comments (and also your confusion) were exactly what I needed. Sadie Rittman, my second editor (and Fran's daughter), for providing your eagle eyes and the final push to polish and sculpt this memoir. I am so lucky to have found this editorial duo, both expats themselves *and* mother and daughter, to take on this mother-daughter expat narrative.

My podcast guests, for sharing your own stories with me and confirming again and again that telling our stories matters. You never know who needs to hear your specific experience.

My trial readers and my online and personal expat community: your insights, depth, humour and vulnerability have inspired me to share my story and encouraged me to keep going. Sometimes, it was just little things you said (Nikki, Maria, Catriona, Mariam, Iliana, Vanessa, to name but a few) that made a huge difference to my confidence.

My coaches, Sundae and Monique, for helping me believe in my potential. Creating a podcast, writing a book and putting myself out there are all huge endeavours. You kept me on track when I needed it the most.

My friends all over the world: the ones I kept, lost and gained along the way. It's hard to maintain relationships across time and distance, and I can't tell you how grateful I am to those who stayed by my side over the years and decades, even though I'm not the best at keeping in touch. I know you appreciate the effort when I turn up or send you a message, and I want to thank you for ignoring the months or even years of no contact. To those I've lost along the way: it was fun being part of your story for a while. Please know I never take friendships lightly. I appreciate the time we had, even when things didn't last. Fi and Nhi, for listening to my ranting and processing throughout the years, and for *always* making time for me when I visit my old stomping grounds. I still fantasise about getting the two of you together one day. You're each other's versions on different continents. Marcsi, for being my first friend in America, and for sticking around for this whole journey (and especially when things got hard). Niki, for being my oldest friend and the one who will always keep me firmly rooted to my origins. Donna and Simone, for jumping in with the spiritual side of things when I needed guidance that wasn't practical or rational.

My teachers: Mr Maslanka, my 8th grade English teacher, for telling me I had a talent for the language. Telling me I was good at something. I will never forget how proud you made me feel. Mr McEwen, my interpreting teacher at college, for really seeing me and knowing when I needed to be pushed and when to back off. You were also the first American I really liked. Ms Gutmann-Patchett, my science teacher at college, for inspiring me to apply to your own alma mater, the University of Kent at Canterbury, and for warning me about English men. I only remembered your words – 'They may look harmless, but they're absolutely not' – when it was too late. Ha!

My sister and my sister-in-law, for not moving as far away from my parents and parents-in-law as we did. Also, thank you for always making an effort to maintain a relationship with my children, even if they're far away.

My parents-in-law, for always helping out, no questions asked, and for never making us feel guilty for taking your grandchildren to a foreign land, corrupting their accents.

My grandma, Ama, for passing on your adventurous spirit and your love of languages and other cultures to me. I know you were reading over my shoulder as I wrote this book. I swear I felt your hand on my head from time to time.

My parents, for giving me strong roots but even stronger wings. You always encouraged my sense of adventure and let me roam and explore without restrictions. And for never once making me feel guilty for leaving Germany and raising your grandchildren in other countries. Now that my own children live far away, I really appreciate how hard that must have been. I hope the fact that my children love speaking German and staying with you whenever they can makes up for it all somehow.

My husband, my *ride or die*, my partner in crime, for encouraging me and making things possible so that I could take the time to write this book. For still being here after 25 years and for never giving up on us, even when we hit rock bottom (and for putting up with all the drama). For being the best dad to our children I could have wished for. I can't believe I had to go all the way to England to find you ;-)

My children, for encouraging me to tell this story, and for giving your okay to share parts of your past. You are so brave and strong, and I am fiercely proud of who you both are.

And last but not least, my pets, for never leaving my side during those long hours I spent writing and swearing and crying at my desk, and for never failing to remind me to take breaks. I've asked your advice a lot. You know everything

About the Author

Born and raised near Munich in Bavaria, Germany, Stephanie moved to the UK in her twenties, where she gained a Master's degree in literature and an English husband. They lived in London and Kent for just over a decade before moving to the US with their two young children.

Now an empty nester, Stephanie currently lives in New Jersey with her husband, dog and two cats, who keep her from being a full-time nomad. Of course, she already has her eye on the next move.

Transcontinental Overload is her first book.

More about the author:
https://linktr.ee/stephaniexcook
www.transcontinentaloverload.com